WITHDRAWN

W9-BRN-206

3 1611 00052 6290

THE LEADER WITHIN

L THE EADER WITHIN

An Empowering Path of Self-Discovery

HOWARD HAAS

with Bob Tamarkin

GOVERNORS STATE UNIVERSITY
UNIVERSITY PARK
IL 60466

HarperBusiness
A Division of HarperCollins*Publishers*

HD 57.7 .H33 1992

Haas, Howard.

The leader within

293090

THE LEADER WITHIN. Copyright © 1992 by Howard G. Haas and Bob Tamarkin. All rights reserved. Printed in the United States of America. No part of this book may be used or reproduced in any manner whatsoever without written permission except in the case of brief quotations embodied in critical articles and reviews. For information address HarperCollins Publishers, Inc., 10 East 53rd Street, New York, NY 10022.

HarperCollins books may be purchased for educational, business, or sales promotional use. For information, please write: Special Markets Department, HarperCollins Publishers, Inc., 10 East 53rd Street, New York, NY 10022.

FIRST EDITION

Designed by Francesca Belanger
Illustrations by Maxwell Group, Inc., Chicago, IL 60661

Library of Congress Cataloging-in-Publication Data

Haas, Howard.
    The leader within: an empowering path of self-discovery/Howard
Haas with Bob Tamarkin.—1st ed.
    p.   cm.
    Includes index.
  ISBN 0-88730-561-X
  1. Leadership. 2. Executive ability. I. Tamarkin, Bob. II. Title.
HD57.7.H33   1992
658.4′092—dc20   91-58504

93 94 95 96 97 AC/RRD 10 9 8 7 6 5 4 3 2 1

To my father, Adolph R. Haas, an immigrant from central Europe at the beginning of the twentieth century, who made the most out of what he had and understood that moving from one culture to another is a born-twice experience from which one can grow, transform, and find personal renewal.

Contents

Foreword by Noel Tichy   ix

Preface   xv

Acknowledgments   xix

Introduction   1

**Part I. The Tapestry of Leadership:
           Building the Warp**

1. The New Realities Require New
    Leadership   13

2. The Roots of Leadership   36

3. Managership, Leadership,
    Followership in Balance   55

4. New Strengths from Old Wounds   70

5. Role Models, Relationships, Networks   85

Summary. Acquiring Warp Threads   108

**Part II. The Tapestry of Leadership:
            Creating the Weft**

6. Vision and Mission—A Balance
    Between the Fresh and Familiar   115

7. Ethics and Integrity Are Not Options   140

8. Vision Becomes Reality
          Through Communication   159

9. Total Quality Management
          Mandates Total Quality Leadership   176

10. Gordon Segal Weaves
          the Warp and Weft of Leadership   189

11. Mastering the Craft of Leadership   209

Appendix   215
Notes   223
Index   235

Foreword

The 1990s are a turning point in American history. We must creatively destroy and remake most of our institutions, both public and private. We live in the post-Cold War geopolitical world in which capitalism has won a very short breathing space to prove that it is indeed the better alternative. At this time the world faces unprecedented challenges, both physical and human ecology issues that threaten our physical, social, and psychic well-being.

As a nation we are either at the end of the American century, which portends a future of continuing decline, leading us to be one more of the societies that Paul Kennedy wrote about in the *The Rise and Fall of the Great Powers*, or we are the one that breaks the mold and goes through Toynbee's revitalization. Our institutions are suffering far greater dry rot than John Gardner ever could have imagined in 1968, when he wrote his frame-breaking book about self-renewing organizations. The missing ingredient at all levels of society is leadership.

In 1986, my co-author, Mary Anne Devanna, and I dedicated our book, *The Transformational Leader*, to our children because we were concerned about the quality of life in the world of the twentieth century. At the time we knew that the task of revitalizing institutions was an awesome one but one that we held some optimism could be successfully accomplished, albeit not without considerable trauma. It is now 1992 and things are worse. Many of the transformational leaders we wrote about in the mid-1980s have failed and their organizations are in worse shape than they were almost a decade ago. The country is in worse shape and the world is not taking advantage of the great opportunities to build a new order for the twenty-first century.

Why?

There is something wrong when a society has to have a riot in Los Angeles to recognize that the issues of racism, poverty, and urban decay are problems. Or when the board of directors at General Motors has to intervene directly and remove the president and strip some of the power of the CEO to mobilize change. Or when leaders of institutions receive historically unprecedented amounts of money while the standard of living of the average citizen declines and while employees in their companies are laid off or paid flat incomes.

The leadership challenges are extraordinary. American industry is still lagging in productivity gains and is slipping in the competitiveness of many technologies. There are serious macroeconomic, political, and cultural problems in the United States, which will continue to make the task of creating world-class competitive firms difficult. Nevertheless, global competitiveness must be the top item on the agenda of business leaders in American firms.

Listed below are major areas that business leaders need to consider in forming their 1990s agenda:

Human Capital Issues

The United States faces a demographic crunch in the 1990s from an aging population with a declining number of qualified entrants into the workforce. The work structure is rapidly changing to one in which the high-value-added knowledge worker and jobs requiring skilled, flexible, constantly trainable employees are the norm. A smaller demographic pool, coupled with a deteriorated educational system, means that companies face human capital challenges in their role in society (how to help improve the U.S. educational system), as well as in the efforts that will go into recruiting, training, and constant retraining of the workforce. Finally, the cultural diversity of the workforce will continue to change rapidly: white males will be the minority.

Environmental Challenges

The 1990s have ushered in an era in which world opinion and political power are rallying around global environmental issues: the greenhouse effect, acid rain, tropical rain forests, and so on. The development of environmental policies—within the company for its own workforce, in environments where the company operates, and in terms of product and service strategies—is high on the list of business leaders' concerns. The challenge will be to deal preemptively rather than defensively. A company like Exxon, with its Valdez spill, has done itself great harm both with its own workforce and its image in society.

Government Relations, Industrial Policy

In the mid-1980s there was much debate about the need for industrial policy in the United States. The advocates of industrial policy lost to the conservative "free market" advocates. As the 1990s emerge, the issue does not go away. In the last few months, executives such as Andy Grove, CEO of Intel, have been calling for the government to help the semiconductor industry. Ironically, the industry that was nonsupportive of the auto industry's call for help in the 1980s is itself now calling for government help. Government's role in enhancing U.S. industry competitiveness is one that will continue to be debated, especially if the U.S. debt and trade imbalance problems persist in the midst of worldwide pressure on capital availability. The business leader's agenda will need to include careful strategizing regarding government's role in global competitiveness.

Development of Global Strategies: Product/Service/Market

As companies look more aggressively to world markets, they are faced with developing world-class products and services at world-class cost. This means changes in product and service design, production, distribution, and marketing. The leaders must be able to implement new forms of product lines and service design, strategic use of sourcing, and the development of world-class standards for design, service, and performance. The requisites for global competitiveness are painfully difficult to implement, and progress to date in the United States is not up to par with that of the best companies in the world.

Developing Strategic Alliances: Partnering

In order to deliver on global strategies, more and varied alliances— partnerships that are needed to gain market entry, price competitiveness, update technology, develop new learnings about management and regions of the world, and so on—are emerging. The success of these alliances depends largely on a set of human factors, such as proper prescreening of partners, proper negotiation, the right conditions for partnering and good day-to-day operating mechanisms for successful coordination and integration.

Developing the Competitive Organization: The Human Dimension

The 1980s can be viewed as the "hardware" decade of rapid transformation, in which much of the organizational change in the United States was done via massive downsizing and restructuring. Even where there was massive investment in technology and new plants and equipment, the human organization was not yet transformed by 1990. GM, after a decade of investment, is still struggling with a slow-moving, inflexible bureaucracy that must go through a radical transformation in the 1990s. Productivity gains in the 1990s must come from a constantly innovating workforce. Taking heads out, doing it with "hardware," is going to be replaced with doing it with "software" investment in people development and cultures that can constantly innovate.

The U.S. business leader is struggling to develop the appropriate global form of organization while simultaneously working on new "micro" forms of organization. By "micro" forms we mean organizations that are much leaner and less hierarchical. This is requiring a total rethinking of management process, human resource practices, and organizations design.

Developing New Global Staffing

There are challenges at both the top and the bottom of the organization. At the bottom, or entry level, U.S. companies face a set of demographic facts of life. The pool of qualified entry-level candidates is shrinking. Part of this is due to the aging of the population, but another increasingly troublesome cause is a deteriorated educational system. This is requiring business leaders to address the role of the company in public education as well as alter training capabilities within the company.

The top of the organizational challenge is focused on how to grow world-class leaders. The traditional career paths will end up reproducing yesterday's domestically focused and nonglobal leaders. The future requires revamping career tracks for management as well as selection criteria. The leaders of the future will need global mind-sets and global team and leadership skills, as well as global network skills.

Developing a Culture That Can Continuously Transform

Perhaps the greatest challenge of all is to develop a culture that can repeatedly creatively destroy and rebuild itself—that is, a self-transforming culture. Given the rapid changes in the global economy and the intensifying competition, all competitive organizations will be continuously bombarded with forces requiring large-scale change.

The true world-class competitors will be capable of rapid transformation. This requires an ability to quickly create a sense of urgent change within the organization, deal with resistance to change, create a new vision, gain commitment, and redesign the organization to fit the new vision.

Having proposed that these are the agenda items for senior

business leaders in the United States, let me expand the challenge to be more globally inclusive. The bigger world leadership challenge is "global citizenship," that is, the leaders of business enterprises throughout the world taking on a deep and enlightened self-interest in the environmental and human capital issues facing the world.

This point was driven home to a group of thirty-two executives in the Michigan Global Leadership Program in 1991. This group of Japanese, U.S., and European executives spent five weeks in an intense action-learning program, which included two weeks to carry out a country assessment in China, India, Brazil, or Russia. Part of the program included an immersion in global citizenship issues; visits to homeless shelters; volunteer work in drug rehabilitation centers; encounters with poverty in China, India, and Russia; as well as extensive debate and study regarding the role of the global corporation in dealing with these issues. When we calculated the sales of the companies in the program, they were well over $835 billion, more than the combined GNP of China and India. The challenge was to think of the implications of the power and wealth wielded by thirty-six companies in relation to almost two billion people surviving on less wealth. As we look toward the twenty-first century, who will play the key roles in the world?

Howard Haas's book points us to the answer, namely, leadership, leadership, leadership. There is a growing need for businesses and societies to tap that all-too-scarce resource. The encouraging part of Haas's message, conveyed through thoughtful analysis and actual case illustration, is that we all have the potential for great leadership actions in our own spheres. As he so aptly points out in his introduction, leadership is based on "exceptional personal commitment." Howard Haas demonstrates that quality personally as a role model and as a teacher through this exceptional book on leadership.

Noel Tichy
Ann Arbor, Michigan
September 1992

Preface

*T*he day after the long Thanksgiving weekend in 1986, as I drove to work, I found myself stuck in traffic among the other returning vacationers. Suddenly, I heard the news blaring over the car radio: Sealy, Inc. had been sold to Ohio Mattress Company, a publicly held corporation. I had worked for Sealy for twenty-seven years, serving as president and chief executive officer for nineteen of them. The acquisition had sealed my fate.

Obviously there was no place for two chief executive officers in the "new" Sealy. So shortly after the merger papers were signed a month later, I cleaned out my desk and started down the path of a second career that included lecturing at the Graduate School of Business at the University of Chicago, consulting, and serving as a director on the boards of several private and public corporations.

I had walked away from Sealy with a great deal of pride and satisfaction. Here was a company that had to be reinvented three times over the years in response to the changing antitrust laws only to end up as a highly desirable acquisition target for an aggressive corporation. Sealy had come a long way since I joined it in 1959 when there were only thirteen employees and a net worth of $600,000. On January 1, 1987, when I had left, Sealy employed eighteen hundred people and its net worth had grown to $60 million. Two years later the integrated Sealy was sold in a leveraged buyout for $1.1 billion.

Although I remained as busy as ever, my new career gave me time to reflect. I thought about the things that had made Sealy work—and didn't. How, I wondered, did other CEOs feel about the kinds of issues I had faced? About managing? About leading? About following? I started by delving into the literature to see what the academics and business writers were saying. I eventually worked my way to the University of Chicago's Regenstein Library, where I browsed the stacks for leadership books, ending up on the second floor in the social science section. There I discovered the trove: scores of books on leadership dated 1907, 1924, 1937, and so on. As I was reading the light suddenly went on: It hadn't been more than fifteen years that the concepts of leadership, managership, and entrepreneurship were well defined. In all the early writings, however, these terms were interchanged, mixed into the same pot like a hobo stew. That is, until 1978 when James MacGregor Burns produced his seminal book called *Leadership* in which he defined the subject in a business context. Most of the previous leadership studies were essentially historical analysis of what others had done, in both the business and political realms. Burns sharpened the focus between leadership and managership that has since been written about in a host of popular and academic articles and bestsellers.

For years the debate over what makes for leadership often stumbled into a philosophic muddle. The conceptual focus remained fixed on the challenge of becoming a leader. Aspiring leaders, for the most part, were encouraged to ape their superiors, to use them as role models for demeanor, speech, management style, and even dress.

The methodology used to discover significant patterns of behavior among business leaders (most of them CEOs) used for this book was through vigorous investigation and analysis. The students in my classes over the past two years conducted more than 150 face-to-face interviews that were purposely unstructured. The interviewees, for the most part, were spontaneous and open in sharing their hard-won leadership experiences. We have selected thirty-one leaders whose verbatim comments are used to amplify the concepts and principles introduced in *The Leader Within*. The intent has been to distill from the literature on leadership—and the original verbatim interviews—a focused flow of information with each source reinforcing the other to delineate more clearly the points we wished to make. Most of my observations and conclusions are summarized in "Reflections" at the end of each chapter and in chapter 11, titled "Mastering the Craft of Leadership."

Today, the views of leadership go well beyond the take-my-word-for-it wisdom of executives who reached the top. Leadership concepts have grown remarkably more inclusive and accurate. Indeed, there is a distinction between a leader and a manager. The stuff of leadership is vision that produces change, transformation, and new direction. It is, in effect, a process that aligns people, ideas, systems, communications, and technology. Vision is risk. A vision of the future, however, can't be accomplished—and appreciated—without a glimpse of the past. This is something people who are part of the same corporate culture should know. The past, then, plays a pivotal role in the way vision and values are transmitted by the leader, who seeks change.

Managership, on one hand, creates order and consistency through planning and budgeting, staffing and organizing. In short, managers cope with complexity, monitor, and problem solve. They are the mortar of a business organization, because they provide consistency and coherence.

One without the other, as we shall see, doesn't work. It's impossible to have strong leadership with weak management. The two functions play off one another to produce creative sparks: Leadership upsets orderly planning; management discourages risk taking.

As for entrepreneurship, aspiring entrepreneurs can be both good leaders and managers. They cannot, however, work within the context of an organization and are, therefore, willing to take more risk than a company normally will allow. So they go off on their own in a different mode. But eventually, when their companies grow big enough, they will have to change their attitudes if they intend to ensure leadership continuity. All too often solo leadership style catches up with a company when the founder steps down as chairman without having groomed a strong successor.

No one has all the answers to the leadership code. But after analyzing the personal factors, the process, the objectives, and disciplines of leadership, I have come up with this certainty: Anyone can be a leader. True, no one can be taught leadership in response to the demand to "make me a leader," but anyone can indeed learn to lead. We all have the right leadership stuff, only most of us don't know it. It takes a little hindsight, but mostly insight into yourself to gain your perspective on reality.

The kind of leadership I'm talking about is what Burns called "transformational," the process of changing the context of where we are and how we operate rather than "transactional," which is the task of getting someone to buy a product or service.

Although the leaders interviewed for this book uniformly reported that they did not set out to be the CEOs of their respective enterprises, they all agreed that the freedom to lead and accomplish new things was both satisfying and rewarding. Moreover, these extensive interviews, laced with my experience and the observations of others who have studied leadership, confirm what I had always suspected: *You can be appointed to the position of boss, but you can never be appointed to the position of being a leader.*

There is a premium on self-expression and creativity in American business today. Without a large dose of new leadership, the management tools of the 1960s, 1970s, and 1980s won't work in the twenty-first century. We are on the threshold of change: the decline of communism, the emergence of "Fortress Europe 1992," the integration of both the global goods and financial markets, the restructuring of Third World debt, the transformation of the workforce as the Baby Boomers hit middle age, the backlash to the excesses of the 1980s. Every nation, it seems, is trying to take hold of its economic destiny in a business environment where value-added services are becoming just as important as value-added manufacturing. The prospect for leadership has never been riper.

Remember, this is not a feel-good book of lists but, rather, an examination of the factors of leadership. As you read, pause and remind yourself of the dogsled metaphor: "If I'm not the lead dog, the view never changes."

Acknowledgments

*I*t was shortly after Dean Harry Davis offered me the opportunity to join the faculty at the Graduate School of Business (GSB) at the University of Chicago that the idea for this book was born.

Nine months later, Business Policy 467—Leadership in Business was completed in response to Dean Davis's proposition that I could teach anything that I wanted to in the business policy division as long as it was not currently being taught at the GSB. Part of that research resulted in this book, and I offer deep gratitude to Dean Davis for the chance to parlay my experience as a businessperson into a highly rewarding teaching experience.

I also want to thank the more than 150 leaders interviewed (they and their organizations are listed in the appendix) whose observations shape the concepts that are dealt with and emphasized through the thirty-one selected quotations used in the book. Many of these leaders took time out of busy schedules to respond to follow-up questions. I especially want to express my appreciation to Gordon Segal for allowing me to use verbatim his long and meaningful interview that appears in chapter 10. I must also add my appreciation to Morris Kaplan, William Walzer, Jerome Rotblatt, Richard Roe, Michael I. Kaplan, and Douglas MacMillan, all my associates at Sealy, Inc. who for three decades provided me with the opportunity to find and develop my *leader within*.

I owe an intellectual debt to James MacGregor Burns, Warren Bennis, Noel Tichy, Abraham Zaleznick, Peter Drucker, and John Kotter, whose research and thinking inspired me to integrate real-world experiences with their important discoveries and observations on leadership.

I wish again to thank Harry Davis and Deputy Dean Albert Madansky for reading and then providing insightful comments on the work in progress. I also wish to acknowledge Professor Wayne Baker, who so carefully reviewed the initial drafts. Such peer review was most helpful.

To my students who interviewed more than 150 leaders and transcribed hundreds of hours of comments to provide a rich body of research material from which conclusions and quotes for this book have been drawn, I wish to express my heartiest appreciation. Without them, this book would not have had its unique quality. I especially want to thank Susan Stevens, who was both a student in my class and a research assistant, helping me with the organization of the tapestry of leadership as well as doing her own work on the symphony metaphor, along with her associates Robert Glowniak, Matthew Samelson, Philip Martin, Gail Gordon, and Janice Smith. I also wish to thank the student researchers who helped me with the chapter on ethics and integrity. They include Dan Lagermeier, Mark Lawson, Rose Martin, Dean Matt, and Jeff Vekony.

To Dr. Sherman Feinstein for reading chapter 4, "New Strengths from Old Wounds." And to Dr. Wendy Deutelbaum for her insights on heroes and myths and for introducing me to the work of Joseph Campbell. To Maryanne Martinez, whose computer skills and patience have been demonstrated time and again as she labored hard and long on the word processor, entering the original draft and then making corrections from both Bob and me.

To my co-author, Bob Tamarkin, a skilled professional writer who is patient, dedicated, insightful, challenging, tireless, a believer, and a skilled collaborator. He created a powerful synergy by adding depth and insight as well as superb literary style to the book.

Finally, to my mentors and role models, Dr. Bernard L. Greene, Bernard A. Mitchell, James W. Alsdorf, Earle Ludgin, and especially my brother, Albert Haas, who believed in me and gave me the encouragement to meet a wide spectrum of professional challenges.

And to my family—to my wife, Kaye, who keeps me in focus and my feet on the ground and who is always there with support and encouragement; my daughter, Jody, a skilled librarian who organized my files so I could find references and research materials from the mass and clutter of facts I had accumulated over the years; and my son, Jon, a musician who encouraged me to develop the symphony metaphor presented in chapter 8.

Introduction

Strange how Adam Smith's invisible hand deals the cards in a game where rules change constantly. For that matter so does the game itself. We got through the decade when conspicuous consumption was the signature vice and corporate America lived on a rapacious diet of bravado and borrowed cash. The Wall came down. East embraced West. The cold thawed. And the once-mighty Soviet Union is postured like a forlorn derelict in a soup kitchen line ready to hock ideology for three squares. We even fought a Middle East war, replete with heroes and villains, to make sure the scales of precious energy tilted in our favor. The world's debt load may have outrun its collateral. Star Wars could now be replaced by Trade Wars in a world where Europe is retreating into "Fortress 1992" and Japan is on a mercantile conquest with an arsenal of electronic marvels.

If there was ever a time for business leadership to step forward, it's now. Yet, in an era when America's work ethic appears bruised and battered, everywhere you turn there seems to be a leadership vacuum. Clearly, business is overmanaged and underled. Business schools are partly to blame. They teach management, not leadership, and most professors are comfortable with theory, not practice. Like fast-food chains, the nation's business schools have churned out cookie-cutter managers by the thousands since the 1960s. Between 1963 and 1988 the number of MBA graduates rose from 5,787 to 70,000. Today there are more than 1 million MBAs. Yet, as *Newsweek* columnist Robert J. Samuelson points out, "The MBA explosion has coincided with a deterioration in the performance and stature of corporate America."

1

The elite business schools argue that they are educating managers. Critics dismiss the high-cost schools merely as expensive employment agencies, noting further that taking risks, creating valuable products, motivating people, and satisfying customers is tough to teach in a classroom.

Indeed today's MBAs are ill-prepared to lead in a dynamic marketplace. Most of their schools focused on management and finance, serving up a blueprint of sorts for planning and budgeting to produce predictable results. Thus graduates aspire to become financial tacticians who, like chess players fighting time and strategy, ponder the effects of volatile markets on risk. They become a breed of phone jockeys tucked away in the corner of a corporation unencumbered by politics. They are, in a phrase, efficient machines of short-term bottom-line performance. Their tools are mathematical models and fast computers that track exchange rates tick by tick. They rearrange the sand on the beach, but avoid building sand castles—the creative aspects of business planning.

Recently, I attended a day-long seminar billed as "the business event of the year" to garner gems of leadership wisdom from a trio of motivators on the stump. They were instructive, humorous, inspirational, and even entertaining. And most of the fifteen hundred businessmen and businesswomen in the audience took notes as if they were students in one of those huge college lecture classes. When it was over, I had lists of dos and don'ts and a litany of management tips. I even felt good. But the encounter was like the Sunday sermon that vanishes from one's conscience by Monday. The presentations had been too slick, too neatly packaged. They lacked that one element a person needs before he or she can change, or is willing to change: introspection. To gain insight into your leadership potential takes some intellectual maneuvering. It is a process, not a checklist or a tip sheet.

The word *leader* conjures up the image of King Arthur sitting at the round table, a mutton loin in one hand, Excalibur in the other; or George Washington perched in the prow of a small boat thrusting against the frigid waves as he and his men make their way across the

Delaware; or Franklin Roosevelt, Winston Churchill, and Josef Stalin posed before the camera at Yalta shortly before they were about to divide up the postwar world; or the skin-and-bones profile of bespectacled Mahatma Gandhi in the nonviolent bid for India's independence. Such are the images of hero leaders that have filtered through the ages from the pens of poets to the shutters of photographers. It's a word practically as old as civilization itself, rooted in the ancient Persian language, meaning "to go, to travel."

The saga of leadership has always drawn psychologists, academics, and historians to ponder the stuff of leaders. Are leaders, like kings of yore, anointed with divine providence? Or is the golden spoon of leadership handed from father to son? Or are leaders products of their times, shaped in character by the ebb and flow of the events that surround them? Although the public generally believes that great people do make history, the truth of assumption, according to James MacGregor Burns, has never been demonstrated.

It is a myth to think that leaders are born. Or that they are bred for the role. Anyone can be a leader. There is no entitlement to leadership. It makes no difference where you buy your clothes or if you make it through the grand slam of education—Andover prep, Yale and Harvard law school—or who your father was or still is. President Harry Truman, once called by Dean Acheson "the greatest little man in history," was a poker-playing, whisky-drinking, small-town politician with a high-school education who failed at the haberdasher's trade. Yet, when the time came, he slipped into Franklin Roosevelt's presidential shoes as if they wore the same size. Three months later he made what is perhaps one of the most crucial—and agonizing—decisions in history: to drop the atomic bomb on Nagasaki and Hiroshima.

More recently, consider the Oxford-educated Margaret Thatcher, who fell from power as England's prime minister. Her political heir was the forty-seven-year-old John Major, a high-school dropout who rose from humble beginnings. A shy child with few friends, Major led a picaresque existence. The son of a circus trapeze artist and onetime mercenary in Brazil, Major grew up in a two-bedroom apartment in a poor London suburb and left school at sixteen to help support his parents. In quick succession he worked as an accounting trainee and as a concrete mixer; at one point he went on the dole for nine months. Although he never went to college he drifted into banking and eventually local politics with a whirlwind style that got him elected to Parliament in 1979.

People with normally endowed intelligence have the right leadership stuff. But getting them to realize it is quite another matter. I've seen it in the classroom and the boardroom: The notion of leadership seems so remote to many aspiring businesspeople that they ignore the possibility of someday becoming the head honcho. They see themselves up against the odds, clashing with older-generation managers who think that if the shoe doesn't fit, you should wear it and walk funny. Unfortunately, there are too many individuals quitting on leadership before they start, at a time when market forces are conspiring in their favor. When mature industries find themselves loaded with fifty- and sixty-year-olds and a strong demand for people to replace them. When U.S. manufacturing— once the most productive machine in the world—needs an overhaul. When headhunters are scratching their own heads in a scramble for executives who can do business across borders.

Leadership can be learned but is seldom taught as part of the graduate curriculum at business schools. Many students, in fact, treat the concept of *leadership* as an enigma, like trying to find the meaning of *Rosebud,* the last cryptic word squeezed out of the dying Citizen Kane. Obviously, most students who leave my class will not become great business leaders, but they do gain an understanding of the source, process, and practice of leadership. People can be empowered, but not motivated. And you don't have to be a boy genius or a wonder woman either. Most people have the right stuff to become leaders, but they believe the folklore and don't even try. As for those bestselling management books, most are loaded with brave new words in the form of leadership jargon rather than leadership language. They lack leadership wisdom but not leadership lists.

That's why this is not a how-to book. There are plenty of those books around that give you the ten easy steps up the corporate ladder—and the ten down. They would have you become a Hun or a shark. Or a Machiavelli with a stiletto wit. Such formulas are merely combination punches, thrown by individuals for whom the path of leadership is nothing more than bobbing and weaving through the corporate mean streets. Usually, they end up shadow boxing. I'm not promising a knockout punch. Rather, think of this book as a guide to a personal odyssey, requiring insight, creativity, risk taking, and flexibility; the kinds of qualities that aren't nurtured in a motivational seminar with hundreds of people crammed into a hotel meeting room.

What I hope you will find is the leader within you. It's never too early or too late to start on the path of leadership. It's a hard journey, but eases as you learn to read the highway markers along the way. Indeed *leadership* is the kind of word that reminds management consultant Fred G. Steingraber, chairman and CEO of A. T. Kearney, Inc., of a comment once attributed to Supreme Court Justice Potter Stewart when asked to define *obscenity*. Stewart apologetically said he couldn't define it, but knew what it was when he saw it. "Leadership," says John Gardner, in explaining its nature, "is the process of persuasion by which an individual induces a group to pursue objectives held by the leader or shared by the leader and his or her followers." Bart Giamatti, the late commissioner of Major League Baseball, defined leadership as the assertion of a vision, not merely the exercise of a style. Consultant Steingraber believes leadership is the process of converting unknowns into knowns. He says,

Leaders are the beacons. They chart the clear courses in the rough waters or through the foggy nights. They're risk takers. They deal with the unknowns. They have to rely on instinct and not always analysis. Leaders have to articulate their institution's values. Leaders understand the importance of innovation and not just imitation. They understand the difference between wealth creation and wealth dissipation.

They know how to balance the short and the long term. Good leaders set stretch goals and they're dedicated to continuous improvement.

Leadership is discovery. Not the discovery of a set of principles as practiced by Atilla that promise to blow the boardroom door off its hinges. Nor is it a one-minute cram course tinged with philosophic observations. Nor is it the Machiavellian way for clawing up the organization with an anything-goes-if-it-works mind-set. Nor does it mean mimicking the Churchills, Roosevelts, Fords, Sloans, or any other twentieth-century leaders.

Leadership means self-discovery, getting a better yield out of your attributes. Strip away the veneer—the abstracts; the formulas; the buzzwords such as vision, mission, values, transformation, and paradigm—and instead follow a simple premise: Because each person is unique, each person has to find the qualities he or she needs to develop his or her own leadership style. Once you see how others have done it, you can, too. Don't mistrust your initial instincts. Leaders are the sum of their experiences, which make them much more than mere organization men and women.

Even the twenty-something generation can't seem to find a role model for leadership inspiration. Recently a *Time* survey revealed that the young generation could find no figures in the present who compared with such 1960s heroes as John F. Kennedy and Martin Luther King, Jr. Even the wanna-be leaders seem unable to maintain their stature. They either self-destruct or are decimated in the press, which trumpets their faults and foibles with headline-grabbing relish. For a while there were the Wall Street movers and shakers—the junk-bond icons—but they vanished when the bubble of greed burst, ending the Decade of the Deal that had given rise to a get-rich-quick mentality and a spending culture to match.

That's not to say that ambition has been mothballed. University of Southern California's leadership pundit, Warren Bennis, points out that eighteenth-century America was notable for its leaders—the likes of Washington, Jefferson, Adams, Hamilton, Franklin and

Madison—who emerged from a population of only five million souls. During the nineteenth century came the adventurers, entrepreneurs, and scientists, and in the twentieth century, the bureaucrats and managers. Passion, Bennis writes, has been replaced by ambition at a time when Oliver North, who insists he was patriotically following orders as a key Iran-Contra player, has become "the thinking man's Rambo." There are those such as Ralph Stayer, the CEO of Johnsonville Foods, who argue the change in leadership texture has come with a fundamental shift in business history: entrepreneurial capitalism yielded to managerial capitalism, which is now giving way to what he calls "intellectual capitalism." The next may be the last stage of the industrial revolution, whereby today's artisans are using their heads, not their hands.

So where will the next generation of leaders come from? Who will they be? How will they develop? If *Fortune* magazine is right, the so-called baby-busters (the babies born in 1965 and after) are beginning to arrive in corporate America, recasting the rules in line with their demands. It's a breed that shuns workaholism for the traditional lures—money, title, security, and ladder climbing. Yet these busters indeed covet job satisfaction, but not at personal sacrifice for the sake of the corporation that feeds them. Family, lifestyle, and the pursuit of new experiences are as important as work. As a generation, however, they don't seem to have a sense of themselves, neither social activists nor political gadflies. The big question: What kind of leadership will they respond to?

The answer depends on the competition and how the business environment shapes up. And the changes in society itself: Americans born through the mid-1960s were the last reared in homes where moms reigned and the dads dominated the workplace. The 1970s and 1980s produced the "latchkey" children with both parents holding down jobs. In any case, it is futile to search for a single type of leader. After all, leadership doesn't come in a size forty suit or size eight dress. There are a range of styles, and identifying a particular one depends on the context of the enterprise and, of course, the makeup of a particular individual.

But hold it a moment. Before we can expect a fresh crop of business leaders to guide us into the next century, we're going to have to return to the basics, to the practical necessity of creating wealth. We need more than conservators and paper shufflers. We need a bunch of willing risk takers who want to see around corners, the kinds of individuals who not only know it's okay to draw outside of the lines but who draw without lines. They should lead business in a way similar to how, say, a Michael Jordan plays basketball. "He reinvents the sport every time he rises in the air," observed one sportswriter. "He plays the game without cliché."

You may, if you want, call me an eternal optimist, mellowed by the classroom experience of shaping the minds of the next generation of business leaders. But in my time I've also been called a hard-as-nails businessman with an instinct for the jugular. In truth, I am a blend of the academician and the practitioner, aged with a dash of cynicism and a pinch of vision. It's a mixture that works fresh alchemy on old elements. Already, we are beginning to see the comeback of a new kind of leader who is less greedy and more sensitive, with humility and a social conscience. But I warn you, don't search for leadership as a tourist; it's not a stopover for the curious before moving on. It's a long-term proposition. Be prepared to settle in. Remember, *to become a leader doesn't require exceptional personal intelligence but, rather, exceptional personal commitment.*

PART I

The Tapestry of Leadership: Building the Warp

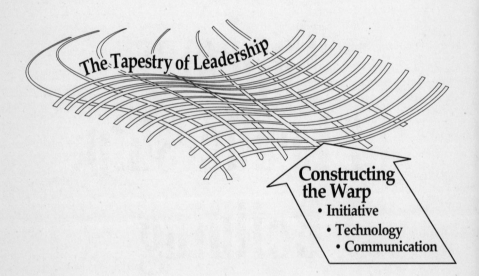

The Tapestry of Leadership

**Constructing
the Warp**
• Initiative
• Technology
• Communication

A useful way to see one's personal development from an apprentice to a craftsperson of leadership is to think about the process and, one hopes, realize that leadership is a lifetime endeavor that develops incrementally like a stunning woven tapestry. To better understand the process, let's turn, for the moment, to weaving as a metaphor. Why weaving? Weaving itself, according to Ella Dobbs, is an educative process, producing varied expression on the part of weavers. "Some differences will be incremental or accidental," Dobbs wrote in *The First Steps in Weaving,* "but they will stimulate real thinking, cause satisfaction or dissatisfaction, and lead to new choices. Through these choices original ideas are born."

The weaver uses warp threads—the lengthwise strands first set up on the loom—and weft threads, the crosswise intersecting strands. Historically, warp and weft had social and symbolic meaning in many cultures. In China, where the word for *warp* also means "king," the warp attached to the loom represents the immutable forces of the world, and the weft, as it moves back and forth between the warp threads, stands for the transient affairs of humans. In Africa, almost all of the weavers are men; in Nepal, mostly women.

11

In India, the weft strands relate to the stages of life, whereas the warp threads are the external factors that shape a person. The warp threads of the fabric symbolize the male persona and the weft, the female.

Now let us gather all the strands—those attributes we learn, those we're endowed with, and those we gain from introspection—on the loom on which we created the tapestry of leadership.

Because the combination of warp and weft leadership threads produces a unique pattern for each individual, the elements of human character never appear in any two of us in the same combination. *Everyone's path to leadership learning is different, and each person's style of leadership is unique.*

Leaders weave their own distinctive fabric, starting with the warp threads of personality that are acquired throughout life. The source of warp threads—the vertical strands—are made up of skills and attributes acquired genetically, environmentally, and socially as well as through schooling.

Among the warp threads of leadership are gender, race, intelligence, physical stature, energy level, social skills, parental influence, ethics and integrity, intimacy, identity, self-esteem, motivation, interpersonal skills, communication skills, reading skills, writing skills, math skills, complex reasoning skills, industry knowledge, market knowledge, and competitive knowledge.

1

The New Realities Require New Leadership

Nothing endures but change.
—HERACLITUS

*E*arly in the twentieth century, science began to transform people's vision of reality. Marie Curie discovered radioactivity and X rays become a popular curiosity. Albert Einstein created new concepts about space and time, matter and energy. Sigmund Freud probed the unconscious mind as a source of healing. The Europeans were fascinated with foreign cultures from African tribal life to cowboys and Indians. In France—where the Eiffel Tower as a spectacular symbol of progress loomed over Paris—the artists of the day were caught up in the vanguard world of change; change in human nature and the nature of society. New structures and machines titillated the senses to height and speed, while science—the metaphor for change—had literally penetrated the body and mind.

The world would never be seen or felt the same way again for those who lived in it. It was being transformed before everyone's eyes, including those of the artists. Many of those artists like Pablo Picasso and Georges Braque lived in the Montmartre section of Paris at the time, struggling to create a new reality through their paintings. The Spaniard Picasso called the Frenchman Braque "Wilbur" and

13

Braque called Picasso "Orville" in reference to their heroes, the airplane-inventing Wright brothers. The two artists would also soar in reputation on a new—and radical—artistic vision that came to be known as Cubism, one of the most important movements in twentieth-century art.

What has this to do with the origins of leadership? In a word, change. In inventing Cubism, Picasso and Braque had shocked the art world with their startling use of lively geometric forms applied to their subjects. In doing so, they had broken with the past. But what got them to break away in the spirit of inventiveness? They were affected by the dramatic changes in their context: The introduction of the automobile, the invention of the airplane, the focus on speed. You could see inside a person's body with X rays and probe the dark wells of their psyche. The world was no longer the way they had perceived it before, the way everyone saw it. Their definition of reality had been transformed. Picasso and Braque asked, How then should we in this world paint life? And Cubism was born as their new view of reality.

Enter the 1990s. So much is happening in today's world that essentially calls on us to see things differently, just as Picasso and Braque had recognized in the early part of the century. Rarely has a decade opened to such rapid change and renewed vigor in politics, technology, communications, and business. Look around you. The experts call it a revolution in an age of boundless mobility. John Welch, the chief executive officer (CEO) of General Electric, makes no bones about it. The heroes and winners in the 1990s, he says, will be entire companies whose cultures relish change instead of fearing it. Listen to author Burt Nanus describe it: "Everywhere around us are accelerating change and uncertainty, global complexity and ambiguity, turbocharged organizational tempos, and in stability that comes from perpetual restructuring at the most fundamental level. Nothing is permanent; all is in flux. These are the realities with which the new age of leadership must deal."

Vanguard of Change

Again we are at the vanguard of change—quick change—that calls for new vision and new leadership. Power indeed has shifted and there now are independent Baltic states and a united Germany, unimaginable a few years ago. The breakup of the Soviet Union shattered the myth that capitalism would forever remain isolated and opened the possibility that perhaps it could become the dominant system of organizing people's economic activities. And it was a strident lesson in the dynamics of leadership as well: Throughout its history the Soviet Union was haunted by the demons of leadership— overmanaging and underleading.

While Eastern Europe struggles to realign itself into a pre– World War II map, Western Europe is busy changing itself economically for the twenty-first century. By 1993, Napoleon's fantasy of a united states of Europe may at last begin to take shape when twelve nations become one market of 320 million as the "hidden hand" reaches across European borders. We are told that goods, services, labor, and capital will move freely. Call it "EC92" or "harmonization" or "Fortress Europe" or the "New Europe," by any name it's a monumental deregulatory movement with a single aim: to counter the industrial might of the United States and Japan.

Thus the notion of twelve countries forged into one barrier-free market has endless possibilities, with all the grandeur of an economic melodrama. Historic battlefields have been replaced by boardrooms in England, France, Germany, Italy, and Spain. The single European market will have a combined gross domestic product comparable with that of the United States and twice Japan's. No wonder General Electric chairman Jack Welch told shareholders not long ago that "the nineties will be a white-knuckle decade for global business . . . fast . . . exhilarating."

From London to Madrid companies are jockeying for position as they consider the new business realities that take advantage of the elimination of border controls and a common currency needed to lubricate the new economic machine. Some companies are merging, others are paring down to run more competitively. Still others are seeking joint ventures. Most companies have concluded that they can no longer dominate domestically, hence they are repositioning themselves around the world. Indeed, corporate alliances— like pre–World War II treaties—are beginning to reshape the traditional European business landscape. For instance, Germany's Siemens teamed with Britain's giant General Electric Company to acquire Plessey Company. This match brought together two key and critical industries that will play a highly significant role in tomorrow's Europe: telecommunications and defense. Like a Napoleonic offensive, the merger was swift, decisive, and unexpected.

The reason for swifter consolidation is obvious. The failure to achieve a common market under the original Treaty of Rome in 1957 cost Europeans a fortune in lost opportunity and brought the word *Eurosclerosis* to our dictionaries. It is fear of being labeled terminally uncompetitive that is pushing Europe toward harmonization, toward the creation of an area without frontiers. The fear is also guiding Fortress Europe toward a protectionist bent. After all, Europe isn't building a single market to turn it over to hungry foreigners any more than General Motors, Ford, and Chrysler are prepared to turn over their domestic market to the Japanese automakers.

Then again, everyone may not have an appetite for the European Community. Several years ago a Booz-Allen Hamilton survey of planning executives among major U.S. corporations with business interests in Europe revealed that many companies were ill-prepared for the new alignment of market forces. Less than one-third of U.S. firms had formal strategic plans for Europe 1992, according to the survey. And fewer than half the firms had even read the European Community Commission's white paper on 1992. This was surprising, because 103 of the *Fortune* 500 companies surveyed have significant European operations. Their European counterparts, the Booz-Allen survey concluded, were further along in the process of mobilizing the opportunities and responding to the threats associated with the establishment of a single European Community market.

Not all of corporate America is dawdling. Ford, for example, has moved into Italy aggressively; will give its key European model, Escort, a face lift by 1993—two years earlier than planned—and is spending $2.5 billion on a joint venture to build minivans in Portugal with Germany's Volkswagen. And General Electric (GE) plans to build a new $1.7 billion plant in Spain. GE is among those U.S. companies that have a grasp on what it will take to compete in borderless markets. Its answer: a "boundaryless" company. To move toward what General Electric's Welch calls a "winning culture," GE is breaking down barriers between functions like engineering and marketing and between employees. The lines of communication between hourly personnel, salaried staff, and management are opening up. Like Economic Europe, geographic barriers are vanishing, too. The GE workers in, say, Delhi and Seoul must be as motivated and informed as they are in Louisville and Schenectady. To get the kind of reflexes and speed GE says it needs, its managers must learn to do two things: simplify and delegate. Explains Welch, "A company can't distribute self-confidence, but it can foster it by removing layers and giving people a chance to win. We have to undo a hundred-year-old concept and convince our managers that their role is not to control people and stay 'on top' of things, but rather to guide, energize and excite."

A. T. Kearney's CEO Fred Steingraber sees the companies of tomorrow as "pan-global" concerns, whereas *Business Week* calls them "stateless" corporations. By whatever name, the pan-global, stateless, or boundaryless company is not tied to any single home country. Its shareholders reside in every part of the world. Likewise, its executives along with its sourcing and manufacturing come from everywhere, too. And between 30 and 50 percent of its revenues will come from outside the home market. The alliances already foretell of the trend. Steingraber uses the automotive industry to illustrate: Chrysler owns 11 percent of Mitsubishi and, through Mitsubishi, a share of Hyundai. Ford—with 33 percent of its sales outside U.S. borders—owns 25 percent of Mazda and Jaguar. Mazda makes cars for Ford and Ford makes trucks for Mazda, and each owns a piece of Kia Motors in Korea, which produces the Ford Festiva. Ford and

Volkswagen have a joint venture in Latin America that's exporting cars back to the United States. General Motors owns Sweden's Saab, 42 percent of Japan's Isuzu, and 50 percent of Korea's Daewoo Motors while at the same time teaming with Toyota to make cars under both labels in the United States and Australia. It's only the beginning.

In 1959, a pair of critical landmark reports by the Carnegie and Ford foundations incited a revolution in business education, which had been characterized as weak and ineffective. As a result, a river of grant money began to flow—some $35 million between 1954 and 1965—nourishing the MBA renaissance and teaching of management. "That initiative was probably the single most important element in a pervasive reorientation of American business education," observes John E. Jeuck, professor emeritus at the University of Chicago Graduate School of Business Administration. As admission standards rose, professors began more rigorous research, some having an impact on business itself. And the popularity of business schools soared.

It has taken our nation's business schools a generation to realize that there's more to success than economics, finance, statistics, marketing, and accounting. Today's MBAs have to be ready to cope with rapid change: new economic realities, dramatic global shifts in political forces, and changing ethical and regulatory concerns. They have to be informed and conditioned for stiffer competition. As B-schools have been busy trying to fill the pipeline with promising talent, they have become the boot camps of manager training. At least their 1987 recruitment catalogs would have had you believe it. Here's a sampling:

> *University of Chicago:* "The MBA curriculum is designed to prepare students for significant careers in management."
>
> *Stanford University:* "The primary purpose of the Stanford Master of Business Administration is to provide men and women with the expertise they need to become effective, professional, high-level general managers."

Columbia University: "We are in an excellent position to prepare the manager of the future with the skills and perspective necessary for success."

Harvard University: "The primary mission of the Harvard MBA program is to prepare its students to assume general management responsibilities."

Dartmouth College: "The principal goal of Tuck's MBA program is to produce graduates who have the motivation, ability, and education to perform effectively as high level general managers."

"These statements run together as though they had been composed by the same computer," comments University of Chicago's Jeuck, who also has taught at the business schools of Harvard, Stanford, Dartmouth, and the University of North Carolina. "Moreover, the catalogs make ubiquitous claims to 'pioneering,' 'innovative,' 'path-breaking' programs packaged in hyperbole that puts the much maligned Madison Avenue huckster to shame." By the 1990s many of the business schools reassessed their programs, with an emphasis on leadership, replacing the term *manager*. For instance, in the spring of 1991 the University of Chicago restated the basic mission of its MBA program: "The objective of the MBA program is to prepare students for positions of business leadership on a foundation of academic excellence." Nevertheless, today's business schools are calibrated to turn out managers. Thousands of them. Seventy thousand—a quarter of all the master's degrees awarded—in 1991. Given these impressive numbers, the question asked by business educators themselves remains: Are students receiving the right education? But an even more important question that industry is asking is: Where are the leaders? During the 1970s and 1980s, business favored strong management in response to such factors as deregulation, high interest rates, leveraged balance sheets, and privatization via leveraged buyouts. Government policy and competition put the premium on controlling issues and meeting cash-flow requirements—narrowing management's focus on short-term results.

Critics of management education complain that the B-schools are producing number-crunching bottom liners that are more akin to, as Stanford University management professor H. J. Leavitt puts it, "the professional mercenary soldier—ready and willing to fight any war and to do so coolly and systematically, but without ever asking the tough pathfinding questions: Is this war worth fighting? Is this the right war? Is the cause just? Do I believe in it?" Henry Mintzberg of McGill University is more blunt in his assessment: "Our management schools have done an admirable job of training the organization's specialists—management scientists, marketing researchers, accountants, and organizational development specialists. But for the most part, they have not trained managers."

Industry is giving us the same message. I hear the constant complaint from recruiters: Today's business school graduates lack dimension, creativity, people skills, foreign language proficiency, and the ability to speak and write with clarity and conciseness—things far removed from the bottom line. Scott Whitlock, executive vice president of Honda of America Manufacturing, Inc., recalls a few years ago when the welding department manager was promoted to assistant plant manager: "He succeeded me in our auto plant in Maryville. The first thing he did after the promotion was to let me know he was taking off for three days to take a course in public speaking. He instinctively knew what he had to do. He doesn't enjoy giving speeches either. But he knew he had to master the skill and become good at it."

To add new dimensions to their curricula, some schools are featuring studies in conceptual and interpersonal skills that are considered crucial in today's dynamic business environment. In the fall of 1989, for instance, the University of Chicago kicked into gear its Leadership Education and Development (LEAD) program aimed at imbuing MBA candidates with interpersonal skills by promoting a stronger sense of community and self-awareness. It is a touchy-feely approach—known in academic lingo by the more formal term of *interpersonal dynamics*—using eclectic methods. Students learn to dissect leadership styles as seen in movies like *Patton, Gandhi,* and *Wall Street.* They spend two days *attending* a presentation and session on nonverbal communication led by members of Chicago's famous Second City, a comedy troupe that specializes in improvisation. LEAD teaches the students the art of communication and how to work in teams, increasingly the practice in today's workplace. Thus some business schools are tilting toward a hands-on clinical approach: Cornell students have summer internships with companies in nine countries on three continents. The New Product Lab course at the University of Chicago places some fifty students a year in such companies as Motorola, Zenith, and Oscar Mayer to experience the process and problems of conceptualizing new products. Carnegie-Mellon has its Operations Management Projects; Harvard, its Creative Marketing Strategy, which provide real-world experience.

But even such programs are not enough. Consequently, more companies are retraining by running their own in-house schools rather than shipping their managers off to a campus. That means corporations themselves are in hot competition with the business schools. Why pay a premium for an MBA when a company can hire bright students with engineering degrees or liberal arts degrees and then teach them business or a specialty?

What, then, do companies want from business schools? Those schools that ask—and many of the best ones are doing so—increasingly hear the same answer. Firms want short courses tailored to each firm's specific needs and taught to its own senior executives by the school's star teachers. The soaring demand for closed, tailored courses is splitting business schools, according to some observers. Based on its recruiting efforts, consultant McKinsey & Company also believes there is more to life than MBAs. In 1990 McKinsey hired 226 consultants overseas, most of them foreign nationals without MBAs, compared with 180 in the United States.

With demand for MBAs wavering, a growing number of business schools in both the United States and Europe are pushing executive education in the form of short courses geared for up-and-comers. In 1992 America's twenty biggest business schools active in executive education collectively offered some forty thousand places. Aimed at senior managers in their mid-thirties to early fifties, such courses can last from two days to three months and are being tailored to fit the schedule of the businessperson, similar to the way the cruise ship industry offers a cruise for virtually every taste, pocketbook, and the time one can afford to spend. At Dartmouth, for example, there is a week-long program for minority entrepreneurs at a cost of $2,400. Harvard's Advanced Management Program for senior managers runs eleven weeks for $29,000 and Wharton's International Forum consists of twelve days of seminars on three continents for $33,000.

The European business schools have latched on to continuing education as key profit centers. Such courses at France's INSEAD accounted for some $25 million, or 53 percent of its total income in 1991. At London Business School the proportion is 45 percent. And American schools such as Wharton and Carnegie-Mellon have seen revenues from their executive education programs triple in recent years. The executive education market is far from being saturated. And although some executives see value in the broadening experience, others say case studies are irrelevant or too theoretical, or courses are too long or too expensive when the loss of the executive's time is factored in. Yet, in our survey, no one argued against continuing education, although some like Quaker Oats Chairman and CEO William Smithburg preferred a less formal approach because there are things that cannot be taught in a classroom. He reflected on his experience:

> Frankly, I went to a lot of seminars when I was younger because I thought it was part of my job. But I'd generally find them boring and I wasn't getting anything out of it. Whether it was a formal seminar or just dialogue with others, if I didn't like it, I'd quit. I wouldn't stick it out for three days just because I was supposed to. I turned, instead, to self-education. For instance, when I became president and chief operating officer, I had very little background in how to finance an acquisition. But I had friends who were invest-

ment bankers whom I called upon for advice and information. When I became president of the Breakfast Division in 1971, I had to do some self-educating to learn new things about marketing. You've got to force yourself into situations that aren't always comfortable. It's human nature to go back to the womb, to go back to what is comfortable. Sometimes I want to say to our younger managers: "Would someone come up with a great idea and fail."

The approach to integrate management theory and training in the 1990s calls for a return to creating value, instead of manipulating value through leveraged buyouts (LBOs) and junk bonds. Business schools are sensitive to the change. But are employers? I believe they are, despite the fact that corporations cast mixed signals in the job market. While recruiters still search campuses for accountants and marketing mavens who can land in those positions running all out, the CEOs—the leaders—talk about the need for visionaries who can understand their business and its relevancy in a dynamic world.

The CEOs of the future will begin to look more like globe-trotting secretaries of state as they scour the world in search of potential investors, venture partners, and untapped foreign markets. Today, the revenues of global conglomerates are greater than the gross national products of many small countries. These challenges will require a creative balance of leadership strategies and management controls. Our leaders must be as concerned about the external global issues today as they are about the internal dynamics of our own enterprises and our nation's economic future.

As the world economy shifts toward democracy and capitalism, the definition of capitalism may have to change in what former Citicorp chairman Walter Wriston calls the "Age of Restructuring." Industrial giants such as General Motors, IBM, and Xerox won't be the companies they were a decade ago as they drastically slash workforces and shed layers of middle managers. Consequently, no longer will the transition from apprentice to general manager take as long. Why? Because companies will be less hierarchical and more fragmented into smaller units where managers make their own decisions. Moreover, the capitalism we have known in the past is not the capitalism—the use of capital—that the twenty-first century will call for. Rather, the capitalism best suited for the United States is the capitalism of creativity—the currency of the future—that translates into talent. "Talent is the number one commodity in short supply," says Wriston. "You can't have enough good people in your organization. Because the terrible truth is that good people can make bad systems work. And bad people can ruin even the best system."

Short Run Versus Long Run

On the home front, change has been equally dramatic. The 1980s were a time, as *Newsweek* put it, "when avarice got respectable, poverty expanded and wealth became a kind of state religion." In 1990, Drexel Burnham Lambert Group—the 152-year-old titan with fifty-three thousand employees and $3.6 billion in assets—vanished almost overnight in the biggest failure in Wall Street history. Drexel's demise brought an end to the era of junk bonds, those debt instruments that paid high interest rates because of the relative shakiness of the investments they funded. The notorious junk bonds helped turn the financial world topsy-turvy and set the tone for the money lust that gripped America in the 1980s.

The focus was short term: How can we make money now? There is enormous pressure on CEOs of publicly held companies to increase quarterly earnings. *Unfortunately, this one-cent-a-share mentality filters down the organization to managers who set their sights on short-term earnings rather than long-term gains.* The result is that many a chief executive becomes a St. George slaying the maiden instead of the dragon. Part of the problem lies with the shareholder. Thirty years ago when widows in St. Louis and dentists in Omaha locked their stock certificates in safety deposit boxes to collect dividends and dust, the short-term drive by CEOs for current earnings was not as intense. Today, one in five Americans—more than fifty-one million people—own stock compared with one in seven a decade ago. But at least half of them own shares through mutual or pension funds. In fact, professional investors—the fund managers—control more than 60 percent of common stock and 25 percent of all corporate shares traded. Every move in the market they make is scrutinized like some laboratory specimen by companies, financial publications, and analysts. In a given quarter, if their investments, say, increase 3 percent and the *Standard and Poor's 500* stock index increases 7 percents, their clients will give them negative reviews. Thus their objective is to record quarterly increases that outperform at least one standard market measurement.

Their income depends on it. In this age of volatile markets institutional investors tend to be quick-draw artists who play the market with hair-trigger nervousness. "To say that an institution that buys and sells stocks every few weeks is a stockholder," says Martin Meyers, "is akin to calling a fellow who specializes in one-night stands a romantic."

Because investors often have a different agenda than employees and managers who work for a company, tension builds. An individual manager looking for a long-term commitment might be asked to relocate, to move his or her family across the country at the company's request. That manager has a vested interest in the company's future; he or she wants to be sure that it will grow and prosper. Similarly, the corporation itself needs time to accomplish its objectives: two years in which the manager can learn the company's business and culture and another three years to launch important programs. Here's where management's needs and investor demand clash. The institutional investor might give a company more than a quarter, but not much more than two years. If the company fails to produce projected earnings, the fund manager will turn a cold shoulder on the growth prospects.

Not all institutional investors, however, are quarterly myopic. Some willing to stick with companies that perform below quarterly expectations as long as the light at the end of the tunnel isn't from an approaching train. In this regard the Japanese have a decisive edge. Philosophically they are long-term players. For instance, the big Japanese banks, which are among the biggest holders of common shares in Japanese companies, are interested in the creation of wealth on a long-term basis rather than in short-term profits. The difference in that attitude has a remarkable impact on both domestic and global strategy and on the environment in which leaders are called on to perform.

So ingrained is the short-term in the American corporate psyche that companies are reticent to talk about the future. Naturally they don't want to tip off competitors, but shareholders—and indeed employees—deserve an inkling of where a company intends to go. After all, that is what the stock market deals with—future events, not the present. The best way I can think of for a company to show its promise is through a mission statement. A decade ago, only 30 percent of the American companies had such written statements. And some of those were locked in a secretary's desk drawer or relegated to the corporate archives, only to be hauled out on founding day anniversaries. There will be more on mission statements in a subsequent chapter, but suffice it to say that they should be used in stockholder reports and securities analysts meetings as a valued communications tool. By conceptualizing the corporate mission, investors, especially anxious ones, are getting far more than words. They're getting a vision of the future, which during a poor quarter could buy management time.

The huge leveraged deals of the 1980s didn't do much to quell investor angst. By the 1990s these megacorporations required financial sustenance in great draining gulps. Selling off valuable corporate assets may have helped to pay down the overwhelming debt, but it left few options for long-range planning. W. Edwards Deming, the American who introduced quality control to the Japanese but was ignored by American industry, says,

> We all have motivation. And we all have self-esteem. And we all have dignity. And we all have eagerness to learn. But the system in the United States crushes it out of us. People don't have an aim. They don't have a long-term objective because they are spending their time managing and not

thinking about the future. We should be preparing for the future. Management needs to be an expert in one thing and support all the other parts of the enterprise.

Deming's voice is one of a small, but vocal, group of critics who believe big executive paychecks and incentive schemes destroy teamwork at many of America's big companies, setting worker against worker, manager against manager. "The kind of people who make good leaders are not obsessed with money," insists Harvard Business School professor John Kotter. The new paragon is an executive who can envision a future for the company and inspire his or her colleagues to join in building that future.

Many of the intangible losses during the 1980s couldn't be measured in traditional terms. Not only was business highly leveraged but so was our entire culture. Only the wealthiest 20 percent of Americans significantly increased their real income during the Reagan era, and the poor slipped further behind. After adjustment for inflation, the real average hourly pay for U.S. workers went from $8.55 in 1973 to $7.54 in 1992.

Greed seems to have gone out of style with the spectacular failures of such 1980s heroes as Michael Milken and Donald Trump, who discredited the era's role models. Some say the new mind-set actually began with the stock market crash of 1987, which gave people second thoughts about the Roaring Eighties. A recession that began in 1990 forced people to cut back on borrowing and spending and to put away the plastic. Then the Gulf War came along, a life-and-death reality that seemed to make the pursuit of glitz and status even more trivial. America pulled together during this period and the can-do spirit caught on. Then, some Americans gave up Gucci for Sears, traded their Jaguars for jeeps, switched from veal Orloff to soy burgers, and shelved their wingtips for ducks. Power ties, power lunches, and power walks were passé. The change in sentiment was highlighted in the popular press in such magazines as *Time*, which featured an April 1991 cover story titled "The Simple Life Rejecting the Rat Race, Americans Get Back to Basics."

But no one can really reject the world's problems unless they cloister themselves in a monastery somewhere. The homeless, the search for an AIDS cure, the savings and loan crisis, global debt, the shambles of American cities, an education system that begs for reform, and environmental issues are among the complex social issues. These are times when people look to their leaders for inspiration. In *Managing as a Performing Art,* Peter Vail says, "All true leadership is indeed spiritual leadership. . . . Leadership is concerned with bringing out the best in people. As such, one's best is tied intimately to one's deepest sense of oneself, to one's spirit." The spiritual aspect of leadership even has crept into the nation's boardrooms. "The language of the pulpit has become the currency of the executive suite," observed *Fortune.* Business thinking in evangelical terms? Herman Miller, CEO of Max DePree, calls it a "covenant" rather than a contract between company and employee as the basis for management framework. Going one step farther, James Autry, president of Meredith Corporation's magazine group, believes that "good management is largely a matter of love . . . a calling . . . a sacred trust." And as Mikhail Gorbachev struggled with the economic and political upheavals in his country at a time when freedom became a global obsession he mused, "The Soviet Union is in a spiritual decline. . . . We were one of the last to realize that in the age of information science, the most valuable asset is knowledge—the breadth of mental outlook and creative imagination."

Over the years, the Soviet leadership allowed its imagination to become rusty. It happens to most governments—and businesses—at one time or another. Leadership begins to decline when an individual becomes parochial or complacent. A leader does not fear change, but rather embraces it and creates it. New leadership challenges will require a creative balance of strategies and technologies beyond mere words. There are too many politicians lip-synching to the words of special interests in the world's capitals. On his visit to the United States, Poland's president Lech Walesa told Congress that there is a declining world market for words. The only thing the world believes, he emphasized, "is behavior, because we all see it instantaneously." Czechoslovakia's Václav Havel, too, personifies this new leadership style. For Havel, a man who deals in words as a playwright, strong political leaders are far more than dynamic orators. As he explained: "When Thomas Jefferson wrote that governments are instituted among men deriving their just powers from the consent of the governed, it was a simple and important act of the human spirit. What gave meaning to that act, however, was the fact that the author backed it up with his life, it was his deed as well."

There is a need today for leaders with a creative spirit and the power to communicate. It became obvious when Czechoslovakians elected Václav Havel, a playwright, to lead them and Lithuanians chose Vytautis Landsbergis, a music teacher. And in 1981, Americans picked Ronald Reagan, the aging actor who could finesse a speech like a script. Historians have since rated Reagan as "below average," along with five other presidential mediocrities that include John Tyler, Zachary Taylor, Millard Fillmore, Franklin Pierce, and Calvin Coolidge. Yet the scholars all agreed that Reagan had a rare knack for getting people to follow him wherever he wanted to go. Although few professors liked where he went, chalk up his ability to attract followers to solid communication skills.

If the 1990s reflect anything at this point, it is change. New realities appear like old trolley tracks that bleed through the asphalt of auto-worn streets. We are reminded of the past and at the same time the present. We see democracy replacing socialism. We see corruption in the form of a black market as the only free market that has existed in the Soviet Union for years. We see that capitalism works because it produces economic success. *We see that leadership can make a difference. We see intellectual power rising in the modern corporation. We see a new kind of capitalism in the making, the capitalism of creativity. In the grammar of leadership, ideas are verbs.*

Incubator of Creativity

America has always been the incubator of creativity because of a diversity strengthened by waves of immigrants. They bring a new vitality to our shores. People came here because they could focus on new opportunity. In making the journey they took risks by separating themselves from their environments that seemed to encumber them. Europe had all the structure and history that pinned people down. In most Asian cultures conformity came first, before individual growth. Although there was bitter disappointment for many immigrants, once they got past the Statue of Liberty, when they found that the roads in America weren't paved with gold, they eventually discovered something more important: a society in which creativity leapt the boundaries of class.

There is perhaps an even more important characteristic in America's ethos that both natives and immigrants learn early: The United States is a country where failure is not a scarlet letter. Steve Lazarus, the CEO of Arch Development Corporation, Argonne National Laboratory's scientific dream machine that uses venture capital to market Argonne's inventions, explains:

> If you fail in the U.S. and come away from the experience with your reputation intact, there will be people willing to let you try again. That's not true in Europe or Japan. It is a fascinating cultural difference that other countries have no respect for failure. In fact it would be a desperately foolish risk for anybody to deliberately put themselves in the way of failure. And that's why you're not likely to have the same kind of venture industry in Europe, and certainly not in Japan, which you have in the United States.

Today the United States is no longer a frontier of unbridled immigration and natural resources. Its vitality as a production machine churning out everything from shoes to steel has long been drained. And for sure it has its problems; a decline in productivity, a decline in capital investment, a decline in savings, a decline in the quality of education, a decline in the pool of qualified workers. But all of these problems can be seen as opportunities. America's basic problem is one of will, not structure. If Americans chose to commit themselves, they could increase productivity or savings. The question remains whether the policymakers have the will to lead. Is the climate suitable to cultivate leaders who seek to serve society, not themselves? It's hard to build fervor where there is abundance. Ordinary people with full stomachs seldom hunger for incentive to change. Business philosopher Robert Greenleaf calls the Walesas and Havels of the world "natural servants" because they are ordinary people who are called to a leadership role through the strength of their beliefs. "Leaders must help people believe that they can be effective," writes John Gardner, "that their goals are possible of accomplishment, that there is a better future that they can move toward through their own efforts."

Not long ago Henry Johnson, former chairman of retail catalog house Spiegel, Inc., shared some of his thoughts on the creative process and change with my students. "Corporate dreams just don't happen," he said. "They evolve over time, shaped by observations and experiences." Even before he joined Spiegel in 1976 he focused on the changes affecting society:

> I noted the progress women were making: I would have to be
> blind to ignore such things as the Equal Rights Amendment,
> the feminist movement, increasing number of women in po-
> sitions of power within government and industry, the growing
> number of women with advanced degrees. There were other
> trends . . . the gas crisis, causing many people to curtail the
> use of cars; the growing consumer demand for quality prod-
> ucts. . . . It struck me that working women would make ex-
> cellent catalog customers. If a catalog were created with that
> specific market in mind . . . it would be enormously success-
> ful. It was a great dream. When I arrived at Spiegel, I found
> an organization where I could translate the dream to strategy.

Johnson's dream turned into what he called "the most beautiful department store in print," lifting sales from $250 million a year to more than $1 billion within five years after he became Spiegel's chief decision maker.

The one thing leaders of every ilk share is commitment. Explains John Gardner, "Your identity is what you have committed yourself to—whether the commitment is to your religion, to an ethical order, to your life work, to loved ones, to the common good, or to coming generations. Today we have to build meaning into our lives, and we build it through our commitment." *So, commitment is part of the leadership identity that recognizes a higher ideal.* The difference between a job and a career demands commitment. A job is what you do every day to get paid. On the other hand, a career is an emotional commitment—made voluntarily—to the future of an enterprise. It is not necessarily a two-way street. By that I mean, you may give your all to a company only to end up with the empty feeling of an unrequited lover. But remember, if you can't open up and commit yourself to the company you believe in, then you forever remain a daily paid worker, a working stiff, in street vernacular. "Commitment requires hard work in the heat of the day," believes Robert Greenleaf. "It requires faithful exertion in behalf of chosen purposes and the enhancement of chosen values. In return it gives meaning to our lives and joint endeavors and lends dignity and continuity to living. Commitments motivate. Values motivate."

Greenleaf may have added one more requirement for the would-be leader: a risk-taking appetite. Not a huge one. Just big enough to make climbing the corporate ladder tasteful. And above all, you've got to like what you're doing, and it is hoped with the zest of a Warren Buffet, the shrewd investment sage and CEO of Hathaway Industries who proclaims: "I love what I do. All I want to do is what I am doing as long as I can. Every day I feel like tap dancing all through the day." Now there's a man who obviously relishes what he does. And few will dispute that he does it superbly.

If, indeed, you are serious about developing your natural talents for leadership, it's time to pause, step back, and do some critical looking at who you are, where you are now, and where you're heading. Not an easy task. That's why I ask my students on the first day of class to write a short paragraph about themselves and the promotion they will receive five years into the future. It gets them out of the present-day mind-set and into doing some gazing at—and thinking about—their futures.

If we are really serious about nurturing leadership in America today, we have to renew our own spirits and begin to renew the soul of our country. There are still plenty of optimists around who believe in the state of American management. One in particular is former Citicorp chairman Walter Wriston, an elder corporate statesman turned business philosopher. "This is the only country in the world that renews itself every day," he says. "The hydraulics of the mind is what is transforming the entire world. Intellectual capital is becoming relatively more important than physical capital."

When I think of Japan—with 120 million people crammed within a landmass the size of New Jersey—I think of human gridlock. Japan, which imports 90 percent of its energy and most everything else, has learned to manage its single most valued natural resource: people. That's why the country has fostered a collective mentality; the Japanese act as a group, their culture demands it. In Japan, it's better to be on a winning team than to shine as an individual hero. Japanese students can't take my class on leadership back to Japan with them because their business culture won't permit individuals to assert themselves in a leadership role. It is a myth to believe that Japan has better business leaders than other nations. True, they have better resources as managers in a business system that grants them support from not only the big and powerful banks but the government as well. But they lack business leaders because Japanese life is focused on consensus, not creativity.

In truth, brilliant leaders are not always brilliant team players. That is why their companies can often fall short of their goals. They can become soloists or too narcissistic, locked inside their own talent. The object of leadership is to empower others to see the goal and concentrate their energy on reaching it. This is demonstrated in sports all the time. Who could forget Bernard Malamud's baseball classic *The Natural*, in which rookie home-run slugger Roy Hobbs with his handmade bat "Wonderboy" empowers his team to climb out of the cellar "like a rusty locomotive pulling out of the roundhouse for the first time in years"? It happens in real life, too. On a so-so basketball team in the 1990–1991 season, Chicago Bulls superstar Michael Jordan inspired his teammates with not only his superb offensive skills, but with his ability to involve everyone by frequently passing the ball. Instinctively, he knew that a pass to someone less strong could make the team stronger. The result: a world championship in 1991 and a repeat championship in 1992.

Why leadership now? Because, I believe, people are ready to make a difference in their lives and in their economic futures. I see it among the corporate boards I serve on. I see it in the classroom, bantering with my students about the job prospects they face on graduation. I see it in the business schools that have vowed to teach so-called soft subjects like leadership as seriously as they do macroeconomics. There is a collective tension out there building among those who appear ready to make a passionate commitment at a time when the 1990s demand strong and decisive business leaders who will manage corporate organizations—with fewer managerial layers —in an emerging business world in which there are no superpowers.

Reflections

Who will weave the tapestry of leadership in the twenty-first century?

The path to leadership is about leveraging most of what you've got into everything you can be in an incredibly rewarding, yet punishing, business environment. There's no need to talk further about the process of why the rules of the game, and in fact the game itself, are changing dramatically. Nor do we have to review the disorientation and lack of direction that have spread throughout the world's business communities. What seems so evident is that we are faced with a leadership vacuum that the present and future business practitioners must fill.

There is an old saw in selling that says, "There is no such thing as a marketing vacuum." The opposite, however, is true when we look at the growing chasm between management and leadership. The very products of leadership—vision and simplicity—are more precious today and will become more so in the future than the styles and elements of managership that dominated the decades of the 1980s.

Later, when I ask you to discard the myths of leadership—

especially the time-worn concept of a "born leader"—I'm inviting you to give yourself a chance to earn the satisfaction associated with leadership as you help others obtain their goals. In effect, I'm asking you not to cheat yourself before you start on the empowering path of self-discovery. Yes, I know *empowering* is one of those buzzwords that sounds as if one person had control over another's fate and by some means could dispense a potion (or a memo in the case of business) to enhance ambition. If empowerment were such a great anodyne then generals wouldn't lose wars and companies that were managed properly wouldn't go out of business. But that, of course, is not the case. In this book the E-word by itself is a non sequitur unless it's used with *self-discovery*. That's the logic of *The Leader Within*—it provides *a means of empowering yourself as you explore your natural, educational, and professional attributes in sizing up your leadership prospects.*

By becoming a part of the leadership pool of talent you become a participant in the unleashing of America's greatest untapped natural resource—creativity—that will allow you to make an important difference inside and outside of the business world.

Other points to consider:

> *Definitions of business reality are changing* because of a united Germany, the breakup of the Soviet Union, the formation of the European Common Market, the increase of pan-global companies, and the restructuring of business.
>
> *Talent is in short supply.*
>
> *The focus will be on creating wealth* for the long term rather than on quarterly earnings.
>
> *Long term will require more of an executive's day-to-day thinking.*
>
> *Your identity is what you commit yourself to* in work as well as in family life.
>
> *Renew yourself as you renew the vitality of America.*

The Roots of Leadership

The quality of a person's life is in direct proportion to their commitment to excellence, regardless of their chosen field of endeavor.

—VINCENT T. LOMBARDI

*B*efore we can explore leadership through the weaving metaphor, first let us consider the myths associated with leadership:

- Leaders are born with special skills.
- Leaders are naturally endowed creative spirits with unique gifts.
- Leadership can't be learned.

Such are the misconceptions. To understand the essence of leadership we begin with the views and experience of Jack Reichert, chief executive officer of the Brunswick Corporation.

Jack Reichert to this day remembers the advice of a friend who took him aside back in 1957 and said, "Come to work for Brunswick. They need a bright, hardworking young guy like you. Who knows, someday you could become president."

Brunswick Corporation? The family-owned-and-run maker of bowling balls and billiards founded by Swiss cabinetmaker John Brunswick in 1845 after he came to America? Become president of Brunswick? Fat chance, believed Reichert. Forget that Reichert's father was a champion bowler. Or that Jack Reichert by the age of fourteen had become an ace pinman himself. Forget even the possibility of becoming a CEO. Besides, in 1957 the twenty-six-year-old Reichert had a pretty good job with General Electric, where he had already spent seven years, and he had his sights set on a GE vice presidency. Despite the odds as he calculated them, however, Reichert took his friend's advice and joined Brunswick.

Reichert recalls, "It was a tiny company when I first started there. You needed to like bowling or you didn't work for Brunswick. Right at the beginning during an interview I was told it would be impossible to be president of the company since no one but descendants of John Brunswick had ever run the company. I thought to myself, 'There has to be a first.' "

By 1971, at age forty, Reichert became the youngest president in Brunswick history. A decade later, in the wake of Brunswick's battle in warding off a hostile takeover bid, Reichert scored an even bigger strike: he was chosen chairman and CEO. In gaining the top post, he became the company's third CEO who wasn't related to the Brunswick family. Almost overnight he changed Brunswick from a highly centralized to a highly decentralized company. Reichert explained the strategy: "There is a fundamental difference between people who create wealth and people who preserve wealth. The role of the corporate staff is to preserve wealth and the role of the divisions is to create wealth. You don't want either entity to get in the way of the other."

After a vigorous program of downsizing, belt-tightening, and excising management layers with the precision of a surgeon, Brunswick ran leaner and meaner. It now focused more of its people in research and development and in manufacturing and fewer in administration. Today the corporate staff of 120 is about half of what it used to be, and sales since Reichert took over climbed from $1 billion to more than $3 billion. Brunswick has 25 percent less people, generating three times the sales volume.

Reichert's journey to the top shows the business traveler how to bypass the dead ends of corporate machismo and avoid the blind alleys of self-pity. His father died when Reichert was twelve years old, and his mother died the day before his sixteenth birthday. Money was scarce, forcing Jack and his brother and sister to scramble for jobs as they looked after one another. One of Reichert's first jobs was as pin boy in a bowling alley. An inkling of leadership came during high school when he was an editor of both the newspaper and yearbook. He didn't attend college until after he returned from the Korean War because he couldn't afford it. The GI Bill gave him the opportunity. In 1957 he graduated night school at the University of Wisconsin Milwaukee campus and began his career as a Brunswick sales trainee.

From that point on, he headed along the CEO track propelled by single-minded commitment and communication skills. "I guess if there was any characteristic that I had at that time it was that I worked very hard and was totally committed to what I was doing. I could also conceptualize ideas easier than others, but I'm not sure that is any particular skill."

Reichert's rise to the top at Brunswick convinced him of at least one thing. "I believe you can mold leaders," he says emphatically, "it is not an innate gene."

Jack Reichert is not alone in his belief. The sobering fact that there is no such animal as a born leader was shared by nearly all of 150 American business leaders exclusively interviewed for my class, Leadership in Business. No chief executive believed he or she was going to be a CEO at the start of their career. Moreover, they collectively felt that leadership can be learned through opening oneself to the possibility of doing important things. That means seeking change in yourself and in your environment.

McDonald's Corporation's CEO Michael Quinlan certainly wasn't born with the silver spoon of leadership dangling from his mouth. Reared on Chicago's West Side in a middle-class neighborhood, Quinlan began working when he was twelve. Just before starting at McDonald's in 1963 as a mailboy, Quinlan was a truck driver for the Coca-Cola Company in a predominantly black area on Chicago's South Side. "It taught me what it was like to be a minority," he says. "It was valuable experience that I still carry around with me today."

Quinlan, who prides himself on being a careful listener, worked for the hamburger chain part-time until he completed his MBA from Loyola University. He then took a full-time position as an assistant buyer and eventually worked in nearly every department. "I was able to gain invaluable experience in many dimensions of McDonald's operations early in my career that would have been very difficult to acquire later on," he recalls. "That coupled with the fact that I grew with the company probably accounted for my quick ascension to where I now am. The company never seemed complex to me because of this."

As to his notion of leadership, he explains:

> I think leaders are made. You have to be smart. You have to be open. And you have to have a pretty good foundation in your home life as you are growing up. My parents didn't have a lot, but somehow they provided for me and allowed me to go to an extremely good private high school. Even as I look back at graduate school in pursuit of my MBA, I can't give you a list of what I got out of it. But it helped the way I think about things and helped me become a student of those individuals I interact with all the time. The learning process never ends. In fact, I've become more of a student than I ever was before because the business environment has undergone constant change.

William D. Smithburg, chairman and CEO of the Quaker Oats Company, learned an important lesson long before he joined the big food marketer in 1966 as a brand manager: to go beyond the traditional parameters of a job. He explains as if he were chanting a management mantra:

> When you go to work for a company they're going to have a job description and the Human Resources people are going to give it to you to read so you can understand it because

that's your job. Then tear it up, because if you limit yourself to that, you've failed. You will never be able to be creative, never be able to be a leader if that's all you do. You have to go beyond that. But you must have someone who can talk to you privately, who can counsel you and encourage you to come up with ideas and listen to them. And if you've learned to be smart, if you understand your business through deep study, and I don't care if you're twenty-five years old or fifty-five years old, when you attend a meeting you've got to feel as if you know more about a product than anyone else in that room. Then you feel that whatever you say comes from the authority of knowledge—not from the authority of a box on some organization chart. I was fortunate to work for people who were receptive, who listened to my ideas. In my early thirties I presented ideas to Quaker's chairman and president. I didn't worry that they could reject them. The best baseball hitter in the world doesn't get a hit every time up. You don't always have to hit home runs. . . . One of my old precepts is "I'm going to make my boss's job easy." I don't want to be constantly in there with a headache for him. He's not there to cure my headaches. I'm there to cure his headaches. He's not there to make my life easy. He's there to give me a challenge because my job is to make his easier, and if I make it hard I don't get anywhere. That was my attitude.

When I became president of the breakfast division in 1971, I had to go out and educate myself over matters such as investment banking. Force myself into things that were not familiar to me. That's another important principle. People have a tendency to go back to the womb, to go back to what's comfortable. As human beings, we constantly tend to retrench rather than go beyond the normal parameters. That's one of the greatest problems I have with the business schools. They are not turning out people who are creative, who are innovative, who understand the proper balance of risk and reward, who understand how to nurture large organizations and how to make contributions to the organization.

Big companies have money, resources, and yet we create people and systems that restrain creativity rather than
enhance it. We had a tough year in 1990 because many of
our people were not taking risks. They were taking what they
perceived to be the least risk of all.

When Smithburg became chairman in 1981, he cast his vision
where most business leaders should: toward the future.

They don't pay me to sit around and worry about quarterly
results. If I don't have division presidents who can make
quarters and financial people who can nurture them along, I
have no business running this company. The first trait of a
good executive is to see the future. All other things follow
from that.

If you don't have a vision of the future—at least five
years out—you are never going to do all the things you have
to do. A marketing department won't give you all those answers. I spent my first couple of years in market research, I
know its strengths and weaknesses. It gives you a snapshot
in time. When we researched Gatorade in Italy and the U.S.,
the response was always negative. People would say, "Who
needs that? We've got water." The market was there, however; but it wasn't researchable. No one knew what an elec-
trolyte was in 1982. Nevertheless, I had the vision for
Gatorade. Because it was physiologically needed. It was part
of a healthy lifestyle trend, part of the rapid growth in sports.
That's what made it succeed.

There is, then, a common element in every leader: a strong
need to prove oneself. But there is far more to leadership than that
single desire. There is self-determination, too. "Only people who
believe in themselves generate believers," observes Harvard University professor Theodore Levitt. What most people lack, however,
is the confidence to give themselves permission to practice leadership development. Such permission has been denied because of the

folklore of leadership that has reverberated through the ages and in one's mind: the notion that leaders are born, not made. There are no such things as leadership genes, at least not yet. Most people are taught to believe they are not leaders. In the past people saw leaders emerge out of a crisis situation. This view became the basis for their belief that leaders were born to the role. However, a more careful analysis shows that ordinary men and women became leaders due to circumstances often well beyond their control. Take, for example, Winston Churchill. Behind those raised pudgy fingers giving the victory sign, the big cigar, and the Victorian lisp was a life of ups, but many, many downs—before World War II thrust him into a crucial role. As a youth, Churchill entered Harrow with the lowest marks in the prep school. He failed three times before he got into Sandhurst, where he ranked 92nd in a class of 102. The first time he ran for Parliament he lost. In 1911 he became First Lord of the Admiralty, and he was dismissed in 1915 over a strategic blunder in World War I. Between 1922 and 1924 he ran for election to Parliament three times—and lost each time. He even managed to lose most of his family's fortune in the crash of 1929. In 1938 he almost failed in business, but was bailed out by a friend. He finally won a seat in Parliament, but in 1939 some of his disgruntled constituents tried to oust him from it. On May 10, 1940—nine months after Hitler invaded Poland to set off World War II—Churchill became prime minister and eventually one of history's greatest wartime leaders. He was sixty-six.

What are we to learn from Churchill's life? Simply, that leadership is not a position. "A person may be appointed to a high position," says Harvard's Levitt, "but never to leadership." Rather, leadership is a role. Forget about the so-called great man theory of leadership embedded in most cultures like a mythic saga. Are the larger-than-life figures, with their indomitable power that shaped history, born leaders? "The truth of this assumption," writes James MacGregor Burns in his classic study called *Leadership*, "as a general proposition has never been demonstrated. Nor has that of the opposite assumption—that history is made by masses of people acting through leaders who are merely agents for the popular or majority will."

However, one need only look into the lives of history's political leaders such as Gandhi, Lenin, and Eleanor Roosevelt to see personalities as diverse as their backgrounds. Yet, they encountered experiences in their early lives that seem to have molded them for their future leadership roles. The great pacifist Mohandas Gandhi, for instance, was reared in a rather seedy home with an authoritarian father who had been married four times, a saintly mother, brothers, sisters, and five uncles and their families. Not surprisingly, the crowded confines enabled Gandhi to learn the power of mutual tolerance. He loved and feared his father, according to psychobiographer Erik Erikson, but his parents allowed him as much freedom as he needed. A college dropout after several months, Gandhi gave no inkling of his future capacity to lead.

By contrast, Vladimir Ilyich Ulyanov, who would become known as Lenin, came from a secure and affluent family. The mother was resourceful, and although the father was devoted, his business took him away from the family for weeks on end. The long absences seemed especially trying for Lenin, who identified with his father. Lenin was slow learning to walk, falling down constantly and crying often. Aggravating the undercurrents of his life was the execution of his older brother for his opposition to the czar. As we shall see in chapter 4, trauma of this magnitude has a profound impact on one's leadership potential.

Alienation played a role in the early life of one of America's most dynamic first ladies, Eleanor Roosevelt. Her childhood years were marked by desertion and loneliness. Eleanor's mother, who had always been cold and aloof, died when Eleanor was eight years old; one of her brothers died a year later. Her father, whom she adored, spent long periods of time away from home. He died when Eleanor was ten. After her father's death she retreated to a dream world in which she was the heroine and her father the hero. Reared in a gloomy house by her grandmother, nurses, and governesses, she grew up with all sorts of fears, from dogs to the dark. During the

White House years, she was virtually deserted by her husband. Yet, she carried on with serenity and compassion as a noble first lady and a champion of the United Nations. "Did she succeed because of or in spite of the unhappiness and insecurity of her early life?" asks Burns. That's impossible to answer.

Obviously none of the world leaders discussed entered life with exceptional genetic endowment. Nor were their future roles as leaders preordained. "Whatever natural endowments we bring to the role of leadership, they can be enhanced," write Warren Bennis and Burt Nanus in *Leaders*. "Nurture is far more important than nature in determining who becomes a successful leader." What the psychobiographies, however, do point out is the fact that the future leaders underwent some form of trauma in their lives. And out of those experiences grew insight and vision along with a will to change things. Although biology may help shape destiny, it does not predetermine it.

Neither is it necessary to master the principles and language of Freud, Skinner, and Maslow to learn leadership. It's more important to master yourself.

Most of the theories floating around ignore what Burns calls possibly the most important force in shaping leaders: learning from living. We learn from other leaders, from followers, from personal victories and defeats, from experiences, and from those unique events in our lives. Each of us processes the learning experience differently, depending on our backgrounds, motivations, and capacities to understand what works and what doesn't. Life becomes a vast maze of rewards and punishments and our responses determine our progress. At times our emotions may be reduced to reactions, like the muscles of a frog that twitch to an electrical jolt. Or we may reach into the dark wells of our own beings to find strength and self-control. Take, for example, two people responding to the same event. The passive person accepts the way things work, shrugs, and says, "That's life." In contrast, another person may feel anger and ask with a clenched fist, "Why?" The latter individual has already begun a process of discovery to find answers through the *Three I's:*

inquiry, information, and introspection. The byproduct becomes personal growth, part of which is the accumulation of experiences you can tap into later on. Think of it this way: If life is going to deal you a bad hand, you'd better draw until you get a better one.

Leadership Motivation

No one, then, starts out to be a leader and paves a way through the wilderness directly to the top. No CEO started out to be the CEO of a company, according to our findings. All were highly motivated with a drive to prove themselves. Formal education was not the crucial factor. Nor were natural gifts. And finally, all were curious; they're self-taught. They seemed to be learning on a daily basis throughout their lives to satisfy a wanderer's lust of seeing for themselves what's on the other side of the mountain. "Successful leaders are those who continue to grow and mature, those who continue to learn every step of the way," insists Robert Malott, CEO of FMC Corporation. "When you stop growing and stop learning, it's over."

A good place to start is with yourself. Everyone has the raw material of leadership within them. But to create a leadership persona is hardly a slam-dunk process. It begins with the given attributes and circumstances in your life.

There's the physical, including your gender, race, size, energy level, and basic intelligence. These endowments are given at birth and nurtured in the family. Naturally good health is important to leadership, because it determines physical capacity to perform at high energy levels, stamina to maintain that performance, and dependability of presence. Sometimes what hasn't been endowed or has even been taken away can be augmented, as we learned in the case of Polish Olympic runner and immigrant Derek Probas: "A couple of years before I got into sports, I was living with my mother in an apartment building. One night she heated up a large pot of water and put it in the bathroom next to the tub. When I finished dinner and went to wash my hands, I tripped over the vat of scalding hot water. I was in the hospital for three months. They wanted to amputate one of my legs. I had to learn how to walk again. I had to grab the walls to support myself. I had to learn to do a lot of things all over again. I was only nine at the time, but I never gave up." Probas went on to win an athletic scholarship to Kent State and to earn a master's degree in international relations from Thunderbird and an MBA from the University of Chicago.

Then there's the emotional side, which includes trust, autonomy, initiative, industry, identity, intimacy, care, and wisdom. These are the traits that give basic strengths such as hope, will, purpose, competence, and fidelity. Here I've drawn on Erik Erikson's scheme in understanding one's self, which is based on eight classic stages of human development: infancy, early childhood, play age, school age, adolescence, young adulthood, adulthood, and old age. In each stage there is a crisis to overcome that leads to a dominant personality trait and the formation of a person's total identity. In the earliest stage, for example, the crisis is one of basic trust versus basic mistrust. If the dilemma is resolved, the basic strength developed is hope.

Why should we really care about coming to terms with our emotions? Because emotionally healthy people usually have the ability to understand and read the feelings of others. And that ability is critical to any leader. While Erikson's life-stage model recognizes the importance of biological and environmental influences on one's personality, it teaches that life is a continual learning process and that skills are accumulated toward leadership development. So for the leader, introspection is an ongoing process, requiring discipline and commitment to improving yourself. Or as Socrates said, "Knowing oneself is the task of a lifetime."

Every leader needs the ability to relate to a broad range of people in both a business and social context. It all begins at home. Harvard psychologist Howard Gardner illustrates: "Much of the social savvy youngsters bring with them to the playground results from how they are treated at home. If you watch kids with little social intelligence trying to enter a game other kids are playing, they jump right in and ask if they can play. They're puzzled when they get rebuffed." However, children with high social intelligence enter the game step by step. At first, they may stand around and watch, then they make comments about the game or those playing it. Finally, they ask if they may join in the next game. These kids have taken the time to notice the relevant social cues, like the expressions on the faces of the others or how they are dressed or the kind of words they use. They also do some quick-minded interpretation of those cues to determine perhaps the two key aspects of dealing with a new set of playmates: Are they friendly? Are they ready to take another kid into the group? Gardner concludes, "Socially aware children will often heighten the rapport they are establishing by moving into the same physical level as other children; for instance, getting on the ground if they are playing jacks."

In today's society, leaders seem to be as uncommon as heroes are because we attribute qualities to them that are larger than life, the kind that ordinary people never have—such as special insights, special knowledge, and special strengths. Don't lock yourself into the cult of the original genius. Yes, Mozart was a prodigy. But he was well trained in music and his father was an accomplished composer and musician. Notwithstanding his genius as depicted in the movie *Amadeus*, Mozart struggled to compose his music. So what harm is there in creating the myth of genius? *New York Times* music critic Donal Henahan tried to answer the question when he wrote:

> The illusion of original genius is, at least in music, our century's curse. The need to be perceived as a wonderworker with no antecedents, which is rooted in the Romantic era's view of Beethoven, once may have served a purpose. But for the last 50 or so years, it has served to block novice composers and delay their maturity. . . . Musical masterpieces do not often, if ever, come out of the egg but are the result of an artist's standing on the shoulders of previous artists. Record-jacket notes to the contrary, Haydn did not "invent" the string quartet, nor did Wagner "invent" music-drama with Tristan.

In other words, exalted bigger-than-life role models can have a negative impact on future generations. They discourage beginners who desperately need models whose growth they can trace as a gauge to their own development. Neither Beethoven nor Mozart composed a classic every time they touched the piano keys—even after they were established as masters.

As leaders emerge out of crisis situations and crucial events, we call them gifted rather than learned. This is nonsense. Leadership is self-expression and creativity coupled with the ability to share these qualities with others. The leader, as Robert Greenleaf sees it, becomes a servant. How much more ordinary can an individual be? Greenleaf's servant as leader is based on a Herman Hesse book called *Journey to the East,* in which a band of traveling men are accompanied by Leo, a servant. While Leo caters to their every whim, he also sustains them with his spirit and song. When Leo disappears, the group falls into disarray and the journey ends. Clearly, they cannot continue without their servant. After years of wandering, Leo is found and taken into the religious order that sponsored the journey. Then reality strikes: Leo, who had been known as a servant, was in fact the titular head of the order, "its guiding spirit, a great and noble leader." Thus the two roles of servant and leader, concludes Greenleaf, can be fused into one. There's another lesson in the Leo parable: that leaders go beyond themselves in showing others how to improve their circumstances.

Robert Galvin, former chairman of Motorola Inc., agrees with Greenleaf's notion that the leader is a follower, too. "The paradox is that a leader needs to perform to the standards and expectations of the organization," says Galvin. "To lead would appear to be always following. But that is a matter of fact; the wisest leader is the wisest follower. But it is also a wise act of leadership to know when not to follow."

No Born Leaders

The message is clear: Be careful as you journey along the road of leadership. Culture kills the incentive to be a leader. The folklore essentially says: You are not going to be a leader unless you're

Alexander the Great. Most of us are conditioned to believe we are not leaders, nor will we ever become leaders. That empty feeling that you aren't naturally endowed or have the capacity to manipulate your way through a set of socialized circumstances discourages a lot of people. Remember this: Intelligence is relative and experts like Harvard psychologist Howard Gardner are constantly discovering new forms of it. In findings published nearly a decade ago, Gardner proposed there are other important kinds of intelligence beyond the abilities for, say, mathematics and language. There is, for example, social intelligence. Gardner explained the concept in a *New York Times* interview: "Your intelligence can be in other people, if you know how to get them to help you. In life, that's the best strategy: mobilize other people. . . . We're finding much of people's effective intelligence is, in a sense, outside the brain."

The leader's mandate, then, is to locate and clarify a common identity. No corporation can exist as an entity without common references such as a mission statement, goals, and a leadership vision the key managers buy into. Most important, it's up to the leader to allay the fear of change that so often undercuts a company's progress. That requires more than coming up with brave new words in the form of such platitudes as "breaking the rules" or "figuring out how to compete." In essence, it requires change. From the top down. But as with many big companies, change can be a slow and painful process. "Some executives underestimate the time and effort it takes to drive change through a large organization," Keith Hammonds wrote in *Business Week* in 1991. "Some don't, and that's why they opt for quick, painless fixes."

Listen to one of history's early masters of change describe the process: "It must be considered that there is nothing more difficult to carry out, nor more dangerous to handle, than to initiate a new order of things." Although it may sound like the wisdom of a McKinsey consultant, it's straight from the lips of a no less princely adviser than Machiavelli. No one ever said change wasn't taxing, wrenching and risky.

"Change lies at the heart of what we expect our leaders to

produce," Hammonds observes. "But the creation of new values, of different ways of thinking and acting, is the most difficult pursuit any leader can undertake."

The Boiled Frog

More often than not, management is slow to recognize the need to change. Lulled by creeping profits and dulled by the same tired strategy, problems aren't discovered until it's too late. The phenomenon has been described many ways. But none hits home as well as the clichéd boiled frog story. A pot of water is placed on the stove at room temperature into which a live frog is placed. The frog will swim around. If you raise the temperature of the water 1 degree every thirty minutes, the frog will continue to stay in the water and swim around until it is boiled. Why? Because the frog cannot sense the fact that the environment is changing around it. If, on the other hand, you take another frog and first heat the water to 180 degrees, then drop the frog in the water, it will jump out immediately before you can snap your fingers. Most American businessmen are boiled frogs. They are in the water. The temperature of the water is changing. They can't feel it. They just keep swimming around. They can't respond to change. This metaphor demonstrates what University of Michigan professor Noel Tichy calls the "just noticeable difference threshold." Managements respond in a similar manner because their threshold of awareness is set too high. During successful years, management consultant Richard Pascale points out, "managers perfect the formula that made their achievement possible. If firms begin to lose momentum, efforts are made to reinvigorate the slackening pace—usually based on what has worked in the past . . . in most instances, these have little lasting impact." Pascale calls it "managerial mind-set." When things go wrong, management will often retreat by going back to basics: trying to do what it was that made the company successful. What is seldom taken into account, however, is the fact that the environment is changing around managers, and just following the same strategy with more intensity leads to the self-destruction of a frog in slowly heated water.

No one denies that change takes time, but it requires a well-articulated vision further afield than simply the desire for increased profits. I am talking about the kind of leaders who do something about the boiling pot so the company doesn't end up as boiled frog. The frog metaphor reminds me of a story that George H. Conrades, senior vice president of IBM Corporation, tells about two elk hunters who were flown into a remote region of Alaska.

They had bagged four elk, but when the bush plane returned to take them back the pilot stepped out and said, "We've got a problem here. This plane can only hold two elk."

In a fit of outrage, the hunters responded by recalling the same trip they had taken the year before. "We were here last year," they countered. "We had four elk; the weather was the same, the plane was the same."

Sheepishly, the pilot backed down. "Well," he said, "I guess you know best."

They loaded up everything and took off, but within minutes the plane began to sputter and it crashed. As they stumbled away from the wreckage dazed and disoriented, one hunter asked the other, "Do you know where we are?"

The other replied, "I don't know, but I think it's about a mile from where we crashed last year."

The moral: It's dangerous to keep doing the same thing when change becomes a matter of survival. Remember, says General Electric's Jack Welch, the winners of the 1990s will be the companies that have developed cultures that do not fear change but relish it.

Change also requires, as Keith Hammonds notes, "a network of compensation systems, human resource policies, and most important, sound business plans to support the vision." One other consideration that should be required as well: unlocking the chains of creativity.

To do that requires an understanding of how creativity has been virtually schooled out of us. Think about it. Recall those grade-school days when the classroom was full of fidgety children. There is order in the room. Desks are in rows, posters and charts are tacked up neatly on the walls. A bubbling fish tank stands in one corner, a terrarium in the other. The teacher at the head of the class is authoritative, instructive, too often dispensing discipline like spelling words. There's the rub. In classroom situations where teachers have to spend most of their time trying to keep order, they become role models of control. Unfortunately, the notion of control is essential, but it also works against the spontaneity of personal expression and creativity. The tapes stay with us and we spend our subsequent school years learning how to control facts, ourselves, and those around us we can influence. In the business world we are rewarded with big salaries for exercising control. We seek to become masters of control instead of masters of creativity. Simply, the creative play gets schooled out of us as early as the third or fourth grade in many cases. But, like a recessive gene, the germ of creativity always remains. It merely lies dormant somewhere inside ourselves waiting to be stimulated.

Spontaneity, then, becomes the stuff of creative combustion. How else could Michael Faraday, with only grade-school mathematics, become one of the founders of modern physics? Indeed, his greatest tool may have been ignorance. Faraday developed simple, nonmathematical concepts to explain his electrical and magnetic phenomena. In doing so, he broke ground rules of which he was unaware, rules that would have stopped professional mathematicians in their tracks. Thus Faraday's ordinary background proved no barrier for extraordinary performance.

College dropout Paul Fireman, chairman and CEO of Reebok International Ltd., identifies with the Faradays of the world. "Reebok is a company in which ordinary people did extraordinary things," says Fireman, who left Boston University after his freshman year. "Ordinary people went way beyond themselves only because they were allowed to do it." His unique ability to spot trends early paid off for both Reebok (1989 sales: $1.8 billion) and Fireman, one of the nation's highest paid executives, whose annual salary and compensation package in 1989 totaled more than $11.4 million. Capitalizing on the U.S. aerobics boom in the early 1980s, in just eleven years, Fireman transformed a small England-based company that turned out nearly twenty-one thousand pairs of Reeboks a year into a global powerhouse that churned out seventy-five million pairs a year.

"Was it dumb luck?" a business student once asked him.

"No," Fireman quickly replied. "It was smart luck."

In reality, there are only a few people who don't have the right stuff to build on. Be practical, even logical, in assessing your attributes. It stands to reason people aren't born with enlightenment, bravery, and charisma. Risk taking isn't genetic. And for heaven's sake, stop listening to what you aren't or can't do. Leadership skills can be amplified physically, emotionally, and intellectually. Take an inventory of your strengths and weaknesses and start building from there. *And never forget: Ordinary people make extraordinary leaders.*

Reflections: Acquiring Valuable Warp Threads

Finding the leader within starts with your belief that you possess the foundation on which to build. Remember:

- Leadership can be learned.
- Leaders are totally committed.
- Leaders are super listeners and excellent communicators.
- Leaders are students of their respective industry, company, and its people.
- Leaders have "the authority of knowledge" and are better at one thing that adds value than anyone else.
- Leaders have a strong need to prove themselves.

People who are defeated before they even start have bought into the myth of original genius instead of the reality of hard work and self-expression. Neither the muses nor genes stand up to the stark light of examination in the search for the headwaters of creativity. Those business leaders we interviewed, in their own emphatic words, debunked the born leader concept. There are no born leaders. *Rather, preparation, hard work, and an ability to synthesize and rearrange facts that others see as confusion are some of the learned skills that make up the stuff of leadership.*

Leaders are not born with creative genius and special endowments. Nor are they preordained to accomplish great things. And they make mistakes—and learn from them.

When we realize that leadership is a role and not a position, we come to understand that leadership can be learned just as professional musicians, actors, and artists master their crafts over a lifetime of practice. Although it takes formal and professional preparation to acquire the necessary skills, it also takes serious introspection in an effort to learn something about ourselves.

Leadership learning begins when one seeks further self-understanding and constructively deals with frustration. *Tapping one's reservoir of passion gives the leader the energy to transform the present into a more successful and promising future.* Be creative, simplify, clarify, and understand that complex problems often do not have a single right answer.

You don't have to be skilled to know how you feel. You have to be in touch with yourself to know why you feel as you do.

Managership, Leadership, Followership in Balance

To be a leader is to enjoy the special privileges of complexity, of ambiguity, of diversity. But to be a leader means, especially, having the opportunity to make a meaningful difference in the lives of those who permit leaders to lead.

—MAX DEPREE

*T*he decade of the 1980s brought into sharp focus a fact of corporate America that was also confirmed from our research: Most companies had been overmanaged and underled since the 1970s. A rainbow of deals that included leveraged buyouts, management buyouts, hostile takeovers, greenmail, white knights, and red herrings arched over the business landscape. But the pot of gold eluded most deal makers, who found themselves mired in debt that squeezed cash flow to a trickle. Instead of creating wealth through a long-range outlook, financial engineering zeroed in on next quarter's financial performance and put the premium on control.

Ever since the early 1960s, when IT&T's wily CEO Harold Geneen proclaimed "managers must manage," there has been a great deal of confusion over managership, leadership, and followership. Before going any further, it will serve us to clarify these terms.

To understand what relevant information we need to give aspiring managers, we first have to understand management itself, its nature and focus and its interaction with leadership. What makes a manager? What makes a leader? What is the difference between a manager and a leader? Can one function without the other? It is as if we were out to reconstruct character, using two portraits of human nature to do so. There are no recipes to follow, other than to point out that change alters character. The history of business, says former Motorola, Inc. chairman Robert Galvin, is the history of surprises and the failure of almost all companies to adapt to them. People need to anticipate the consequences of surprises—like the computer, transistor, fiber optic—creatively and then, as Galvin puts it, "do imaginative things about them with commitment." To carry that commitment forward requires the tandem effort of a leader and a manager.

Let us now consider management. Henry Mintzberg argues that it is greatly exaggerated to characterize managers as reflective, systematic planners. Rather, he says, managers "work at an unrelenting pace, that their activities are characterized by brevity, variety, and discontinuity, and that they are strongly oriented to action rather than reflective activities." And don't be so quick to rely on words like *judgment* and *intuition* to describe the attributes of a solid manager because, as Mintzberg notes, "they are merely labels for our ignorance."

Management is really all about control. As I previously pointed out, leadership and management are necessary, but not necessarily compatible. They are the corporate ying and yang. Leadership upsets orderly planning while management discourages risk taking. Yet these elements play off one another to create a balance of sorts. They must. For without management and its short-term focus, there can be no long run, the domain of leadership. Managers, then, produce orderly results, concentrate on the short run, seek consistency, and solve problems. Leaders, on the other hand, produce significant change, concentrate on the long run, establish new directions and produce new opportunities.

In *Force for Change*, John P. Kotter describes how leadership differs from that of management. Management is planning and budgeting, organizing and staffing, controlling and problem solving, and producing predictability and order. Let's take each separately.

A well-defined plan should be like a road map of sorts: a layout of the terrain with timetables of what to expect at certain intervals in the forthcoming fiscal year, with forecasts and results based on past performance and anticipated changes in economic factors that impact a company. To carry out the plan, the manager becomes an organization person: He or she builds staff, sets goals, allocates resources, revises policies, sets up the pecking order—all in the name of delegating. In essence, one is building the human network in line with those policies and guidelines that shape the organization's political, cultural, and technical architecture. The manager, then, is in control, assigned the role of problem solver as he or she monitors the company's performance against its forecast, making small adjustments here and there in line with the annual plan. The ship is tight, the course is set, the future predictable. That's how a manager likes it. No surprises, thank you.

Why should a manager be so offended by something unforeseeable down the pike? Because it upsets order. Often there is not enough time to deal with surprises. Thus solutions lack analysis and verification. Remember, predictability is the goal of management. "Managing," IT&T's Harold Geneen once remarked, "means that once you set your business plan and budget for the year, you must achieve the sales, the market share, the earnings and whatever to which you committed yourself. Management must manage! . . . is a very simple credo, probably the closest thing to the secret of success in business, in professional life, in almost everything you undertake."

Sounds pretty clear—just the way a manager likes things. But if you were to ask Henry Mintzberg what do managers do, he'll respond by saying, "Even managers don't know." Mintzberg further observes that managers prefer live action to delayed action; managers are key in obtaining "soft" information, then passing it along; managers are low-tech communicators who prefer the spoken word through telephone calls and meetings rather than memos and spiffy management information systems; managers allocate the most precious of all resources—time.

Naturally, a manager's performance depends on how well he or she understands and responds to the dilemmas of the job. Mintzberg's description of that job includes "a number of important managerial skills—developing peer relationships, carrying out negotiations, motivating subordinates, resolving conflicts, establishing information networks and subsequently disseminating information, making decisions in conditions of extreme ambiguity, and allocating resources. Above all, the manager needs to be introspective in order to learn on the job."

There are, of course, managerial pitfalls to sidestep along the way. The last thing a corporation wants to do is to create a routinized manager who reacts and responds like a Stepford wife. Harvard's Theodore Levitt reminds us that there are "few things as bad as breeding people to managerial routines that equate order with rationality and careful study with true knowledge." At the same time, Levitt warns, an aloof management leads to irresolution, mistakes, and quick calamity. In the final analysis, it takes great effort to stay in contact with the nitty-gritty of a business on which decisions must be made.

So managers push the company forward, gaining power as they make their way through the corporate ranks. Their authority and responsibility come by fiat. Their power comes by information, by position in the hierarchy, by control over decision making, by dispensation of rewards and punishment, and by allocation of resources. But their success depends on their ability to maintain a delicate balance: They must blend tough-minded persistence and hard-nosed analysis with a tolerance that engenders goodwill.

By contrast, these same traits may be eschewed by leaders who are preoccupied with creating a long-term vision rather than with implementation. FMC Corporation's CEO Robert Malott, who made *Fortune*'s list of the ten toughest bosses in America, admits that

> people skills are not my strongest point. I've been tough, and it's known that I have a low tolerance for incompetence.
>
> I don't mind my reputation for toughness. One of the most important things a business leader does—in fact, a

business leader's most fundamental responsibility—is to make tough decisions about people. Some of those decisions are going to hurt peoples' feelings. But a business leader must have the internal fortitude to address inadequate performance. For example, I had to demote two senior vice presidents because they were not performing. It hurt them, it hurt their families, and it wasn't fun for me to make those decisions either. But let me add that both of these individuals went on to have successful, productive, and happier careers with the company. One of the strongest moral arguments for toughness—for confronting problems head-on—is that you can often salvage a career that way. And, of course, if you don't make those decisions your business will suffer.

Leaders

Leadership is far more than occupational. To some degree, it can be inspirational. I don't mean Moses standing on a mountain grasping the Ten Commandments while his tribes look up from below in hero-worshiping awe. Of course, when Moses descended the holy mountain the tribes were in disarray. He had lost the trust of many of his followers to, of all things, a golden calf. Not only Moses was miffed, but God was as well. For the kind of inspiration I mean, one need only recall the guts-and-glory speech given in *Patton* by George C. Scott in his Oscar-winning portrayal of World War II's legendary and irascible General George Patton. Here is a role model of a powerful communicator, using words and pictures and the soldier's language as he talks about the war from their point of view. Garbed as a hero, he is offering himself to be their leader.

Dwarfed by a huge American flag in the background, Patton steps forward before his troops on the eve of battle against the Nazis, sporting a pearl-handled pistol and a medal-bedecked chest as he begins his warrior's homily:

I want you to remember that no bastard ever won a war dying for his country. He won it by making the other poor dumb bastard die for his country. . . . Americans traditionally love to fight. All real Americans love the sting of battle. . . . Americans love a winner and will not tolerate a loser. Americans play to win all the time. I wouldn't give a hoot and hell for a man who lost and laughed. . . . An army is a team. It lives, eats, sleeps and fights as a team. This individuality stuff is crap. . . . We have the finest food and equipment, the best spirit and best men in the world. . . . We're not just going to shoot the bastards. We're going to cut out their guts and use them to grease the threads of our tanks. . . . Some of you boys are wondering if you're going to chicken out under fire. Don't worry about it. I can assure you, you'll all do your duty. . . . Now another thing I want you to remember. I don't want to get a message that we're holding our position. We're not holding anything. Let the Hun do that. We are advancing constantly and we are not interested in holding on to anything except the enemy.

True, being the boss reflects a person's position and power. But being a boss doesn't necessarily mean that the boss is a leader. *Simply, the power of a leader comes from those who follow. One finds a reciprocity between a leader and follower based on mutual trust. "You trust me," the leader asks of the follower who accepts the vision and change. "I trust you," the leader tells the follower in closing the circle of power and empowerment.*

ARA Services chairman Joseph Neubauer puts it another way: "You cannot lead by yourself. You have to lead through people."

Just as there is an art of leadership, there too is an art of followership. Organizations prosper or fail not solely on how well they are managed and led, but on the quality of the followers and how well they follow. Carnegie-Mellon's Robert Kelley in *In Praise of Followers* says, "Bosses are not necessarily good leaders; subordinates are not necessarily effective followers . . . and the reality is that most of us are more often followers than leaders."

What, then, differentiates effective from ineffective followers? There are several factors, Kelley believes, including enthusiasm, intelligent participation, and willingness to pursue organizational goals without star billing. But followers also have to be independent thinkers, people who think for themselves and carry out their jobs with energy and assertiveness. They are well-balanced responsible people who can succeed without strong supervision. They build their own confidence and somewhere in their plan of self-development is embedded the need for continuing education. Finally, effective followers are believable and courageous, insightful and candid, keeping colleagues honest and informed.

Hail to the leader! Not quite. Followers don't blindly worship leaders. They respect them. And leaders respect followers. "Instead of seeing the leadership role as superior to and more active than the role of follower, we can think of them as equal, but different activities," emphatically states Kelley.

The leader is the architect, the individual who designs the strategy; the follower is the engineer, sleeves rolled up, pencil behind ear, who walks along the scaffold to make sure the plan is carried out by the carpenters, electricians, and myriad craftspeople it takes to build the dream. The leader, as we shall see, needs the gift of gab, not the fast-talking kind, but the kind that can charge people with enthusiasm—the win-one-for-the-Gipper kind of homily that rallies them in a common cause. The leader needs consensus. Without it, the team falls apart. If the leader sees the forest, insists Kelley, then the follower sees the forest and its trees.

Overmanaged and Underled

Yet too much leadership or too much managership can kill a company. There needs to be a balance. Most companies today are overmanaged and underled. Why? Because of the dynamic nature of the world we're in, it's often difficult for leaders to picture where the company fits. In the past, the huge U.S. market allowed medium-size companies to be inward and parochial. According to the Commerce Department, only one-third of the U.S. companies that could have been exporting did so in 1991. Many companies are just starting to feel the heat of global competition, but if they don't respond fast enough, they'll self-destruct as their counterparts in Europe and Japan invade American markets. Companies that successfully compete abroad are usually winners in their home markets, too. Deregulation had also become a fly in the corporate ointment by creating easy leverage. In fact, for many corporations leverage turned out to be a fraying rope bridge swaying above a deep gorge. It forced management to focus on the short term in response to anxious banks demanding interest payments that could eat up a year's worth of cash flow. That kind of thinking can be devastating to a company like 3M Corporation, where researchers spend at least 15 percent of their time on projects that won't pay off until they are far down the road. Too much short-term thinking can work against the creative flow of a company to break down morale among followers, many of whom are a source of new ideas that are the lifeblood of an enterprise.

Followers can be loyal, hardworking, and even uncreative, but that doesn't necessarily mean they take orders without questioning authority. On the contrary, the sought-after follower is an independent critical thinker who can challenge the leader. Such a challenge, for example, took place on December 20, 1990, when Soviet Foreign Minister Eduard Shevardnadze stormed out of the Russian Parliament in protest of perestroika, surprising his close friend, fellow reformer, and boss, President Mikhail S. Gorbachev. "The reformers have gone to seed," he shouted at the Supreme Soviet. "Dictatorship is coming . . . I am resigning . . . do not respond and do not curse me—let this be my contribution, if you like, my protest against the onset of dictatorship." Eight months later, Gorbachev was nearly ousted in a failed coup led by hard-liners he himself had appointed to high office. Shortly thereafter, as we all know, came the Second Russian Revolution, dissolving the Soviet Union and Gorbachev's position with it.

If the leader's actions are never questioned by the follower, then the leader's mistakes are often magnified. So the follower can boss the boss. Why not? The follower is usually closer to where the action is, focusing on the substance of the business and what keeps it working. "At Wal-Mart," says CEO David Glass, "our philosophy is that the best ideas come from people on the firing line." When Merck Corporation hit a new-product drought in the early 1980s, CEO Roy Vagelos, a physician and biochemist, turned the company's talent scouts loose, recruiting hundreds of research scientists to reignite Merck's labs, which have discovered ten new major drugs since 1981, each accounting for $100 million in sales. Remember, in the end what wins in the business wars is the value-creating idea. Often the best ideas come from where reality is, and reality isn't in the executive suite.

Please don't misunderstand me. I'm not advocating revolution in the management ranks when you don't agree with your boss. But it serves no purpose to seethe with resentment. Followers are responsible individuals, and although they have to believe in the leader, first and foremost, they must believe in themselves.

Leadership satisfies such basic human needs as achievement, belonging, recognition, self-esteem, and control over one's life. Leaders touch followers deeply and powerfully by articulating their vision—a vision that appeals to common values. See it big and keep it simple. Developing that vision creates a new pattern out of old facts. Motorola, Inc.'s former chairman Robert Galvin uses three terms to describe how companies are run: running the business, managing the corporation, and leading the institution.

"The runner of the business and the manager of the business operate within the activity zone or charter of the institution," Galvin says. "The leader of the institution takes the institution elsewhere. The new direction doesn't have to be geographic, doesn't have to be a new business. Those, of course, are manifestations. Changing the expectation level, starting a training program, anything that takes the organization to a new elsewhere, that is leadership."

As the facts are diligently gathered and assembled, the leader looks for new patterns, tests new directions in an effort to refine the vision and to move the enterprise from the present to the future. Words then take over. They don't have to be strong or mellow or witty or long or short—but exact. And there doesn't have to be a lot of them, just enough to convey the message. Some leaders use symbols, others phrases, and still others metaphors composed of simple images or words that communicate powerfully. When, for example, Mary Kay prodded her sales force to sell more cosmetics beyond their goals, she reminded them that "a bumble bee has a body too big for its wings and should not be able to fly—but it does." In any case, leaders must communicate in clear language that can be understood at all management levels; their mouths cannot seem to move independently of the words, like one of those eerie Anima-tronic Disney robots. They must be direct, using words as if they were smart bombs hitting precise targets. Then repeat the words. Repeat. Repeat. Repeat.

Scott Whitlock, executive vice president of Honda of America, insists that "in communicating the vision there is one rule: repetition." Whitlock recalls an early experience as a plant manager when one of his associates came to him with a problem:

> Another associate in his team was not understanding one of the company's policies. I asked if he had explained the reason for the policy. He said, "Yes, three times I've explained the reason." The next thing that popped out of my mouth was, "Well, I think you have about six more to go." That became what we informally refer to as "the rule of nine." If you want somebody to hear you once, say it nine times. It helps relieve the frustration when someone doesn't hear you the first or second time. It reminds management to repeat messages to make sure that they are understood. Repetition is important in everything we do. If you look at the Honda advertising campaigns on television—and go back and look at them every year for the last fifteen years or so—you will see a remarkable consistency in the message. The message is fundamentally the same over long periods of time.

The responsibility for communication at Honda is with the person who has the information—not the person who receives it.

"Until the listener understands fully, the person with information has not done his job," Whitlock says. The most important thing that the heads of his company do, he emphasizes, is to listen. And you don't necessarily have to have ears to do that. Sometimes, eye contact is enough to cross even the language barrier. Whitlock explains:

> One of the things I have learned in looking at plants in Japan and looking at our plant is the tremendous strength of non-verbal communication. There are point-out posters, drawings that point out what we've got to do to prevent a quality defect. I sometimes get accounting sheets from Japan where I know from the layout of the sheet exactly what those numbers mean and exactly what they are trying to communicate to me. We have found as we get into computerized design that one of its big advantages for us is not the fact that it helps automate the design process. One of the big advantages is that it gives us a system whereby an American engineer and a Japanese engineer, neither of whom speak a word of the other's language and who are located halfway around the globe from each other, can communicate together regarding the design of a part without learning any language other than the computer language.

So the common thread that links the manager to the leader is communication. A number of years ago Motorola's Robert Galvin was on a panel dealing with communication in business. After the other speakers had given their remarks, he stepped to the microphone to present his views. "Business communicates by the written word, by the spoken word, by a special process called the rumor," he said. "Thank you very much." With that, he began to return to his seat, startling the chairman of the panel with such brief comments. But before the chairman could react, Galvin quickly returned to the dais and added, "And by impression."

Then he confided to the audience of businesspeople, "I don't know whether I've created a good or bad impression, but that's not of any concern to me. In a few days none of us will remember the content of what was said here, but possibly you will remember that an impression is an extremely important aspect of communication."

Thus the key word here is *communication*. Some experts estimate that only 10 percent of CEOs are effective communicators. Others say the number is too low. Regardless, many corporations communicate with high-tech gadgetry from voice mail and videocassette to videoconferencing and satellite transmission. Of the various whiz-bang media available to them, Mintzberg points out, "managers favor the verbal media—namely telephone calls and meetings." The competent executives today, he adds, "are fundamentally indistinguishable from their counterparts of a hundred years ago. The information they need differs, but they seek it in the same way—by word of mouth."

The importance of the spoken word in the corporate culture is no different from that of any other culture. All anthropologists know that indigenous knowledge among tribes disappears when oral tradition breaks down. The villagers of the Penan tribe on Borneo used to watch for the appearance of a certain butterfly that marked the arrival of a herd of boar and the promise of good hunting. Now most of the Penans cannot remember which butterfly to look for. The reason: The village youth stopped talking to the elders. Language is doomed when there are no children to speak it. And when language disappears, knowledge vanishes with it. Leaders and followers must talk—and listen—to keep the culture alive.

It is through communication, among other things, that a leader builds credibility. Consistency between words and deeds must constantly be verified in the minds of the followers who painfully scrutinize the leader's personal track record. Integrity and trustworthiness, of course, are crucial in aligning managers, too. But in final analysis, leaders get power through their performance, which is based on the value of their vision to the enterprise and its publics, the ability to produce change as the environment changes, the skill to empower the followers and develop a strategy for achieving the changes, and the willingness to take the necessary risks to accomplish the new goals.

Trust is the force that keeps leadership rolling because, according to Warren Bennis and Burt Nanus, it implies accountability, predictability, and reliability. Arthur Knight, CEO of Morgan Products, Ltd., sums it up:

> The capability to build trust among constituencies and to gain the commitment of those constituencies to attainment of the vision are corollary competencies. My belief is that vision, trust, and commitment are crucially interdependent and that one without the other will not succeed. In my opinion, leaders at every level build trust in a few simple direct ways. By being honest with people. By openly communicating with people. By being nonmanipulative. By recognizing that different constituencies within the enterprise have different agendas and interests and by balancing those agendas and interests without hidden agendas or manipulation. Honest, open communication . . . doing what you say you will do . . . constancy . . . that builds trust.

Clearly, there are distinctive differences between the manager and leader, differences that have been written about and discussed for decades. By its very nature, leadership is long run, risk taking, and upsetting to management's predictable work, and it creates dislocation in followers. It can, for the followers, even create fear and anger of the unknown, a period of disorientation as the signposts of the past are no longer guides to the future. Sometimes it requires altering identity by each person in the entire organization and a rededication to the new vision.

Reflections: Building the Warp of Leadership

Of managers: They are controlling. They are predictive. They take the short-term view. They seek stability and form. They are rigid. They are interested in facts and answers. They are passive.

Of followers: They see both the big picture and the small details. They have the social capacity to work well with others. They have the strength of character to flourish without heroic status. They have the moral and psychological balance to pursue personal and corporate goals at no cost to either. They participate in a team effort for the accomplishment of a common purpose.

Of leaders: They use imagination. They are open. They synthesize. They take risks. They take a long-term view. They are interested in initiative. They are active. They are interested in discovery. They seek alternatives. They are interested in content. They are involved with strategy. They are experimental. They are inductive. They are firm. They are dynamic.

> *Change is the process,*
> *vision is the path,*
> *followership is the means,*
> *leadership is the role*
> *that transforms the enterprise.*

There is still a lack of clarity surrounding the definition of manager and leader. This lack of specificity ends up with labels stretched around business practices of all sorts, blurring the lines between leadership, managership, and entrepreneurship. To illustrate the point, think of business cultures falling into three basic categories:

The managerial culture, in which people are focused on preserving what they have.

The entrepreneurial culture, in which people are focused on creating something new.

The leadership culture, in which people are focused on transforming what exists.

Reflect, for a moment, on the type of culture in which your firm operates as a first step in evaluating the environment in which you have planted your professional roots.

Leadership, managership, and followership are interchangeable roles. These functions are like hats that the same person changes on the same day at different times, depending on which task is being undertaken. When, say, one puts on the follower's hat, the course is set on accomplishing tasks that advance the corporate goal. But that does not mean the follower's hat stays on all day, all week, or all month. Along the way, your technical competence demands that objectives be modified. You alert your colleagues to the new information and they join you in the recast mission. Now you're wearing the leadership hat. The hats are neither hard nor soft, but necessary hats that adjust to fit every head size.

The leader must be the source of the organization's vision and mission statement, acting as an auditor of sorts to make sure the vision meets the reality of the marketplace. The leader is also the chief communicator of the new vision and culture, using images and metaphors to draw analogies. The information should be vivid and spiked with imagination, yet logical and convincing in line with what the leader is asking his or her followers to do: change their behavior to satisfy new hopes, desires, and needs.

The roots of leadership are deeply embedded in each person's need for self-expression and in a developed capacity to integrate a new reality out of the relevant fragments of information that one accumulates. A business professional grows by the authority of knowledge and by being a superb practitioner in the roles of follower and manager.

New Strengths from Old Wounds

The personal commitment of a man to his skill, the intellectual commitment and the emotional equipment working together as one, has made the Ascent of Man.

—JACOB BRONOWSKI

*I*n *Reality Isn't What It Used to Be,* Walter Truett Anderson observes:

The Wizard of Oz is another myth for our time—especially rich in meaning at its conclusion, in which, after a long quest for the great Oz, Dorothy and her friends reach his palace. They are ushered into the throne room and are finally in his mighty presence. Lights flash, and a great voice thunders at them. They are suitably terrified and impressed—until Dorothy's dog, Toto, pulls away the curtain to reveal that behind the awe-inspiring machinery is nothing but an ordinary human being. The wizard is seen at last. Dorothy, in her disappointment, accuses him of being a very bad man. He replies that he is a very good man, but a very bad wizard.

Just like our society, our business community supports the idea that the construction of reality comes from something and someone beyond us—maybe not from God, but at least from a larger-than-life business practitioner with special endowments for seeing the future and making a coherent plan out of it.

Our research, in fact, denies these assumptions.

The wizard is not what we expected—the leader is an ordinary practitioner with some special insights. Leaders are ordinary people that have been forged and shaped on the anvil of reality who like what they see and seek new insights about themselves and about the possibilities and promise of the future. They, in fact, are the creators of their own reality.

Unlike managers who focus on stability, abide by rules made by someone else, and procedures that accomplish forecasted goals—people satisfied with predictable results—leaders are creators of change because they in fact have changed themselves.

Leaders are not disoriented by change. They don't run from change, seeking the present or past for comfort. Rather, they see change as an opportunity, a constant in the equation of life. For them, change is not a threat, but a challenge.

Change requires risk. And why shouldn't it? Man is as old as his arteries, philosopher Will Durant said, but as young as the risks he takes.

A company, like a human being, goes through stages: youth, middle age, and old age. Thus in the latter years there is a tendency to slow down, coast on the momentum of past glories. But for those who perceive moderation as a virtue, others see it as the road to mediocrity. The corporation declines when there is an overemphasis on stability, rules, and procedures. The result: a decreased eagerness to take risks and innovate—and an overall staleness in the organization. It's the job of the leader to make sure that corporate arteries don't harden.

Along with their risk appetites, most leaders have an early-warning mechanism signaling the need for change. It isn't instinctive like the shrill chirping cicada's appearance every seventeen years out of some natural order. Nor is it taught in a classroom. Where, then, does it come from? It comes from living. From the bumps and bangs and painful life cycle events that create the emotional jolts that stay with us consciously and subconsciously. These incidents are the triggers that set off special personal insights that help break the leadership code. To see what I'm driving at, consider for the moment two types of personality patterns.

One type is the adaptive person. This individual goes with the flow, taking life as it comes. He or she is in harmony with the environment, following the path of expectations no matter how they may twist and turn—from family to school to marriage to career—all seem to move smoothly through the life cycle events. This doesn't mean life is without trauma for the adaptive person. Far from it. Adaptive persons are often satisfied to be defined by how others see them. Think, for a moment, what it's like when you walk down the street and your eyes catch your reflection in a store-front window. Hair perfectly combed. Clothes neatly styled. It's you, at least physically. But how about the inner "you" others experience, the "you" that is more than mere exterior, the total persona? Psychologist Charles Horton Cooley says we acquire a sense of our selves through the "looking-glass self." It is not Lewis Carroll's elastic looking-glass through which Alice walked into a world where the laws of nature were repealed. Rather, Cooley's looking-glass self is the process of finding identity through one's self-image reflected back through the reactions of others around us. We accumulate impressions that give us a view of ourselves based on our interpretation of how others see us in all of our activities: at home, at school, and in social situations. For example, identity at work comes from our job title, its position in the management structure, how others view us as well as through performance evaluations. Other people become the looking glass in which we see and define ourselves. The adaptive person is largely satisfied by what is reflected back through the looking-glass self.

The other type is the participant-observer. This individual starts and stops and starts again on an existential highway that seems hostile. He or she has been forced to look inward for meaning in response to some emotionally charged event—a death in the family, sickness, a divorce—beyond their own control. They struggle to sort out the meaning of the disruption from a trauma that has created a feeling of profound separateness, some anger, and disorientation. There is a need to question goals, values, norms of conduct, meaning, and ask the proverbial "Why?" about things never questioned before. The trauma-created anger heightens emotional energy, which can either be turned on one's self in a destructive manner or in a creative burst of energy. In this process, the person becomes an observer and at the same time a participant. One is both an actor in the drama, and a viewer in the audience. At the same time as events are unfolding, the participant-observer seeks separateness for perspective and contemplation to sort out the confusion. Thus the participant-observer gains another dimension from which he or she is able to refocus on events out of a totally fresh perspective. It is hoped that the person sees new meaning—when in the past there was none—while abandoning the childlike notion of immortality. Life now becomes a journey with a sense of urgency to accomplish new goals. Because all change creates risk, participant-observers are necessarily transformational risk takers.

There is an emerging theme here: Leadership is less about sheer talent than about introspection forged from suffering.

Virtually every business leader interviewed for this book had the experience of a participant-observer. At one time or another in their lives, for example, they let go of something that they thought was important. They now seek to clarify for others because they have had to do it for themselves. They speak to the depths of another person because they are in touch with their own deeper conflicts. Finally, they are able to replace set ways with experiment and improvisation.

And although it may be lonely at the top, true leaders act on behalf of the entire enterprise. In a real sense they are generous; that is, they are willing to spend themselves. They work in quiet but irresistible ways as they seek to operate with crisp, well-coordinated teamwork. In short, they seek to communicate a new vision to their followers, who in turn see that vision in their own best interest as well as in the firm's. Out of this mutuality grows an emotional fidelity to the organization that is at the core of a leader's being. Naturally, the leader wants the followers to feel tangibly the same, so all are connected by the same strategic goals. The risk of change, then, is not taken so much in the leader's own self-interest, but in the best interest of the entire enterprise. Thus a critical factor of leadership is the willingness of the leader to use power in the best interest of the followers.

"Business leaders have a professional responsibility to their clients, just as lawyers and physicians do," says Joseph Neubauer, CEO and chairman of ARA Services, Inc. "When you are a business leader your client is the organization. The organization and its needs come first." Neubauer explains:

> One of the toughest things a business leader has to do is judge between the needs of an individual and those of the corporation. Those are not easy issues. They are what I call forty-eight/fifty-two percent issues. I almost always end up asking how a decision will affect the organization. For example, you would like to take care of good old Harry who has been with you for twenty-five years and has worked very hard. You could let him stay in the job for another two years, because he's near retirement. But you must think of the people working for good old Harry, who are frustrated, whose growth you would be stunting. They will not regard you as a good leader if you favor a person, rather than work for the common good of the organization. Decisions like that are among the toughest things that I have to do. They are one of the toughest things that leaders have to learn in the process of becoming a leader.

Twice-Born/Participant-Observer

The idea of the participant-observer has its roots in turn-of-the-century literature that described a concept called *twice born*. Although it might sound spiritual, even metaphysical, it isn't. The premise is simple enough: Leaders grow through mastering painful conflicts—sickness; death of a parent, sibling, or friend; early divorce; rejection by a role model—in their developmental years. That, in turn, creates a sense of alienation, forcing a person to look inward for a redefined sense of identity.

It was a concept espoused by brilliant Harvard psychologist William James in his 1902 book, *The Varieties of Religious Experience,* in which he drew the idea from English scholar Francis W. Newman, who wrote, "God has two families of children on this earth, the once-born and the twice-born." James, one of the founders of pragmatism and the brother of novelist Henry James, had taken the twice-born concept away from the mysticism of religion and anchored it in the logic of the twentieth century. Nearly seven decades later, Harvard's Abraham Zaleznik picked up the twice-born notion in defining leaders and managers. Does the twice-born concept hold up in the practical business world today? You bet it does.

"For a once born personality, the sense of self, as a guide to conduct and attitude, derives from a feeling of being at home and in harmony with one's environment," Zaleznik observed in his classic "Managers and Leaders: Are they different?" written for the *Harvard Business Review* in 1977. By nature, the manager is a once-born personality. "Managers," he continued, "see themselves as conservators and regulators of an existing order of affairs with which they personally identify and from which they gain rewards."

Leaders, however, are twice borns often struggling out of a feeling of separateness. They take nothing for granted. There are disruptions in their relationships, forcing them to turn inward to reestablish or redefine order. They emerge with a sense of clarity and a feeling of renewal. "For such a person," Zaleznik says, "self-esteem no longer depends solely upon positive attachments and real rewards. A form of self-reliance takes hold along with expectations of performance and achievement, and perhaps even the desire to do great works."

After Charles Darwin was selected as the naturalist for the around-the-world voyage of the H.M.S. *Beagle* and shortly before sailing, he wrote: "My second life will then commence, and it shall be as a birthday for the rest of my life." It was a birthday to be celebrated by the entire world. For in his second life, Darwin produced the classic masterpiece *The Origin of Species.*

Instead of plowing through one obstacle and heading for the next, the participant-observer pauses and asks: "What does this mean to me?" Consider the plight of immigrants. Removed from their pasts, they reflect and question most of the new cultural norms as they deal with not only the words but the semantic meaning of a new language, new customs, and new social codes. Somehow they must integrate their past experience with the current environment to define a new world. So it is with the business leader.

Another twice-born encounter may come from combat service in the military. During World War II, every day I got up and climbed into a B-24 bomber, I thought it was going to be the last day of my life. The sunrise looks a lot different on the last day of your life than on a normal day. Norman Mailer, in his gritty war novel *The Naked and the Dead,* talks about how the experience of war matures people. For sure, it changes their perception; it teaches them life can be short and enlarges the value of time. Think about it, twice-born experiences are all around us. They even flicker on our movie screens.

"Some mistakes," says baseball player Roy Hobbs in *The Natural,* "I guess we never stop paying for."

"Well," smiles Iris, the home-town sweetheart he hasn't seen in years, "I think we have two lives—the life we learn with, and the life we live with afterwards."

There are, of course, those who have a twice-born experience that so traumatizes them, they never recover. Most people who do, however, often don't realize the stages they go through, each one as precise as the factors in a mathematical equation: separation, anger, disassociation, reorientation, and reentry. "Why did it happen to me?" Sometimes the anger lasts a lifetime. But the leader—as long as he or she is emotionally healthy enough to master his or her own tragedies—has the ability to come out on the other side of the trauma with the capacity to cope creatively. The personality of the leader becomes extradimensional. Thus, as Zaleznik comments, "Leaders grow through mastering painful conflict during the developmental years. Leaders are born-twice individuals who endure major events and crises that lead to sense of separateness and estrangement from their environment."

When movie director Martin Scorsese was three years old, his mother tricked him. She told him he was going to the circus to see the clowns and elephants. Instead, she brought him to a hospital in Flushing, New York. The nurse, she assured her asthmatic son, was going to take little Martin to the circus. His mother left. Eventually the nurse showed up all right, but she took the child to an operating room where his tonsils were removed. The next morning Scorsese's mother rushed back to the hospital to find Martin sitting on a little bench in the waiting room. "He was livid," she recalled. "We brought him home and he didn't say anything."

To this day, say movie critics, Scorsese may not always know what the truth is, but he's in constant search of it through movies that are riddled with the energy of obsession. Small wonder, the characters from Christ to Travis Bickel the taxi driver suffer a sense of alienation, anguish, and despair. *Raging* and *mean* are the kinds of words you find in the title of his movies. Scorsese the Catholic choirboy instinctively knew the power of imagery. During his sickly youth, he would often pass the time drawing pictures in storyboard form for the movies in his head. There were other setbacks in his youth: He had made a commitment to the church to become a priest, but the church flunked him when he failed Latin.

It wasn't until he was in his thirties when he confronted his mother over the tonsil incident. "Mother, I have something to tell you that I can't hold back any longer," she recalled him saying. "You lied to me. You said the nurse was bringing me to the circus and you lied. Don't ever do that, you should always tell children what you're doing, the truth, because I believed you."

Leo Melamed, a pioneer of the financial futures markets and chairman emeritus of the Chicago Mercantile Exchange, doesn't doubt that events in his childhood have much to do with his motivation. At thirty-seven Melamed had been one of the youngest chairmen in the Merc's history. In 1939, when he was seven, Melamed and his parents fled the Russian pogroms and German blitzkrieg from their home in Bialystok, Poland. They were one step ahead of the Nazis, who had gathered up Bialystok's Jewry, including Leo's grandmother and aunts, and burned them alive in the synagogue. After a Dr. Zhivago–type ride across Siberia, the Melameds ended up in Vladivostok and from there went to Japan. In 1941, eight months before Pearl Harbor, they fled again, heading for the United States. The family reached Seattle, Washington, in April 1941. Then they moved to New York and two months later they moved again to Chicago's northwest side, where his parents taught Hebrew and Yiddish (*melamed* means "Hebrew teacher") at a parochial school. When the shy, young Leo entered Chicago public school at eleven he spoke only Yiddish, which alienated him even more from his classmates. Those early years left Melamed skeptical, wary, and somewhat superstitious. He calls it the Bialystok syndrome: Disaster is always around the next corner, and you invite it when you begin bragging about your success. That was why one time early in his career he sent out letters to friends and colleagues around Chicago excusing himself for sounding bombastic in a local newspaper feature about his commodity trading exploits. As for the notion of risk, he says, "I come from a family of risk takers. I wouldn't be alive today if my parents hadn't taken incredible risks." Small wonder Melamed ended up carving a career for himself in the high-risk, high-stakes game of commodity futures.

Fascinated by the psyche, Melamed attended the University of Illinois, where he received a psychology degree before going on to receive a law degree. To help finance his legal education, he drove a taxicab, worked in the catalog house of Montgomery Ward & Company, and as a clerk for Merrill Lynch on the Chicago Mercantile Exchange. While in law school, he borrowed money from his father and bought an exchange membership. In 1966 he gave up law to become a full-time trader and was elected to the board a year later. His quick rise to exchange leadership was due, in good part, to the fact that as a lawyer he could articulate ideas with convincing ease. That, coupled with a thick-skinned aggressiveness, meant it wasn't long before Melamed had sold the Merc members on the idea of trading the ultimate commodity—money. And in 1972, the Merc became the first exchange to successfully trade foreign currencies through the International Monetary Market and an entire new industry called financial futures evolved.

Melamed's traumatic youth is hardly an isolated case in cor-

porate America. There is Ken West, chairman of Harris Bank, who
was abandoned by his natural parents in Fort Collins, Colorado, and
adopted from an orphanage. And Brunswick CEO Jack Reichert,
whose father died when he was twelve and whose mother died four
years later when he graduated from high school. To this day Wes
Christopherson remembers struggling through a depression-ridden
childhood as the son of a South Dakota dirt farmer before going on to
law school and eventually ending up in Chicago where he ran Jewel
Companies. What do Scorsese, Melamed, West, Reichert, and the
others have in common? A transformational experience that forever
changes their appraisal of events. They've become participant-
observers.

By no means, however, does a trauma alone become the merit
badge of leadership. Far from it. Many people don't have the ability
to turn emotions such as rage and anger into constructive energy.
Inner drive slows to a crawl. Fear often sets in. You get stuck. You
become your own boiled frog in your own pond: You can't get out.
You can't get through the rejection, anger, and pain. Instead, you
lock the door on it.

There's nobody who's going to get through life without a twice-
born experience. Nobody. If you haven't had one yet, don't worry. It
will happen. The experience is different for everyone, because everyone has a different tolerance. Timing also is important. At five
years old, you may not be able to articulate the experience. While
you can't synthesize it, it remains in you somewhere.

Throughout history, myths have encoded the same message: the
journey to discover oneself. There's the sacrifice for perspective.
Then the rebirth with new knowledge and vision. And finally the
return. Myths are the models for understanding your own life, insisted the late scholar Joseph Campbell: "Anybody going on a journey, inward or outward, to find values, will be on a journey that has
been described many times in the myths of mankind." The idea of
a journey inward, every person an explorer and hero facing the inner
self, is as old as the tale of Aeneas, the wandering warrior who
ventured into the underworld in search of his father. He fords the
river Styx, takes on the monstrous three-headed watchdog of Hades,

and manages a conversation with the ghost of his father, who teaches Aeneas things he needs to know to continue his journey and to enhance his understanding of life once he returns from the unknown. His new vision enables him to become the founder of the city of Lavinium and the Latin nation, from which eventually the Romans were descended.

We should be able to identify with Aeneas and his journey. First, there is his disengagement from the past as he leaves Troy and the memories of war behind and the painful loss of his father— twice-born experiences. Then comes the sense of alienation in the underworld, followed by renewed insight and spirit from his father. And at last, vision. Aeneas is proud, brave, devoted to family, and able to submerge personal considerations to the greater good. As a leader, he indeed is too good to be true. But perhaps that's why he's even more of a myth in today's context.

Myths are the software of culture. They open one to mysteries of the world, they validate the values of society, by showing us how to live with risk and overcome trauma. Myths tell us what we don't know because we haven't yet had the experience—"the rapture" of living, Campbell calls it. Myths give us a deeper awareness and clues to our spiritual behavior. But because of the sound-bite world we live in, the myths of the past are hardly remembered today. Culture has become homogenized and the mythic stories of the past are no longer told. We are sort of mythologically blind. The old myths have been replaced by manufactured scenarios of terminators and aliens in big-screen color.

Improvisation

Any jazz musician will tell you what Will Durant said years ago: "Happiness is the free play of the instincts." But you don't have to be a musician to improvise creatively. You need only know how to let go of those certain experiences that may control your life. Indeed, it isn't all that different from the process a jazz musician goes through.

Let's look at the inner process of leadership through the words and thoughts of our jazz musician. Although *improvisation* means "unprepared," it doesn't mean without preparation. The business leader, like the musician who masters his or her instrument, must also be a virtuoso in at least one aspect of his or her business. The business leader must be able to demonstrate that expertise to colleagues before being allowed to lead them into new territory. Improvisers are technical masters. And so are business leaders who master a phase of their business. But, make no mistake, being a technical master does not necessarily mean you are a leader. The improviser must have other attributes. Access to past experiences is one. In addition is the ability to focus intently on the present so that there is a dual awareness: Old memories and feelings are fused to current events. And finally, one must be confident enough to give up total control over the familiar, the comfortable, in order to free-fall with experimentation.

At forty-five, jazz pianist Joel Futterman has recorded fourteen albums described by trade publications as everything from "passionate stuff" to "the most creative music in the world of new music." And although his compact discs sell like hotcakes in the European capitals and Tokyo, he has yet to be discovered by American jazz enthusiasts other than the critics, who herald him with a sense of innovative awe. He plays with his fingers, his head, his heart, and every other sense he can stir when he sits down, shuts his eyes tightly, and creates. "The pioneer of inspiration is being conscious of life itself," he says. Futterman is an improvisationist who, through his music, connects emotions, memory, and intellect with feelings and desires. "I am," he says, "in full communication with myself." Improvisation is not a random experience. In each phrase there's connection and resolution. It's like having a conversation. One phrase leads to another. Conscious listening, then response. It requires a relaxed concentration. In short, Futterman is a master of musical risk.

Hear him rhapsodize about his music:

I'm focused. Some musicians play only what they've learned and end up digging holes for themselves. When they improvise, there are a lot of clichés in the music. True jazz improvisation is when there are total unknowns out there. And you play the phrase without any preconceived notions; you don't know what's going to happen next. I hear it. Then I execute what I hear.

To get to that stage takes hours of practicing and listening for the connection and resolution in all kinds of music. It's a lifelong study. The talent has been developed by playing inside music too, music with set harmonies and chord structures and preconceived melodies that define the tune. First I begin to improvise within a set of chord changes. Then I start experimenting.

So, like the jazz musician, the participant-observer reacts to the past and when he becomes a master of the business, is able to define and redefine his goals and create a new vision. That's why leaders focus on imaginative ideas and are more dramatic in style and unpredictable in behavior than managers. They realize they can't get work done without aggression but relate to people in an intuitive and empathic way. One of the critical jobs of the leader is to overcome political inclinations of conformity while encouraging individual expression of talent.

Vision, then, along with risk and change is yet another element of leadership. Back in the nineteenth century, the Rothschilds, England's renowned bankers, showed a world vision that went beyond the narrow view of those who competed for their empire. Nathan Rothschild floated loans to overcome the Irish famine and helped finance the British government in its defeat of Napoleon. And like today's shrewd investor, he used the technology of his day to get an edge: He learned of the outcome of the Battle of Waterloo within a day, thanks to the carrier pigeon, and scored a fortune in the stock market. Such a historical anecdote demonstrates the need for vision, perseverance, and the long-term view. Perspective is the key here. It, among other factors, separates leaders from managers, as we shall see in the following chapter.

Yes, the participant-observer is really the twice-born person.

He or she has the feeling of separateness, which results in being able to see new ways to make things work. It requires a reevaluation of the process. That in turn leads to a redefinition of the goals. *Participant-observers are technical masters who have shown exceptional competence in some phase of the business. They are able to look at problems with a fresh perspective and let loose the energy and creativity to transform the process or goal.* Leaders can see the flow of events and patterns as would outside observers. At the same time, they feel a sense of urgency based on the understanding that time is the most precious of all resources. They have learned to channel their emotional energy into creativity. And above all, they are willing to take risks, which almost surely results in an invigorating experience of being alive.

Reflections: New Warp Threads from the Struggle of Life

The participant-observer is both performer and a member of the audience at the same time. Participant-observers can see their lives growing in extra dimensions out of personal adversity and the ability to cope with the trauma. The results are new insights and special strengths we draw on throughout our lives. From Newman's born-twice concept to William James's observations of this transformation to Erik Erikson's codification of the stages of life, the process by which we add new strengths is a step-by-step progression.

Although Leo Melamed, Jack Reichert, Weston Christopherson, and many of the other CEOs who were interviewed were able to talk about their life traumas, some were not. From these emotionally wrenching events—death, sickness, poverty, parental separation, and immigration—the leader undergoes a transformation deep within the psyche. Sometimes the leader is aware of the change, but more often he or she is not. Yet we were able to identify specific events that personally had impact on the individual, who came out of the experience changed and energized with special strengths. One of those strengths was an ability to reinterpret in a novel way perplexing problems.

At this point, I invite you to take a personal inventory of your strengths and weaknesses. Do you have persistence, positive self-regard, capacity to empower, the ability to create compacts that bind, an intellectual commitment, the wherewithal to overcome chaos, a willingness toward risk, a command of substance of a particular business, a long-term view, flexibility, and openness?

Now think about your professional goals, core values, and personal needs. Take it one step further by writing down these introspective observations. The result will be a blueprint from which you can compare your current professional status against your expectations.

5

Role Models, Relationships, Networks

> It is one of the most beautiful compensations of this life that no man can sincerely try to help another without helping himself.
>
> —RALPH WALDO EMERSON

*C*all it chemistry or charisma or by whatever name you wish. But there exists an emotional catalyst that causes the apprentice to want to emulate a parent, teacher, or boss by changing behavior. Role models, relationships, and networks are the mechanisms by which important skills of leadership are transmitted.

It doesn't take a Clausewitz to know that a winning battlefield strategy depends on troop movement, firepower, and communication. An army deficient in any one of these elements may win a battle or two, but it is likely to lose the war. Consider the plight of the Iraqi army in the Gulf War. While General Norman Schwarzkopf's troops were taking Kuwait by the back door, the Iraqis seemed to be stuck in the sand. The reason: Iraqi commanders couldn't communicate quickly enough with each other. Sure, they all spoke the same language, but they couldn't understand one another. In fact, some of them couldn't even hear each other. There in the desert they had created their own Tower of Babel.

The breakdown in communications wasn't fully understood until U.S. communications officers analyzed the Iraqi system after the war. They were flabbergasted by their findings. In its military shop-

85

ping spree over the year, Iraq had bought no less than fourteen different kinds of radio systems, most with varied frequency bands that could not be tuned to talk to each other. One Iraqi battalion, for example, had a British system, the adjoining battalion a Russian system. The result was static, not to mention confusion. Without a viable communications network, the Iraqi army was doomed before it could even fire a shot. The notion of many radios set to a common frequency was as alien to the Iraqis as was the desert to the Americans.

The communications plan for the Fourteenth Iraqi Battalion was shaped like a Japanese fan; the apex of the fan was the headquarters and each line represented direct radio communications to a single outfit. There were eleven lines reaching out to eleven pairs of radios keyed on eleven different frequencies. The plan, said the experts, was entirely linear, meaning that the information flowed from the lower unit to the higher unit. Thus commanders on the front line were unable to speak to each other. The American radio configuration looked like a spiderweb with information flowing upward, downward, and laterally.

How many business executives in the same company operate on different wavelengths, cut off from each other by not paying enough attention to networking?

Like a spiderweb, the corporate network extends in every direction, touching individuals at every level of management. It is the primary means of communication, sometimes transcending positions and even titles. Organizations usually maintain two types of networks: formal and informal. Most companies have organization charts and job descriptions that present a formalized statement of duties and responsibilities and varied reporting relationships. It is a diagram of how the parts fit and how they should relate to each other. But the organizational plan is only the tip of the iceberg. What lurks beneath, however, is not a dark icy abyss but another network, a number of communication channels that intersect all levels and outposts of the company. These channels are the nerve endings of the invisible organization. Consultant Ram Charan observes that "networks are designed to build the central competitive advantage of the 1990s—superior execution in a volatile environment." Networks begin to matter when they change behavior. As Charan points out, "all too often, managers invest huge amounts of time and energy to reach agreement on vision without investing in the truly hard work— becoming aligned on the nitty-gritty trade-offs and time pressure required to deliver on the vision."

The network breathes life into the company, serving as a means of cross-fertilization. Expertise and energy are focused on important problems rather than dissipated under a clutter of memos piled forehead high on some manager's desk who is interested only in protecting his or her own turf. A solid network overcomes frustration, cynicism, and complacency. "Agreement without alignment," Charan says, "seldom changes behavior."

Terrence Deal and Allen Kennedy in their fascinating book called *Corporate Cultures* conclude that "in a strong culture, the network is powerful because it can reinforce the basic beliefs of the organization, enhance the symbolic value of heroes by passing on stories of their deeds and accomplishments, set a new climate for change, and provide a tight structure of influence for the CEO." In fact sometimes in a large corporation, they add, the network can be the only way to get a job done. President Franklin D. Roosevelt was said to be the consummate networker. To back that claim, Deal and Kennedy quote historian Arthur Schlesinger, who wrote: "The first task of an executive, as Roosevelt saw it, was to guarantee himself an effective flow of information and ideas. . . . Roosevelt's persistent effort, therefore, was to check and balance information acquired through official channels by information acquired through a myriad of private, informal, and unorthodox channels and espionage networks. At times, he seemed to pit his personal sources against his public sources."

As American companies grew in the 1960s and 1970s they became compartmentalized, which hurt their ability to compete in the 1980s. In recent years, however, executives have been pushing the notion of the boundaryless corporation, breaking down not only departmental walls, but divisional walls as well, and allowing managers from one area to share knowledge with those of another. The result is a cross-fertilization of ideas and information. General Electric paved the way to allow more latitude by sharply trimming management layers. Pepsico encourages lateral movement across divisions along with broadening jobs so a benefits manager, for example, also can take on recruiting and planning. Intel is experimenting with job sharing, placing three managers on teams so fewer people can do more work; even the chief executive and chairman share jobs. At General Motors, Ford, and Chrysler design engineers now work with marketing people in the seminal stages of creating new models.

Networking can also help companies keep their hard chargers energized. These days it will take every strategy in the book to cope with those younger managers on the track to leadership. With companies downsizing and consolidating, the management slots and raises are dwindling at a time when ranks of the aspirants are ballooning; at a median age of thirty-three, the eighty-one million baby boomers are clogging the management pipeline. Business leaders have to recognize and deal with the cultural explosion or risk the wrath of customers and employees alike. "That's the issue," insisted Pepsi-Cola Chairman D. Wayne Calloway at a University of Chicago Graduate Business School conference in 1991. "Let's call it craving for autonomy, individuality and responsibility. Here's the rub: At the exact moment business leaders are trying to gain more control over their businesses, their employees and their customers seek fewer controls and more freedom. It's a big problem, and it's growing bigger by the day."

Value of Networks

Networking offers a means toward coping with the problem faced by Calloway and other chief executives. When ties cross departmental lines, employees share a wider, more rational view and are more likely to cooperate with each other, allowing an organization to better handle crisis. Thus a powerful network can reinforce the vision of the leader because it enables the leader to anticipate roadblocks, resistance, and defects in a program.

"The value of networking has become self-evident," says Ira Levin, an organizational psychologist at Kaiser Permanente, the giant Oakland-based health care operator. "Managers get a broader perspective as well as a sounder footing in the business." At Kaiser, Levin has assisted in the design and implementation of a pilot networking program for assistant directors of nursing to develop nurses who think like CEOs. The nurses, who have spent all their time in clinics and hospitals, now spend six to eight weeks at a stretch in each of several departments, learning financial analysis, information systems, rate planning, facilities planning, labor relations, and materials management. "They work with people they would never have met in their daily regime," says Levin. "They have new business relations. We hope to develop a cadre of generalists who are well-versed in multiple aspects of the business, along with providing lateral opportunities for those who want to redirect or reenergize their careers."

Today's business world accepts more career diversity than it used to. In fact, zigzagging through the corporate ranks broadens managers who in the past have traveled along narrow paths only to find they have a limited understanding of the business because they've spent most of their careers in one function. Attitudes have changed from the top down. No longer do managers have to define themselves solely by the rungs they've climbed. Some companies, in fact, have tried team approaches at the loftiest executive levels. At Intel Corporation, for instance, CEO Andrew Grove shared the president's role with Chairman Gordon Moore and Executive Vice President Craig Barrett in what was called the "Executive Office." Grove concentrated on management issues and product strategy, while Moore focused on financial matters and Barrett on operations.

The passage to the executive suite is cobbled with memos, letters, notes, edicts, statements, flip charts, and other formal means of communication. Deal and Kennedy estimate that 90 percent "of what goes on in an organization has nothing to do with formal events." Instead, they say, "the real business" flows through the company's cultural network. They explain: "Even in the context of a highly controlled meeting, there is a lot of informal communication going on—bonding, rituals, glances, innuendoes, and so forth. The real process of making decisions, of gathering support, of developing opinions, happens before the meeting—or after."

Moreover, there's an amazing efficiency in networking. "Networks," Ram Charan says, "are faster, smarter, and more flexible than reorganizations or downsizings—dislocating steps that cause confusion, sap emotional energy, and seldom produce sustainable results." For nearly a decade Charan helped to create networks in ten companies based in North America and Europe: At Conrail, the Philadelphia-based freight transport firm, a network called the "operating committee" consists of a team of nineteen middle managers who meet every Monday morning to make decisions on a range of tactical issues as well as to work on a five-year plan to create new approaches to important segments of the business. At Montreal's Royal Bank of Canada, a dozen middle managers from field offices across Canada developed a reform program to rejuvenate the bank's retail strategy. At the UK headquarters of Dun & Bradstreet Europe a "development network" works on new products and customization of existing ones in addition to finding ways to ease the tensions of a cross-border, cross-cultural organization.

Using the network to tap into the business culture is virtually a part of our social fabric. "It is back to the old days of using contacts for all they are worth," wrote Elizabeth Fowler in the *New York Times* in the summer of 1991. Lee J. Svete, placement director of St. Lawrence University, estimates that nearly 70 percent of those who found jobs during the white and blue collar recession in 1991 did so through contacts with alumni, parents, friends, and others compared with 50 percent of the class that relied on such contacts the previous year. "If you cannot go in the front door," says Svete, "you go through a side door."

Once you're in the door, it's business as usual. The network responds to all sorts of behavior; sometimes, for instance, it favors the finesse of a golf swing as opposed to the eloquence of words. As long as there have been sand traps, executives have been cutting business deals over the lush greens of golf courses. The network extends well beyond the corporate walls linked by the practice of passing along business cards or making a call on behalf of an old fraternity pal, or the cocktail parties and long business lunches. These are among the avenues where the good-ol'-boy network thrived. All along, however, professional associations and clubs have mushroomed, giving the outside network equal billing with the inside network. For example, as we shall see in chapter 10, it wasn't until Crate & Barrel's Gordon Segal joined the Young President's Organization that he realized the true value of networking. He had emerged from a management cocoon he himself had built as the Crate's founder, entrepreneur, and CEO. It wasn't until he met other young chief executives that he realized they too had problems similar to his own, problems he thought were unique. He no longer felt isolated. Segal had learned an important lesson: Most leaders are self-taught, acquiring their leadership skills by trial and error.

He also learned that involvement in the minutiae of the culture of the corporation can be a drag on a leader's creativity. That in turn can lead to the inbreeding of ideas built on vague perceptions rather than hard reality. No matter how good your controls are, you must constantly look outside your own company. It's a lot easier to be number two in the industry and know you want to be number one. Aiming for the top spot becomes a focused objective. But when you're already number one who do you compare yourself to? A lack of perception becomes a disabling weakness for many companies stuck in their own glory. Five years after Tom Peters and Robert Waterman wrote *In Search of Excellence* (published in 1982), two-thirds of the companies they pegged as excellent have slipped drastically and some, in fact, are out of business.

Networking breaks through a company's self-imposed isolation. But you've got to become a wise networker. That means networking without giving any competitive secrets away. Don't, for instance, get too intimately involved in a trade association because colleagues will pump you for information. Most businesspeople, as Segal discovered, share generic problems. Thus external networks are windows on reality that help to change perspectives. To put it another way: To distinguish between corporate reality and corporate fantasy, the leader must follow the painter's practice of stepping back from the easel to survey the work with critical and self-excluding eyes. The leader who develops this kind of discipline is well on the way to achieving honest perspective.

Remember, a corporate culture is as artificial as the entity it represents—the corporation. Yet, each corporate culture is unique, defining what's important, who's important, what conduct is acceptable, what conduct is discouraged. The culture defines the dress code, travel code, and the way conversations are carried on. Some corporate cultures even create their own language, a kind of corporatespeak that acts as a bond among employees. At bureaucratic IBM, for example, a fairly extensive euphemistic lexicon has evolved over the years. In IBMese, a "tree hugger" is an employee who resists a move or any other change; a "remission" is a new plan, and to "redeploy" is to perform another type of job.

Part of the leader's on-the-job training is to use reason and persuasion. Logic usually wins over heated argument as long you're dealing with rational people. Never face down another executive and unleash a barrage of words that spray like pellets from a double-barreled shotgun. Nobody likes a motor mouth. The art of plain talk is your best weapon. However, if at times you can salt your speech figuratively with metaphor, a statement that conveys an idea through comparison, do so. As long as they're not obscure, sharp metaphors are verbal snapshots that can communicate insight with a wallop.

After a while networking assumes a life of its own like an amoeba taking shape. The stimuli are everywhere. "Leading and managing," says University of Chicago professor Wayne Baker, "are accomplished by cultivating, maintaining, and using a multitude of direct and indirect relationships inside and outside the firm." A CEO deals with not only the board of directors and senior managers but also customers, clients, suppliers, government agencies, the press, and the public. The leader's task is to unify this vast network as a positive force.

The network often extends into the social and civic spheres as well. Indeed, many business executives are bonded together by a tradition of involvement in community affairs. The late James Bere, former chairman of Borg-Warner, remembered his civic baptism, which took place in 1963. An up-and-comer in the executive ranks, he was invited to lunch at the Chicago Club by Robert Ingersoll, then Borg-Warner's chairman and Bere's mentor. "We're considering you for president," said Ingersoll. "I have two questions. Are you willing to pay the price? And are you committed to serving the community?"

Bere answered yes to both questions, although looking back, he admits and says that his response to the first one "came from total ignorance, because I didn't know what the price was." But he knew exactly what Ingersoll meant by the second. "He wanted a person who would not focus solely on the running of the company. Leadership demanded that you be part of the community."

Likewise, Commonwealth Edison Corporation's chairman James O'Connor says he learned from the example of his predecessor, Thomas Ayers. O'Connor, who figures he spends 15 to 20 percent of an eighty-hour work week on civic matters, even took Ayers's place as a trustee of Northwestern University when he succeeded him as chief executive.

It's impossible to say how many deals have been cut behind closed doors of executive clubs, until very recently exclusive male enclaves. But for sure they are a link in the business network. Typical perhaps is the Chicago Club. Membership in the 123-year-old club, any of the city's executives will tell you, is an introduction to business high society. The building with its five floors of private meeting rooms oozes with tradition, old-boy charm, and, above all, power. The Chicago Club has 1,200 members (850 resident members and 350 out of towners) and a waiting list as least as long. In the old days the Big Boys would have lunch or play poker at the millionaire's table. There, sipping port and smoking Havana cigars, could be seen the likes of the meatpacker Philip Armour and Potter Palmer, the hotelier. It was at that very table that Marshall Field, the department store tycoon, causally lent George Pullman the money to build his sleeping cars. Another table served only railroad chiefs, and a third catered to a group known as the little sons of the rich. According to Marshall Field's nephew Stanley Field, "Everything to be done in Chicago was discussed by that group, and then word was passed out."

Unfortunately, businesses have not permitted most women to cultivate the same outreach contacts as their male counterparts. However, recently women have attempted to construct their own networks. For instance, a number of alumnae at the University of Pennsylvania and Cornell University have fashioned councils for which career women serve as mentors and advisers to help women graduates get a start in the business world. In major cities across the country professional women belong to chapters of the National Women's Network, which serves mainly as a means of referrals for business contacts. Although these newly created organizations lack the bonding of an old-boy network of school chums and close friends, the women's networks do indeed serve as a valuable resource, especially in women's efforts to break through the glass ceiling that has blocked promotion for women in many companies.

In *The Female Advantage—Women's Ways of Leadership,* journalist Sally Helgesen notes that women tend to form flat organizations, rather than hierarchies, that emphasize frequent contact among staff members and sharing of information. She terms such networks "webs of inclusion." It is a circular system interconnected by a steady flow of information that moves up, down, and laterally. At the center of this web is the leader who becomes "educated" and "refreshed" by the information from a multitude of both business and social sources that include attorneys, ad agencies, accountants, college roommates, professional associations, consulting firms, churches, temples, social clubs, service clubs, charitable boards, educators, and friends. The web is wide reaching, informal, and well suited for the female sensibility, according to Helgesen, who observes: "We feel, many of us, that women are more caring and intuitive, better at seeing the human side, quicker to cut through competitive distinctions of hierarchy and ranking, impatient with cumbersome protocols."

Some experts are convinced there is a gender gap in leadership. In a provocative article titled "How Women Lead" in the December 1990 issue of the *Harvard Business Review,* Judy B. Rosener, a professor at the University of California at Irvine, wrote that "a second wave of women is making its way into top management not by adopting the style and habits that have proved successful for men, but drawing on the skills and attitudes they developed from their shared experience as women." Rosener further points out that women leaders encourage participation and share power and information. She calls their leadership style "interactive leadership" because "these women actively work to make their interactions with subordinates positive for everyone involved." They don't, says Rosener, covet formal authority and they've learned to lead without it. Women leaders believe that people perform best when they feel good about themselves and their work. They then try to create situations that contribute to that feeling. "Young, educated professionals impose special requirements on their organization," concludes Rosener. "They demand to participate and contribute. In some cases they have knowledge or talents that their bosses don't have. If they are good performers, they have many employment options . . . these professionals will respond to leaders who are inclusive and open, who enhance the self-worth of others, and who create a fun work environment."

Finding a Role Model

Regardless of executive gender, it helps to have a role model when getting started. When Robert Galvin showed up at his first job at Motorola Inc., he wanted to make a good impression. He arrived early and quietly sat on a bench in the personnel department waiting his turn. Across from Galvin sat another man who had arrived even earlier. Galvin had caught the eye of the personnel director, who beckoned to him. "What are you doing here?" asked the director. "Come right on in and we'll take care of you." Galvin cleared his throat, thanked him, and said he would wait because the man on the other bench had been waiting longer. Galvin waited his turn. Forget that Galvin was the boss's son, although the personnel director couldn't.

Robert Galvin, former chairman of Motorola Inc., has never tried to hide the fact that his father was Paul Galvin, the founder of Motorola. To this day he talks with deep admiration about the relationship. "I was his only son," reflects Bob Galvin. "While he wasn't always available for family affairs, he often shared his business experiences with me." The elder Galvin would often take young Bob on business trips and expose him to the inner workings of Motorola. Although Bob didn't know it at the time, he was being groomed as his father's successor. Paul wanted to hand over the reins of leadership as painlessly as possible. He had no intention of being dragged kicking and screaming from the chairman's office. "He was a remarkable operator throughout his life," recalled Galvin. "He expressed a genuine empathy for people. He didn't try to make himself popular, yet he was immensely admired by the organization. He reached out to people, respected the dignity of others. So I learned a lot of lessons from him. The concepts and values of Paul Galvin still exist today. Integrity is a very important factor. We don't need to take advantage of anybody, the customer or supplier. It never works. What my father demonstrated to me was trust. It was the single greatest motivation and I responded to it. That's why I honor trust. Stewardship is not for the preservation of the status quo, but for the preservation of the values of the firm, and the dignities relating to the firm."

Bob Galvin had a unique experience growing up. Paul Galvin was not only Bob's father but his mentor and role model as well. What better situation when you consider that learning about leadership requires on-the-job training, along with a deep attachment to a teacher who can mold the lessons necessary for development—someone who can be emulated. Thus aspiring leaders in the journeyman stage become copycats, imitators long before they craft their own styles. "I'm privileged," muses Bob Galvin. "I have had sufficient wealth to hire private ski instructors for my grandchildren. I choose those ski instructors for their character as well as their skiing excellence. How do my grandchildren learn how to ski? Not much better than anyone else's grandchildren, but they all learn by imitating, by following the role model."

James Bere inculcated Borg-Warner's corporate culture with a sense of strong values toward family. Once Bere reached the top, he made it a policy to be with his family on weekends no matter what. In time, many of the company's top executives began following his example.

Role models are a significant ingredient in leadership development. There is a way of learning by watching for and following role models. Psychohistorian James MacGregor Burns would certainly agree with Galvin's firsthand experience at teaching by role model. "Qualities of leadership emerge out of these imitative, selective and role-taking or empathetic processes," writes Burns. "As persons gain in experience, knowledge and understanding, imitation, intentionality, and capacity for higher moral judgment and as they grow more skillful in accommodation in role-taking, they gain the capacity of leadership that draws from others (needs, roles and values . . .)." Children learn by imitating parents, older siblings, and other admired individuals. It's a process that extends into maturity as a means of gaining knowledge and social understanding.

There has never been a shortage of role models in the business world—positive and negative. In September 1990, when *Life* magazine unveiled its selection of the 100 most influential Americans of the twentieth century, one-quarter of them were businessmen. Although Madonna, Magic Johnson, Clark Gable, Marilyn Monroe, and Joe DiMaggio didn't make the list, Ray Kroc, Thomas Watson, Edwin Land, Henry Ford, Alfred P. Sloan, Jr., John D. Rockefeller, Jr., and Charles E. Merrill were among those businessmen who did.

The mentorship of a powerful banker helped John Bryan ease into the executive life when he moved from West Point, Mississippi, to Chicago in 1974. Bryan, then thirty-seven years old, was executive vice president and a director of Sara Lee Corporation. Tilden Cummings, the sixty-seven-year-old former chairman of the Continental Bank and also a member of the Sara Lee board, took Bryan under his wing. Cummings, at the time of one the most powerful businessmen in the community, introduced Bryan to a number of people and Bryan's network began. The elder statesman Cummings also served Bryan as a role model.

Another executive who certainly appreciates the value of a role model is Elmer Johnson, managing partner of the law firm Kirkland & Ellis and former executive vice president of General Motors Corporation. Johnson's principal role model, however, was not an attorney or a businessman, but a philosopher.

Johnson, a consummate thinker and deeply religious man, was raised in Denver. His twice-born experience came early when he suffered the grief of a lost sibling. Johnson's twelve-year-old sister, Donna, died from polio. After the tragedy, he said, "I just had the conviction I had to make the most of myself, a sense of calling, a religious purpose." Johnson graduated from Yale with a degree in English literature and then received a law degree from the University of Chicago. By 1973 he was the managing partner of Kirkland & Ellis, one of Chicago's biggest law firms, when he got a call from the White House. He was a candidate for the chairmanship of the Securities and Exchange Commission. Johnson had lost out to the Nixon administration's first choice. Johnson was disappointed, not so much over the fact he had lost out, but over how he handled himself during the interview process. "It shattered me," he recalled. "I hadn't had well-conceived answers or thought deeply enough about the fundamental issues."

Shortly thereafter Johnson paid a visit to James Gustafson, a professor of theology and ethics at the University of Chicago. "It perhaps has been the most important friendship of my life," Johnson says today. Gustafson set out to fill Johnson's educational gap by drawing up a lengthy reading list of books on theology, ethics, political philosophy, and the sociology of capitalism. The rest was up to Johnson. From two A.M. to five A.M. every other morning, he read, thought, and took copious notes.

By the time he went to General Motors to head up legal, environmental, government relations, and other staffs, he had prepared a thirty-page bibliography with commentary on the 150 books he read. So grateful for what Gustafson had done for him, Johnson bankrolled the professor for two years at $50,000 a year so he could write a book on ethics. The education of Elmer Johnson gave him a renewed sense of confidence. Never short of ambition, Johnson was a well-disciplined individual with a lot of energy. Although he could be beguiling and open, which gave people confidence in him, he was no pushover. To the contrary, he was focused and knew what he wanted. By1987, he had become executive vice president and a GM director, in addition to serving on two of GM's most powerful committees, the executive committee and finance committee.

He even became a volunteer in his drive through the corporate ranks. In July 1984, he told Chairman Roger Smith he wanted to try to reform the personnel system. His request was promptly granted, and the personnel staff was added to the other responsibilities. His first assignment: Trim the white collar work force by forty thousand employees, a job he carried out with great pain. Increasingly, Johnson was identified as a top candidate for the CEO's office. But like a faulty gear, his experience didn't quite mesh with GM's culture. Smith and the two chairmen before him had come up through GM's financial ranks. And neither did Johnson have the manufacturing experience that Robert Sempel had, the man who was to replace Smith. More important, he began to disagree more and more with Smith's strategies. On July 1, 1988, Johnson returned to Kirkland & Ellis as managing partner.

The leader also learns from failure. Unfortunately, most of us make the same mistakes repeatedly. It's all right to admit mistakes, it's even healthy. No one has all the answers all the time. The important thing is knowing where to find the answers—and to avoid the same mistakes. That, however, takes more than just mental adjustment. It takes a change in behavior; a new attitude, a new way of looking at old problems. Be curious. "Why?" and "What if?" are probably the two most provocative questions a leader can ask. In building a museum that will preserve its institutional memory, Motorola Corporation will showcase not only its winning products, but its losers as well. Why? "There are lessons to be learned from our mistakes," explains Bob Galvin. "This museum will house these mistakes so we can learn from them to prevent the same problems from arising in the future."

An intense desire to do better opens an individual up to change, as does working in an environment that stretches your capacity. When starting out, be a B player in an A game to sharpen your skills—"No strain, no gain." And be a volunteer. By that I mean, don't wait to be plucked from boredom. If you see a situation that you believe you can contribute to or learn from, ask if you can participate. Say yes to new committee assignments, training programs, and special projects. Take the view that it's better to regret the things you have done than the things you haven't. And finally, don't be afraid to look silly. Or, as author Peter Schwartz in *The Art of the Long View* puts it, "Allow yourself to be enthralled."

We can also learn from negative role models. The lesson in this case is obvious: Avoid the CEO disease. That's how *Business Week* described it in a 1991 cover story about executives who fall victims to their own success. The CEO disease can be contagious and even fatal to a career. The telltale signs of this executive malady are as obvious as the symptoms of a nagging flu. They include refusing to admit mistakes; spending excessive time on boards of other companies or civic groups, shuttling to and fro in statesmanlike fashion; being surrounded by yes-people; insisting on making the critical decisions, but not bothering to find out the details; trying to outdo other CEOs with a bigger salary and fleet of corporate jets; becoming obsessed with protocol that dictates where executives sit at meetings or whether people rise when the boss enters the room; relishing media attention for personal gain rather than for the company; and hanging on to the job too long and undermining attempts to find a successor.

Call it what you want—egotism, narcissism, or old-fashioned autocratic bullying—the CEO disease leads to bad blood relationships among executives, contaminates a corporate culture with pettiness, and sends a negative message throughout the organization. Consider the plight of Chrysler chairman Lee Iacocca, a feisty and tenacious man once considered America's model executive. Judging from the millions of copies his autobiography sold, apparently people wanted to hear what he had to say. At one point there was even talk of Iacocca as a presidential candidate. His press was sterling. In the late 1970s Iacocca resuscitated a near dying company, then took on Tokyo and Washington in a crusade to bolster free markets for free people. As the sole spokesperson on television commercials, he became Chrysler incarnate. But something happened. By the late 1980s Chrysler was in a tailspin. In the fourth quarter of 1989 Chrysler had sustained its first loss since 1982. Earnings continued to slide and by 1990 Chrysler's share of the market had fallen by 14 percent. And there were major defections in his key management ranks, including his heir apparent. Unfortunately Iacocca seemed to have ignored the maximum he penned in his 1984 autobiography: "In the end, all business operations can be reduced to three words: people, product, and profits. People come first. Unless you've got a good team, you can't do much with the other two."

What had happened to the once most focused of all CEOs? He had shifted his priorities. Instead of updating Chrysler's decade-old technology, he squandered money and energy acquiring new properties in the face of deteriorating labor relations and managers squabbling over the right to succeed him. "Like Donald Trump and other wildly successful Reagan-era businessmen," writes John Judis in a *Business Month* story titled "Myth vs. Man," "Iacocca fell victim to the Scylla and Charybdis of late-20th-century corporate management: the distraction of celebrity and the promise of power through deal making."

Chrysler faltered when Iacocca began to believe his do-no-wrong image. In short, he seemed to have caught a bad case of CEO disease. Eventually, as Judis viewed it, Chrysler became a kingdom without a king as the lords who had labored gladly and peacefully under him began fighting among themselves for control of the throne. Iacocca's was a management style that nurtured individual drive and creativity. But it needed a strong role model to maintain balance, a person at the top who not only commanded the loyalty of subordinates, but who could soothe their egos and reconcile their competing visions. "When the executive absents himself from the daily goings-on, all hell can break lose," Judis observes. "This is what seems to have happened at Chrysler."

Don't, however, write Iacocca off just yet. There seems to be plenty of fight left in him. "If he pulls another miracle," concludes Judis, "he will be heralded in the long line of immortals—stretching from Paul Revere to the auto-industry whiz Alfred P. Sloan." And if he doesn't pull it off? "He will be lumped with the likes of his nemesis Henry Ford II, who resurrected a company from the dead only to fall victim to illusions of omnipotence and the temptations of celebrity." If so, history will likely deem Iacocca unworthy of his hero status.

So, where are today's heroes? We must search our own mythology for the answer. But where are our myths? Flickering on the movie screens in a fantasy world that parallels ours. Let's, for the moment, consider *Star Wars*. Once described as a hip homage to B-movie ethics and heroism in the space age, *Star Wars* is sort of a cross between *Flash Gordon* and *The Wizard of Oz*. With ethnic myths no longer relevant in a borderless world, *Star Wars* serves us as a modern-day myth. It is a synthetic myth, communicated instantly around the world. By that I mean it is a deliberate creation to help us come to terms with the modern cultural environment. We don't believe Athena sprang from the head of Zeus. Nor are most of us familiar with the trials of St. George and the dragon because we don't believe in dragons. So what do we believe in? *Star Wars*. Luke Skywalker did indeed spring from the head of George Lucas.

Movie producer George Lucas was heavily influenced by Joseph Campbell's thoughts and his analysis of heroes and mythology. There is one mythology in the world. And that mythology is the hero's journey—a vision quest that transforms the world. *Star Wars*'s protagonist Luke Skywalker goes on such a journey. And he, too, like any hero-leader, has a mentor (named Ben Kenobi), a wise role model to help him through the tough times. Luke also undergoes the prototypical twice-born experience. In short, the *Star Wars* odyssey can serve as a metaphor for the road to leadership.

Myths and Heroes

Myths, of course, offer any number of purposes; they may stress religious significance or historical meaning in Greek and Roman history, or they can be analyzed from the point of view of psychology or anthropology. Whatever else a myth may be, it's a story. The Greek word *mythos* means exactly that, a "story." Myths are important because they have become part of our cultural network, interwoven into the arts and humanities. But unfortunately, as Campbell points out, there is no longer a society "as the gods once supported. The social unit is not a carrier of religious content, but an economic-political organization."

For Campbell there is structure to every myth: the hero's restlessness, the hero's separation from home and friends, the hero's need for a mentor or role model for encouragement, the hero's adventure, the hero's descent into the region of the unknown, the hero's confrontation with death, the hero lets go of the past, the hero defines the needs and wants of the group to which he or she returns, and the hero returns with new wisdom. In short, he or she is transformed. When transformation takes place two things occur: The hero lets go of the past and gains new insights. He or she becomes insecure. Why? Because the past is an anchor. Without it, an individual free-floats, bobbing up and down while drifting through life. In the beginning the hero usually has a noticeable flaw in his or her power, strength, or cunning. The hero needs help. After all, the hero's only human. That's when a mentor steps forth, offering stability through wise counsel. The hero's world suddenly looks different. What has really happened? The hero has been twice born and his or her identity has been recast to fit a new reality.

Of the mentor, note Donna Rosenberg and Sorelle Baker in *Mythology and You*, "These figures teach the hero or lend him their shrewdness through an apprenticeship, so that he can ultimately emerge victorious. Their special role in the heroic myths is similar to those of parents or leaders who help the young person develop the skills that enable him to cope with the problems of his existence. As he achieves a sense of autonomy, he no longer requires the guardianship of helpful figures. He is now an active and combative adult."

With that in mind *Star Wars* is not, as Campbell believed, a simple morality play. What, then, is this tale that mesmerized millions with eye-dazzling special effects? "It has to do with the powers of life," Campbell said, "as they are either fulfilled or broken and suppressed through the action of man." It is a modern-day myth, a heroic tale that provides a means of decoding the leadership wisdom in our folklore. To understand what I'm driving at, let's review the story—recalling some of the leadership concepts so far presented:

The saga opens on Luke Skywalker, a callow youth, who has undergone a twice-born experience arising out of the death of his parents. He has become the ward of his aunt and uncle. There is a restlessness about Luke, a need to leave the farm where he works scratching out a living in a hostile land. He is dissatisfied with things as they are. He meets Ben Kenobi, a Jedi knight, endowed with exceptional powers. He is the perfect role model and mentor for Luke. Ben Kenobi is old, with a full recollection of the past, yet he can see the future. He has gained wisdom from Jedi disciples. He exudes honesty, merits trust, and is experienced. Dressed plainly, he wears a monk's robe, conducting himself as a servant. Luke's mentor teaches him about the Force—a power and energy in life used to fight the power of evil in the form of the masked Darth Vader, who is faceless because he lacks humanity. He is, said Campbell, a robot, a bureaucrat living in terms of an imposed system.

Now comes the hero's adventurous journey. From the exhausted atmosphere of his planet, Luke, with assistance from Ben Kenobi and mercenary Han Solo, blasts off for a more promising galaxy. He is, in essence, an immigrant as he travels toward a new world. On the way, however, he finds himself in the middle of a struggle between the dark forces of Darth Vader and those of the white-clad Princess Leia. Soon he finds himself descending into the region of the unknown as Luke, Han, and Leia are captured and imprisoned in the fortress spaceship of the dark galaxy. They escape and make their way through a maze of rooms and corridors while fighting off Vader's troops. Eventually Luke returns to attack the fortress as a "top gun" spaceship fighter pilot, darting and weaving in air-to-air combat. In the climatic moment of the battle, in a mystic revelation, Ben Kenobi says to Luke, "Turn off your computer, turn off your machine and do it yourself, follow your feelings, trust your feelings." He is asking Luke to believe in himself. In a final burst of bravado, Luke destroys the fortress and, he believes, Vader with it. He has accomplished his goal, returning to Princess Leia's kingdom where he is accorded a hero's welcome and receives a medal for his deeds. Luke knows he has changed. He has an enlarged view of himself and the confidence of a person who has met a challenge with undaunted success. Luke has gone through his apprenticeship and emerged victoriously.

The transformation of Luke Skywalker follows the path laid down by his mentor, Ben Kenobi:

> *Let go of your conscious self* to become a participant-observer by becoming an immigrant as Luke traveled from his world to a new one.
>
> *Listen to your gut feeling;* it's all right to act on instinct.
>
> *Stretch your feelings with a willingness to spend yourself for the benefit of others.*
>
> *Don't count on luck or wait for something to happen;* instead be proactive and make it happen.
>
> *Take your first step into a larger world*—leaders take risks.

Believe in yourself as a winner; no one will trust you unless you believe in yourself and demonstrate that you have confidence in your vision of the future.

Reflections: The Warp Threads of Imagination, Mentorship, and Networking

Most of the CEOs we interviewed learned their leadership skills by trial and error in an informal on-the-job training program. Yet they had different agendas that took them to the head of their respective organizations. Somewhere along the way they had profited from an apprentice-master relationship in developing the craft of leadership. They became logicians in a step-by-step learning process that required a high degree of mental discipline. They displayed a thirst for knowledge to satisfy their needs for both intellectual and social growth. The scope of knowledge of an aspiring manager must extend well beyond the technical level of a mentor or role model.

Chief executive officers get their job done through relationships that include the board of directors, peers, immediate subordinates, the subordinates' subordinates, relationships with outside organizations, customer contacts, client contacts, suppliers, competitors, governmental agencies, the press, and the public.

Obviously, learning leadership skills is not solely an intellectual experience. An effective role model can stimulate an emotional and visceral response just as, say, music appeals to a person's aesthetic tastes. *"Music is something terribly special,"* said the late conductor-composer Leonard Bernstein. *"It doesn't have to pass through the censor of the brain before it can reach the heart . . . an F sharp doesn't have to be considered in the mind; it is a direct hit and therefore all the more powerful."* Positive role modeling is also a direct hit and like an F sharp doesn't have to be considered by the mind. Often apprentices mimic the dress, speech, thinking, code of conduct, and other admirable aspects of the role model's persona.

We also learn from negative role models. A pair of intriguing ones were CEO Harold Geneen and General George Patton. Both were fighters on different fronts. Geneen the field marshal of International Telephone and Telegraph Corporation is credited with fashioning the modern conglomerate and touching off the acquisition craze of the 1960s. The so-called Geneen machine snapped up companies like Patton's Third Army swallowed real estate in North Africa and Europe on the way to defeating the Germans during World War II.

When Patton looked his troops in the eye and proclaimed, "All real Americans love the sting of battle," he was as sincere as the American flag behind him. His booming voice and finger-in-the-chest aggressiveness characterized his leadership style, which led to military victories but, ironically, to his personal defeat as well. He was stripped of his command. In the corporate wars Geneen met a similar fate, having been fired as head of the company he built brick by brick. Both men had a global perspective. Both had loyal cadres of followers and power rooted in the detailed grasp of strategic planning. Both were iconoclastic. And both allowed their egos to cloud judgment, which resulted in their downfalls. They were both leaders, the kind who never ducked responsibility, yet told everyone else what to do. Unfortunately, both were their own worst enemies. There are lessons to be learned from them, nevertheless, because both positive as well as negative role models are crucial in defining a person's leadership style.

Leadership craftsmen also expand their skill by networking. The networks can be formal and informal, strong and weak, inside and outside the organization. They help the leader coordinate learning while enhancing self-confidence. In the networking process each person becomes an investor in the new idea and has a stake in working for its success.

Acquiring
Warp Threads

Design in the tapestry of leadership is determined in part by biological and sociological threads. Among them are the following.

Gender
Intelligence
Physical characteristics
Energy/health
Mother as caretaker
Father as caretaker
Siblings
Family position—first or second child
Relatives and relationships.

Some threads, or specific personality traits, are acquired during critical periods of childhood and adolescent development as plotted by Erik Erikson and Jean Erikson in *The Eight Stages of Man.* These traits, too, become part of the warp threads of leadership acquired during each stage.

Infancy—social trust and mistrust; autonomy or shame.

Early Childhood—initiative or guilt

School Age—industry or inferiority

Puberty—industry or role confusion; a universal born-twice event

Some threads are earned by careful study and observation enhanced by an accumulation of facts and skills.

Industry knowledge, including technology, competition, strengths and weaknesses of your company, strengths and weaknesses of the competition

Company knowledge, including culture, history, proven performers, knowledge of where "the bodies are buried"

Internal and external network development

Improvement of your personal skills

Personal growth through learning, including role models and the study of the human experience

Acquiring warp threads throughout one's life is part of becoming a whole person while facilitating growth in a chaotic business climate.

PART II

The Tapestry of Leadership: Creating the Weft

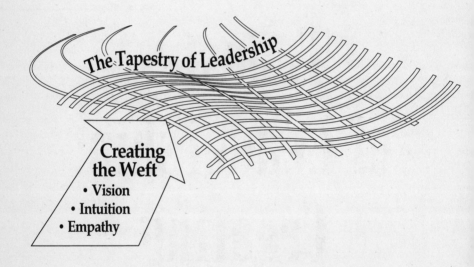

The Tapestry of Leadership

Creating
the Weft
• Vision
• Intuition
• Empathy

*C*reating weft threads—the second essential step in weaving—requires sifting through one's own creative potential, choosing the useful attributes, and making a major emotional, intellectual, and sometimes financial commitment.

The weft threads—the crosswise strands—those intersecting elements that create the pattern and breathe life into the leadership tapestry are *intuition, empathy, creativity, imagination, insight, sensitivity, introspection, curiosity, optimism, confidence, commitment, vision, risk taking, ability to synthesize, sense of urgency, listening, and communication skills.* Many of our warp threads derive from the time when we were children and could still see the wonderment of life. However, freedom to create is sadly lacking in most of our adult activities today. While everyone has creative ideas, the problem arises for adults to give themselves the permission to express themselves on important and serious subjects in a creative way. Why? Because we are not empowered to take risks by schools, our bosses, our friends. We are taught and rewarded to conform. However, having permission to express oneself, combined with the willingness to take risk, are essential elements of weaving the weft threads of leadership.

Creating weft threads also requires shifting through the many creative thoughts one has, choosing the valid ones, and making an emotional, intellectual, and often financial commitment to their realization. *It not only requires giving oneself permission to take risks; it at the same time gives one permission to accept the consequences of failure.*

Oliver Wendell Holmes commented: "There are one-story intellectuals, two-story intellectuals and three-story intellectuals with skylights. All fact collectors who have no aim beyond their facts are one-story men. Two-story men compare, reason and generalize, using the labor of fact collectors as their own. Three-story men idealize, imagine, predict—their best illumination comes from above the skylight."

Weft threads are the skylights of three-story men and women.

Vision and Mission— A Balance Between the Fresh and Familiar

Some men see things as they are and say, "Why?" I dream things that never were, and say, "Why not?"
—GEORGE BERNARD SHAW

*T*he concept of vision doesn't lend itself to easy analysis. Suffice it to say vision is more than perception and cockeyed optimism. Vision in the business world means looking at the long run with a novel response that solves significant problems. A leader looks at the present and sees a different road to the future by tossing out old ways of doing things and capturing the imagination of the whole business. Business leaders, then, are futurists. But their vision must be practical and obtainable. As *Fortune* points out, while the leader must promulgate a vision, "the most brilliant vision statement this side of Paraguay won't budge a culture unless it's backed up by action." In other words, don't count on vision to work miracles without followers who adopt the vision.

Consider railroad baron James J. Hill, who headed the Great Northern Railway back in the nineteenth century. Hill had a vision as well as a strategy: to lay tracks across the continent over which goods from New England and the Midwest could be shipped to Puget Sound and then exported to the Far East. No one had ever attempted

115

GOVERNORS STATE UNIVERSITY
UNIVERSITY PARK
IL 60466

such an undertaking without government subsidy. But Hill, over the protest of his directors, remained committed to his vision of launching trans-Pacific commerce in the spirit of private enterprise. In the end, Hill's vision was realized: American cotton, wheat, and other crops were carried by rail to Seattle and from there by ship to Japan and China. Hill's was a long-term as well as a global vision.

The Declaration of Independence, carefully crafted by Thomas Jefferson and laced with the philosophy of John Locke, and the Gettysburg Address, hastily scrawled on an envelope by Abraham Lincoln, are two of the most famous and widely circulated vision statements ever composed. Together, they are the spiritual constitution of the United States, and at the time they were written, each served a great purpose. Both documents, poetic enough to be literature, mingle the controversy of the time with the broad outlook of a noble appeal for the dignity and rights of Americans. And both are reasoned enough to carry conviction and fervent enough to inspire enthusiasm among followers. In short, they are empowering statements.

Vision

Leaders, according to Harvard's John Kotter, create a pragmatic vision that sets a direction for the future. They align people, ideas, systems, attitudes, and technology toward fulfilling the vision, which is usually a statement of some kind of the corporation's longer-term goals and objectives. We're not talking here about strategic goals, such as return on sales, sales per employee, return on assets, and so on. At the beginning of the 1980s, for instance, Xerox Corporation was up against an onslaught of smaller and feistier competitors whose copiers were cheaper and, in many cases, better. The result: Xerox was losing market share at a hefty clip. That's when Xerox in its end-of-the-decade vision turned quality obsessed. The result: By 1990 it had won back market share and then some to regain its position and stature. Consequently, observed *Fortune* writer Thomas Stewart, Xerox was one of those companies that entered the 1980s "like a lamb and left like a lion."

Every business has goals tied to a vision. Some are intuitive; others are informal, fragmented, obscure, or vague. Some are even loaded with clichés. (But clichés—those soggy nuggets of conventional wisdom—are often true.) Some embrace novelty with an approach to creative endeavors largely unencumbered by tradition. Whatever the dream or its style, it can't be culled from a committee. The vision must be articulated solely from the leader. Like the proverbial buck, the vision statement too stops with the leader. As we will see with Crate & Barrel, Gordon Segal didn't get around to really defining his vision until he had to articulate it to outsiders. But it was his. At the other extreme is Honda of America, which has carefully crafted and broadly published its vision. Honda, in fact, has had a clearly articulated vision written in 1954 by one man, an engineer named Honda. Hanging on the wall of every Honda plant, it states: "We're dedicated to supplying products of the highest efficiency, yet at a reasonable price for worldwide customer satisfaction."

Honda's principles expressed his view of the company vision. Like most statements of purpose, the Honda statement specifies a goal: worldwide consumer satisfaction. "But it goes beyond specifying the goal," explains Honda executive vice president Scott Whitlock. "It also specifies a means and an engineering solution for achieving customer satisfaction. It calls for 'products of the highest efficiency, yet at a reasonable price,' not products of reasonable efficiency at the lowest price. When you look at our design over the years, you will see that reflected in everything we've tried to design over the years—in fuel efficiency, in the aerodynamics, and the way our products operate."

A creative vision, which requires dissatisfaction with the status quo, can be both intellectual and intuitive. But the vision can't be built on smoke. It needs to be fired up with information, lots of it. To assess the possibilities, the leader must have information leverage, the steady flow of facts, figures, and concepts that enable him or her to develop a clear view of the present. By that I mean a business leader must have a demonstrated technical expertise in at least one function of the enterprise as well as a broad knowledge of the industry in which the company competes. Why? Because a leader must be credible and must have the professional respect of those peers and subordinates who are being led. As basic as it might seem, don't expect the organization to go through the trauma of change unless the leader has the confidence of the followers. A leader's vision is not a vehicle for creating blind trust among followers. The experience of Motorola's former CEO and chairman Robert Galvin typifies what others have told us. Galvin explains:

> If a leader is going to take somebody someplace, you have to know where you're going. To that end, one of the critical determinants as to whether a person deserves to be called a leader will be manifest in the leader's ability to make a sufficient number of minority decisions. By that I mean a decision no one agrees with; a leader has to stand up for what he considers to be the best decisions for the company. That does not mean that a leader is arrogant or that he orders people around. These decisions are based on involvement, which means absorbing everything and anything that you can regarding the business. You have to know what to stand for before anyone else knows. . . . The leader has to have a sense of why and how you're going to achieve your long-term objectives and then stick to the commitment. Many institutions are too short term and can always justify why they shouldn't spend the money to finance long-term projects. . . . We have built a museum at Motorola in order to maintain an institutional memory. There are lessons to be learned from our mistakes; this museum houses those mistakes so we can learn from them to prevent the same problems from arising in the future.
>
> It took a great deal of brainstorming to come up with the answer when people were asking the age-old question: How do we make ourselves more competitive? We concluded we needed to be more competitive at a personal level. I had to be as good as Mr. Kobayashi of NEC, my vice presidents had to be as good as our competitor's vice presidents. As soon as we came to that simple proposition, I recommended

that every individual enter a special training program. Many responded that they would be willing to go ahead with such a program if it didn't cost anything and didn't take any time. Well, that was impossible. I decided to go ahead with the program despite their disagreement. This competitive improvement program cost $40 million per year and $10 million for the facility. I was the only one who truly believed in the program. Eighteen months later, everyone was proud of the training program. So how do you lead? Not with a lot of fanfare.

In 1988 Motorola won the prestigious Malcolm Baldrige National Quality Award based on five categories that included leadership.

Leaders can't wait for inspiration from the Muses. They must go about the business of forming a vision that draws simplicity out of complexity and clarity out of obscurity. The corporate mission must support the vision technically, culturally, and politically. Look at it another way. Say a company make machine screws (the technical know-how) that are of the finest quality (the cultural forces in play) and that the best idea in that particular company wins, not the guy with the biggest office and highest salary (the company's political nature). "Vision is anchored in the past and the present," observes Warren Bennis, "but built upon the assumptions and facts that predict a new reality."

The ability to communicate the vision to the followers becomes as important as creating it. The key to Johnson & Johnson's (J&J's) corporate culture, *Fortune* pointed out in 1990, is its credo, a forty-four-year-old, 309-word statement created by Robert Wood Johnson, son of the founder. As with most such mission statements, the credo mentions honesty, integrity, and putting people before profits. "What's unusual," *Fortune* noted, "is the amount of energy J&J's high executives devote to ensuring that employees live by those words." Every few years or so the company gathers its senior managers to debate and discuss the credo in an effort to keep its ideals fresh. "I tell employees they have to take the short hit," CEO Ralph

Larsen says. "In the end, they'll prosper." When, for instance, J&J was faced with the nightmare of the Tylenol case in which eight people died from swallowing poisoned capsules, it quickly recalled the product, despite J&J's belief that the pill was tampered with in the stores and not the factory. The action meant a loss of $240 million in earnings. But biting the bullet short term paid off in the long run: Consumers remained loyal to Tylenol, which has since bounced back as the nation's leading brand of painkiller.

The new reality in business is not based on the old rule-by-the book military chain of command. Superior execution in today's volatile environment depends on networks that underlie and reshape organizations. Consultant Ram Charan believes that networks begin to matter when they change behavior, the frequency, the intensity, and the honesty of the dialogue among managers. "All too often, managers invest huge amounts of time and energy to reach agreement on vision without investing in the truly hard work—becoming aligned on the nitty-gritty trade-offs and time pressures required to deliver on the vision," Charan recently wrote in the *Harvard Business Review*. "Agreement without alignment seldom changes behavior. Instead it generates frustration, cynicism, and complacency."

The leader seeks feedback of ideas and information flowing freely from the bottom to top and back down again. A lack of free-flowing information within a corporation can often paralyze it. To sort out the facts and discard the ambiguities, the leader must approach the task of gathering information with the sensitivity of the participant-observer that allows him or her to stand back and seek new perspectives. In the business mosaic, the leader sees the picture first and the pieces second, whereas the manager sees the pieces as individual parts and then the picture. As they gather insights, weigh the pros and cons, and think of the possibilities, leaders carefully listen because they ask hard questions. Again, leaders draw on their networks to verify the quality of interpretation.

"Information is critical to vision, because without it vision is useless," Scott Whitlock says. For a company like Honda that churns out Accords in its Siam plant in Japan and its Maryville plant in

Ohio, managing information can be tricky. Despite the logistics, Honda does not rely solely on the computer in the high-tech age. "The computer is too inflexible," Whitlock notes. "Have you ever seen a computer that was good with rumors?"

Since information is power in every business, we often find people who hoard information to protect their status. They control and manipulate the outcome of projects for their personal protection. There are many approaches at getting out the word. And as simple as it may seem, the person in the organization with the information is responsible for getting information to the person who needs it. "If you have information," Whitlock adds, "it's your responsibility to communicate it." At Honda, concedes Whitlock, that practice has not always been as easy as it sounds. "Sometimes with great difficulty employees may overcome those organizational barriers that we as managers create and got that information to the person who needed it. . . . You may be riding with the CEO in a car and simply say, 'By the way, there's one other thing you need to know before we visit this customer.' Make sure people get the information across. Making that a fundamental belief, a fundamental principle, is one of the roles of management."

What Scott Whitlock and his colleagues are doing is what Peter Drucker wrote about back in 1946 in *Concept of the Corporation* when he observed that "any institution has to be organized so as to bring out talents and capacities within the organization, to encourage men to take the initiative, give them a chance to show what they can do, and a scope within which to grow." Actually the notion of empowering and networking is as old as the Bible itself.

What Exactly Is a Corporate Mission Statement?

A mission statement should include a clear and concise declaration of the goals, values, and sources of strength as a guide to all stakeholders. It tells the company's constituents what it is capable of and willing to do. A mission statement is really a "value creation"

platform that promotes change in management behavior by differ-
entiating the future opportunities from those of the present. It in-
corporates the company's beliefs and values building commitment to
the long-term objectives. Finally, the mission must be obtainable
and congruent with management's capability for executing it.

In creating either a new mission statement or revising an existing one, these questions will start the creative planning process,
giving it structure and direction:

What is the technological leadership of the company?

What are the profit objectives (growth, market share,
and so on)?

What are the returns on equity (capital) objectives?

What are the most promising areas for developing
future growth?

What is the human resource capability for growth?

What are the cultural and political constraints that
will restrict accomplishing the overall objectives?

What capacity do the organizational structure and
the company's personnel have for adapting to change?

Why are major changes needed?

Is the new mission statement believable, credible,
doable, and measurable?

Does the new mission statement offer each individual a better future than the current program?

Is the management committed to supporting the new
mission?

Will the mission unify the organization and act as the
collective glue that enables the individual to refocus and
retool his or her skills at improved levels of performance?

Let's now consider the focus of several unique and empowering
mission statements that convey how the leader unifies his or her
vision with corporate performance. The comments in brackets are
mine.

BBA Group plc

The United Kingdom–based BBA Group plc, with annual sales of some $2 billion, makes an array of textile products for the automotive, aviation, and industrial markets in Europe and North America. Its statement is the following.

The inertia of history is a powerful influence on corporate philosophy. BBA in its 103 years of existence has strayed little from: Yorkshire paternalism; Weaving of heavy textiles; Friction technology via woven or pressed resin media. The philosophy of BBA for the next few years will be to adapt rather than abandon the inert. [Comment: BBA's corporate philosophy is almost tribal in nature as it combines history and folklore. Yet it is presented with laser-sharp clarity.]

Management—Grit and gumption are preferable to inertia and intellect. The Victorian work ethic is not an antique. One man can only serve one master, to whom he is responsible for a minimum number of succinctly defined tasks. Most companies owned or yet to be acquired possess adequate people waiting to be transformed by dedicated leadership. The effectiveness of an organization is in inverse proportion to the number of hierarchical layers. [Comment: This is a strong value statement that clearly defines BBA's corporate culture as one that covets sweat, hard work, and minimal management.]

Markets—We shall concentrate in markets where: The products are in a state of maturity or decline "Sunset Industries." The scale of our presence in a market segment will allow price leadership. The capital cost of market entry is high. Fragmentation of ownership on the supply side facilitates rapid earnings growth by acquisition of contribution flows. [Comment: This matrix for a sales strategy is highly focused.]

Money—The longer run belongs to Oscar Wilde, who is dead. The key macro and micro variables of our business are so dynamic that poker becomes more predictable than planning and reactivity more profitable than rumination. Budgets are personal commitments made by management to their superiors, subordinates, shareholders and their self-respect. The cheapest producer will win. The investment of money on average return of less than three points above market should be restricted to Ascot. Gearing should not exceed 40 per cent. The location from which funds emanate should be matched to the location from which the profit stream permits their service. We are not currency speculators, even when we win. Tax is a direct cost to the business and, accordingly, should be eschewed. Victorian thrift is not an antique. Nothing comes free, cheap assets are often expensive utilities. [Comment: A set of specific performance guidelines that shows both financial savvy and wit. And although money is no laughing matter, this part of the statement is tinged with humorous patter in such references to Oscar Wilde and Ascot. Yet there is more financial wisdom packed in the few droll lines than in many a textbook on corporate finance.]

Monday—Our tactic is to: Increase the metabolism of BBA through directed endeavor. To increase profit margins by drastic cost reduction. To massage and thereby extend the life cycle of the products in which we are engaged. To become market dominant in our market niches by: outproducing the competition; transforming general markets where we are nobody to market niches where we are somebody; buying competitors. Use less money in total and keep more money away from the tax man and the usurer. Avoid the belief that dealing is preferable to working. Go home tired. [Comment: This statement deals with aspirations and ties the role of each employee into BBA's strategic goals. In a sense it links the entire organization.]

Maybe—The replication of our day-to-day tactic provides long-term growth. We need to address "Monday" this week and what our reaction will be to what may be on "Monday" for the next three years. Three years is, in the current environment, the limit of man's comprehension of what may be. Long-term growth necessitates: Resources—notably men and money. Sustain performance rather than superficial genius. [Comment: This is a succinct summary of BBA's mission and its definition of a realistic time frame.]

Over all, BBA's mission statement is clear, powerful, human, obtainable, and believable. It uses language brilliantly. There's wit, humor, metaphor, all in the context of serious business. Yet there is no business jargon or technical terms to grapple with. It's a statement that can easily be understood—and appreciated—from CEO to mailroom clerk.

Coca-Cola Company

Cola-Cola, based in Atlanta, Georgia, has revenues of $8.4 billion and pretax income of $1.58 billion from its three primary areas of business: soft drinks, foods, and entertainment. Coca-Cola's seventeen thousand employees are led by Chairman and CEO Roberto C. Goizueta, the Cuban-born chemical engineer who fled with his family to Miami shortly after Fidel Castro seized power in 1959. The family, which had owned a sugar refinery, lost everything. About the only thing Goizueta had when he reached the United States was a job with Coke. The fifty-nine-year-old Goizueta has been with Coke for more than three decades and since taking charge in 1981, he has managed to boost shareholders' equity from 21 percent to 32 percent in 1989. His basic formula: cutting Coke's dividend payout ratio from 60 percent in 1981 to 41 percent. The savings were then used to buy equity positions in independent bottlers. At one point, Coke was sitting with some $2.7 billion in cash that included $1.1 billion in proceeds from its sale in 1990 to Sony of a 49 percent interest in Columbia Pictures Entertainment. While Coca-Cola President Donald Keough charts the company's marketing strategy, Goizueta ponders ways to improve the company's value and financial stability. "From the time I get up in the morning to the time I go to bed," he told *Fortune* in 1990, "I even think about it when I'm shaving. But I use an electric razor, so I think I'm safe."

MISSION STATEMENT: STRATEGY FOR THE 1980s

Our challenge—In order to give my version of our Company for 1990, I must first postulate what I visualize our mission to be during the 1980s. I see our challenge as continuing the growth in profits of our highly successful existing main business, and those we may choose to enter, at a rate substantially in excess of inflation, in order to give our shareholders an above average total return on their investment. The unique position of excellence that the trademark Coca-Cola has attained in the world will be protected and enhanced as a primary objective. [Comment: Notice that this mission statement, unlike most, is in the first person, coming, so to speak, straight from the CEO's mouth. It gives the primary objectives through the end of decade of the 1980s. As a first-person statement, it is Goizueta's personal commitment we are hearing, which seems to give the vision more dramatic resonance.]

Our business—I perceive us by the 1990s to continue to be or become the leading force in the soft drink industry in each of the countries in which it is economically feasible for us to be so. We shall continue to emphasize product quality worldwide, as well as market share improvement in growth markets. The products of our Foods Division will also continue to be the leading entries in those markets which they serve, particularly in the U.S.

In the U.S. we will also become a stronger factor in the packaged consumer goods business. I do not rule out providing appropriate services to this same consumer as well. It is most likely that we will be in industries in which we are not today. We will not, however, stray far from our major strengths: an impeccable and positive image with the consumer, a unique franchise system second to none; and the intimate knowledge of, and contacts with, local business conditions around the world.

In choosing new areas of business, each market we enter must have sufficient inherent real growth potential to make entry desirable. It is not our desire to battle continually for share in a stagnant market in these new areas of business. By and large, industrial markets are not our business.

Finally, we shall tirelessly investigate services that

complement our product lines and that are compatible with our consumer image. [Comment: Goizueta has laid out specific objectives by product category of the current business. Then he gives the criteria for performance in the new businesses, reminding us that Coke is both domestically and globally minded and will remain a consumer-oriented company.]

Our consumers—Company management at all levels will be committed to serving to the best of its ability our bottlers and our consumers, as well as the retail and wholesale distribution systems through which these consumers are reached. These are our primary targets. The world is our arena in which to win marketing victories as we must.

Our shareholders—We shall, during the next decade, remain totally committed to our shareholders and to the protection and enhancement of their investment and confidence in our Company, its character and style, products and image.

Our "bottom line"—My financial vision is not complicated, but it will require courage and commitment to attain financial goals consistently and effect growth in real profits, most especially during uncertain and fast changing economic times.

Our strong balance sheet and financial position will be maintained so that the Company can withstand any economic windstorm, as well as enable us to take advantage of expansion opportunities which complement our existing business and that offer acceptable earnings growth and return on investment.

It is our desire to continue to pay ever-increasing dividends to our shareholders. This will be done as a result of rapidly increasing annual earnings while of necessity reducing our dividend pay-out ratio, in order to reinvest a greater percentage of our earnings to help sustain the growth rate which we must have. We shall consider divesting assets when they no longer generate acceptable returns and earnings growth. Increasing annual earnings per share and effecting increased return on equity are still the name of the game—but not to the extent that our longer term viability is threatened.

Our people—Finally, let me comment on this vision as it affects our "life style"—or business behavior—as a viable international business entity. I have previously referred to courage and commitment that will be indispensable as we move through the 1980s. To this I wish to add integrity and fairness, and insist that the combination of these four ethics be permeated from top to bottom throughout our organization so that our behavior will produce leaders, good managers, and—most importantly—entrepreneurs. It is my desire that we take initiatives as opposed to being only reactive and that we encourage intelligent individual risk-taking.

As a true international company with a multicultural and multinational employee complement, we must foster the "international family" concept which has been a part of our tradition. All employees will have equal opportunities to grow, develop and advance with the Company. Their progress will depend only on their abilities, ambition and achievements. [Comment: Like a prudent politician, Goizueta comes to terms with his constituencies: the bottlers, consumers, shareholders, and employees. He knows each group and is sensitive to their interests. He defines them, he talks to them and makes no promises he can't keep. His is truly a platform for all of Coca-Cola's public. There is compassion and commitment in his finely tuned words. He wants to promote an ethical environment and culture out of which Coca-Cola's future leaders, managers, and entrepreneurs will emerge with risk-taking drive. And though he is bottom-line conscious, it is not at the expense of long-term vision.]

Our Wisdom—When we arrive at the 1990s, my vision is to be able to say with confidence that all of us in our own way displayed: The ability to see the long-term consequences of current actions; The willingness to sacrifice, if necessary, short-term gains for longer-term benefits; The sensitivity to anticipate and adapt to change—change in consumer life styles, change in consumer tastes and change in consumer needs; The commitment to manage our enterprise in such a way that we will always be considered a welcomed and important part of the business community in each and every country which we do business; and the capacity in which to control what is controllable and the wisdom not to bother with what is not.

Roberto C. Goizueta

Note that Goizueta evokes solid commitment keyed to performance guidelines that look to the long term. The important word he uses is *change*, which implies a dynamic organization capable of adapting to new circumstances and opportunities that will develop in the future.

Montgomery Ward & Company

In 1985 Montgomery Ward was hemorrhaging with a loss of $298 million. That's the year Bernard F. Brennan took the helm. Four years later Ward's was celebrating record profits of $139 million. In between those years, Brennan had changed Ward's face and focus. First he pulled off the largest leveraged buyout ever by management when he bought the company from Mobil Corporation for $3.8 billion. Then he took Ward's private. Next came the sacred cow: He axed Ward's sluggish mail order catalog—the first and oldest in America—and fired seventeen thousand people, many involved in the catalog operations. Others were laid off because they couldn't buy into Brennan's program, a personal vision written as thirteen planks—detailed and demanding—that was part merchandising manifesto and part rallying cry. For the fifty-five thousand remaining employees, Brennan is somewhat of a hero. "Bernie brought this company back from the brink of oblivion," said Bernie Andrews, president of Ward's home and automotive group. "Now, we have the opportunity to do something the world thought was simply not doable. That's what motivates many of us. We're zealots."

Brennan came from a three-generation Sears, Roebuck & Company family. His brother, Edward A. Brennan, is chief executive of Sears, and his father, mother, and grandfather were all Sears merchandisers. He spent twelve years at Sears before the entrepreneurial spirit drove him to leave Sears for retailing distributor Sav-A-Stop in Jacksonville, Florida. The day after he took that company public in September 1982, he joined Ward's for the first time as executive vice president of store operations. Thirteen months later, however, he left, citing irreconcilable differences with then-CEO Stephen L. Pistner. Brennan left Ward's for Household International, Inc., where he became CEO of Household's merchandising division. Less than two years later, Pistner was out and Brennan was back at Ward's in the driver's seat with the experience that had enabled him to scan the entire retailing landscape.

In Brennan's mind the old-line department store was quickly becoming a retailing dinosaur. Out of that conviction he fashioned a new concept for Ward's. Instead of a dowdy middle-of-the-road general merchandise store, he saw future merchandising promise in an aggregate of specialty stores under one roof. He described the retailing blueprint in his mission statement, along with a code of conduct and a business philosophy. He even stated it in person to his vendors at Ward's headquarters on Chicago Avenue. He actually passed out the document, called "Focus on the Future," which explained the concept of value-driven specialty stores under one roof. Although it was a well-thought-out presentation, most of the vendors couldn't believe it. How do I know? Because, as Ward's major supplier of mattresses, I attended the meeting. The skeptics didn't think Brennan's plan would work, but wouldn't say so out loud. Instead, the attitude was more along the lines of "We've got to humor him because we need the Ward's business." There were at least one hundred vendors in the room and Brennan wanted them to believe in his idea and to support him with their best goods delivered on a timely basis. Moreover, he asked the vendors for extended payment terms of ninety days. This was a crucial meeting that he had made a personal investment in. He had a vision, conceptualized it, then sold it internally and saw that it was implemented. Those who only gave it lip service were terminated, whether you were a Ward's vendor or a manager. This was something Bernie Brennan believed in totally. "When you're in a turnaround," Brennan said, "the issue is survival."

The following is Brenann's thirteen-point mission statement that blends his philosophy, analysis, strategy, and vision for the retailing world today and tomorrow:

1. *Montgomery Ward will become a chain of value-driven specialty stores.* Consumers today are shopping the specialists because they consistently provide strong values, understand customer needs and focus their efforts on meeting those needs. By providing dominant merchandise assortments and rigorous control over the cost of doing business, specialists are also highly profitable. We are going to adopt the same tactics and all our strategies will be measured against this standard.

2. *Our business is to understand and serve customers.* We must think more about consumer wants and needs and provide the goods and services they want—at a profit. Our customers deserve friendly, courteous, knowledgeable service, and we are dedicated to providing it. We are going to listen to our customer and deliver on our promises.

3. *We will deliver strong value through dominant merchandise assortments.* Everything we do must focus on the merchandise. "Value" means providing more for the same dollars. We will become dominant, the first store customers think of when they go to make a purchase in our merchandise categories. We will assure customers a disappointment-free shopping experience.

4. *Being good isn't good enough.* We must be better than the competition. We must beat the competition to take business away from them. Our strategies will be successful only when customers name us as their first choice. We will try new concepts and learn from our customers and other retailers. We will give consumers a clear reason to shop us rather than the competition.

5. *Our stores will be exciting places to shop.* We want our stores to be fun, exciting our customers' imagination and curiosity. Sales people will be trained, professional and customer-sensitive. Satisfying customers must become an obsession, and we will become excellent problem resolvers for our customers. Our customers should want to visit us on a regular basis.

6. *We will become an entrepreneurial company capable of independence from Mobil.* [Comment: Mobil had acquired Montgomery Ward along with Container Corporation during the 1970s.] To become independent, we work hard and work smart. We must become "associates" of this company, making decisions as though we personally owned it. We will reward those who deliver on performance. Success requires all of us to accept personal accountability in our jobs each and every day.

7. *We will redeploy assets to maximize our profitability.* Assets that make money must be allowed to grow; those that do not will be sold or redeployed in other areas. There will be a continuous review of our organizational structure and operating methods to ensure peak efficiency. We must be willing to accept change and eagerly seek our ways to do things better. New growth opportunities will be seized as they arise.

8. *Specialty stores are critical to our future growth.* We have begun the transition from general merchandiser to value-driven specialty store. Smaller specialty stores with strong, compelling merchandise will become our major growth vehicle. We will convert full-line stores to a specialty store format and add new specialty stores in metro and mid-size markets. We will put ourselves ahead of the competition.

9. *We will become a low cost operator.* We will improve efficiency and productivity in all aspects of the business to meet the standards for low cost operations set by the top 25% of our competition. We will develop effective information systems. This means commitment, involvement and teamwork. We will reduce bureaucracy, improve communications and deliver superior results consistently.

10. *Cost minimization begins in the Buying Office.* We must buy merchandise at the lowest possible cost without lowering quality by developing advantageous and aggressive vendor programs. Cost minimization also means better internal controls. We will be in-stock, speed up merchandise flow, improve turnover and improve our forecasting. We must be quick, flexible and opportunistic; tough but fair and honest negotiators.

11. *Logistics means more than distribution centers and transportation.* Logistics is the entire process of getting goods from the vendors to the customers. We cannot let merchandise jam up in back rooms or position it on the sales floor in a way that makes no sense to the customer. Inventory management is critical to achieve inventory turnover levels that are competitive and optimize performance. We must ensure that the right goods, in the right quantity, are in the right places at the right time, all at an affordable expense.

12. *Credit and Signature will play an important role in Montgomery Ward's future.* By offering convenience and choice to customers in paying for purchases, Montgomery Ward has a distinct competitive advantage. Our credit operations will be the most efficient in the industry, and we will continue programs to expand our credit file. The Signature Group will profitably market its growing range of financial products and clubs, including expanding into external markets.

13. *Retailing is a people business.* We are reliant on attracting and keeping good people. Management will be sensitive to the needs of our people. We will provide growth opportunities in a stimulating environment and reward good performance. We must communicate our plans, successes and failures throughout the organization and listen to constructive criticism. We will reward those who make Montgomery Ward the first place customers think of when going to make a purchase and who help us achieve this goal profitably.

From the time he returned to Montgomery Ward in 1985, Brennan has turned a floundering company into a focused one. He did so, he explained, by following six basic principles. Reviewing those principles can help us understand how a CEO thinks when going about developing a strategy to support the vision—with deep thought, care, and creative flair. Let's look over Brennan's shoulder.

First, Brennan created a vision supported by a written strategy. He believed there was a unique opportunity to incorporate the successful concepts of the new so-called value specialists with those of the general merchant. "No one had yet integrated these concepts and to me this represented our opportunity," Brennan said. "I wrote a basic outline of becoming a value-driven retailer before returning to Montgomery Ward. I realized, however, that radical change was needed to accomplish this objective. My job was to begin an immediate process of verifying this strategic position through a thorough review and action plan. But I believed this had to be done quickly—because in a turnaround, your window of opportunity is very short."

Second, he studied the competition. Through a historical analysis, he determined that Ward's had been a noncompetitive company going back to World War II days when the company—then the second largest retailer in America behind Sears—decided to sit on its cash instead of expanding, as its biggest competitor did. "This was a major strategic failure," he concluded. But Ward's grew because retailing through the mid-1970s was a seller's market. Then came the discounters with their emphasis on price and convenient location. For the first time mass merchants and department stores conceded that someone could take their customers away.

By 1985, the competition had been carefully studied. "Instead of looking at our history," Brennan said, "we studied those who were growing the fastest." Brennan's team looked at market share and return on equity (ROE) among some of the best specialists that included The Limited, Wal-Mart, Toys "R" Us, and Circuit City. Some had returns on equity in the 30 percent range. General merchants—the companies that had been Ward's role models—were producing ROEs only slightly more than 10 percent and losing market share. "The messages from the competition were unmistakable—value, low cost, and specialization," Brennan recalled.

Ward's was barely surviving as a mass merchant. What did it

need to overcome the tough times? "We needed to incorporate competitiveness as a fundamental business value of our organization," Brennan emphasized.

The third principle was to listen to customers. The company stopped looking at its competitors through the eyes of a 113-year-old retailer, which had invented the catalog business and indeed was the oldest catalog in America. First and oldest, however, did not necessarily mean best and most profitably established. The Ward's catalog had primarily become a rural merchandising vehicle. Thousands of items were sold through two thousand small stores in small towns to rural customers whose buying power was declining. It was, in effect, a high-cost channel of distribution and the newcomers like Wal-Mart were filling the basic needs of these customers. Ward's was losing its synergy, because its merchants were buying different goods for the urban and rural markets. Brennan realized that Ward's could not efficiently serve both consumer bases. At the same time, through customer surveys, Brennan learned that Ward's shoppers didn't believe its private label goods had the same quality and value as brand names. Soon Ward's stores were displaying an array of brands that included such names as General Electric, Maytag, Zenith, Tappan, Simmons, Sony, and La-Z-Boy.

The fourth principle was to focus on a core business. Brennan believed Ward's could be viable, but only by intensely focusing on a core business instead of dissipating its energies on retail, catalog, discount, credit, and direct marketing divisions. "We knew we had to focus on what we could do best and what the competition and our customers were telling us we had to do—value-driven retailing," Brennan said. Brennan was doing what leaders should do: listen.

So Brennan closed down Ward's $1.2 billion catalog division, a move, he said, that was "a very unpopular decision," along with liquidating the discount business (Jefferson Ward), and selling off the credit business. In six months the company had given up $2 billion in annual sales, one-third of its total sales. Closing the catalog and Jefferson Ward divisions were more than operational moves, according to Brennan. He explained: "If we were going to close every marginal or unprofitable segment of Montgomery Ward, you might as well have closed the entire company. The decisions were strategic, as we needed to redeploy assets to grow a new business."

Out of this redeployment, Brennan noted, "we created something new in American retailing—a value-driven specialty store." Now Brennan was positive Ward's "could compete with the best in the business" by focusing on four key merchandising areas: "Home Ideas," "Electric Avenue," "Auto Express," and "The Apparel Store," which included "The Kids Store" and "Gold 'N Gems," the jewelry store.

By mid-April 1989, Brennan was calling Ward's "a growth company," as he projected plans in the following sixteen months that included 31 new stores (17 full-line and 14 specialty) to the then-current base of 327 stores. An additional thirty locations were under consideration. During the next two years, he said at the time, Wards planned to hire ten thousand new "associates."

The fifth principle was to contain costs. Here Brennan was faced with a retailer's catch-22. Ward's could not become a value-driven merchant, selling quality brand names, if it were not also a low-cost operator. Within three years, Ward's had lowered its cost of doing business by five percentage points, but not without the pain of layoffs. "Our most difficult cost-reduction decision related to people," recalled Brennan. "In order to become more competitive, we had to reduce our work force—seventeen thousand within a six-month period—which proved a very difficult time. I vowed, during that period, never to allow a company that I managed to be placed in this situation."

The consolidation and cost cuts freed up some $1.5 billion in working capital, both to reduce interest expense and to invest in the growth of the business.

The sixth principle was commitment. "If you are going to radically change the structure and nature of your business, you need the commitment of its managers and associates," Brennan said. "This is far more difficult than the quantitative measurements."

The key to that commitment was the mission statement. It stated: "Montgomery Ward will become a chain of value-driven specialty stores." The challenge to Brennan, he said, "was to effectively communicate this strategy—getting people to believe." That took time and patience. Of the effort Brennan recounted:

> We spent the majority of our time in 1985 and 1986 working with management to refine our understanding of our mission and to garner their commitment. Some of these meetings seemed endless, and we hammered out our direction.
>
> It is not easy to recycle attitudes and philosophies. Some people actually learn to accept failure. I knew that Montgomery Ward could not succeed if any of its managers represented that profile. Although it's been a very tough environment, I believe our managers would tell you that winning is a better option.
>
> Commitment to me means something more than coherence of common goals. It means intensity in the pursuit of them. I think my job is to be uncompromising. I think that kind of intensity is not the prerogative but the responsibility of management in today's competitive environment.

Like all leaders—inside and outside of business—Brennan's role was to create the vision, craft it in a mission statement, and to communicate, as he said, "again and again."

It's hard to believe that no more than perhaps 60 percent of American companies have mission statements. There are, of course, times when companies have moved in a particular direction on sheer intuition with a gut-feeling strategy. What immediately comes to mind is the introduction of the Ford Mustang back in spring 1964. More than four hundred thousand Mustangs sold in the first year. The car's design virtually became a cultural artifact. Don Frey, a former vice president of product development at Ford Motor Company during the Mustang years, learned a lesson from the Mustang he carries with him to this day: "I learned the never-to-be-forgotten importance of how a few believers with no initial sanction, no committee, no formal market research, and no funds could change a company's fate." Currently professor of industrial engineering and management science at Northwestern University, Frey also cautions: "Nothing puts a greater drag on innovation than the inertia in your own organization, especially difficult manufacturing reforms or the politics surrounding the security of people's jobs."

What Frey demonstrates is that just a few heroes with vision and commitment can make the critical difference. Billed as "Love at First Byte," two of computerdom's greatest blood rivals—International Business Machines and Apple Computer—decided in 1991 to join forces. Instead of flinging the competitive hatchets at each other, they chose to bury them in a truce leading to shared technology that could reshape the computer industry for years to come. Faced with declining market shares as customers became more concerned about price than brand names or even performance, both companies had stalled in their historical pasts and run out of future. The IBM-Apple combo will result in integrated product lines as well as the development of a new generation of high-powered, multimedia hardware and software. During the 1980s, companies found out that it was more expensive to build than to buy brands. So it is in this case, too. Financial engineering has little to do with this particular alliance. It's strictly a venture of value creation that would never have been thinkable a decade ago. IBM has a lock on the big business market and Apple, with a sales force about one-tenth the size of IBM's, has sold millions of its user-friendly computers, mostly in the school market. If it clicks, the winners, of course, will be the customers.

So the leader hammers out a mission statement, the conceptual road map for the company to follow. It is a clear and concise declaration of the goals, values, and sources of strength to all the stakeholders. It tells them, in essence, what the company is capable and willing to do. It is the fount out of which springs the stuff that creates a corporation's value and the source from which flows the strategic plan.

What, then, is the difference between mission, vision and strategic plan? Think of the differences this way:

> *Vision is what we can be.*
> *Mission is what we want to be.*
> *Strategic plan is how we get there.*

Reflections: Vision—The Singular
Weft Thread of the Leader

As Alice made her way through Wonderland she met up with the Cheshire cat and asked for directions. "Would you tell me please, which way I ought to go from here?" The cat's reply: "That depends a great deal on where you want to go."

In business, a leader asks the same question. However, the leader asks himself or herself because only the leader can answer the question. The most valued product of a leader's task is the vision that becomes part of the company's mission.

The mission statement must be believable, achievable, and measurable and offer a future to each person in the enterprise that is better than the present or the past.

The mission statement should consist of a limited number of priority objectives, goals that can be measured, and identifiable strengths that can be augmented to the advantage of the enterprise.

The mission statement is the "culture glue" that focuses the organization as a collective unity to accomplish the vision.

The mission statement that does not reflect reality can generate cynicism and disillusionment. The statement should act as an inspiration for employees and as a means of communicating the vision to all the stakeholders.

Thus the mission statement is an integration of facts and vision, the probable and possible. It must be realistically in line with the organization's resources and talent. It must be ambitious. And attainable. An unrealistic mission statement, which is not part of the day-to-day behavior of the company or sets unreachable goals, undermines the entire corporate culture as well as the leadership authority.

Vision and mission need true consensus among the top managers who are called on to follow through. Thus a strong mission statement can service as a rallying cry toward team building with a long-term perspective. Although distinctly different, the three mission statements reviewed in this chapter all share key elements: candidness, creativity, and commitment.

Ethics and Integrity
Are Not Options

The price of greatness is responsibility.
—WINSTON CHURCHILL

No sooner had the jail cells of the fallen Wall Street poten-
tates slammed shut on the greedy deals and elaborate scams that
rasped apart like Velcro in the 1980s than the 1990s roared in with
its own ethical storms. Consider the Bank of Credit and Commerce
International, whose influence-peddling and money-laundering
schemes tarnished the golden reputation of Clark Clifford, political
adviser to Harry Truman, secretary of defense under Lyndon Johnson
and above all, as one magazine put it, "a man of impeccable integrity." And let's not forget "Rubbergate," the check-writing scandal
that reached the front pages in September 1991, when the General
Accounting Office reported that the nation's lawmakers—and in
many cases our political role models—had overdrawn their check-
ing accounts 8,331 times between July 1989 and June 1990. If
anything, the 1990s took over where the 1980s left off as far as trust
and integrity go—a pair of bruised values in need of deep healing.
Yet every leader in our survey agreed that there are no shades when
it comes to honesty and moral judgment—inside and outside a
company. No question about it, a business leader must be an ethical
model for the corporation and its employees. In short, ethics and
integrity are not options.

"What is honesty and ethical behavior?" mused Richard Ferris, former CEO of United Airlines. "Think of a chalk line. On one side is ethical, on the other unethical. There are a lot of people who spend their life with a lot of chalk on their toes. They are always crowding the line. I tell my executives that if they ever have the slightest question, get it out on the table. That kind of leadership must come from the top. You have to set a tone. If you don't do it, no one else is going to do it. A corporation has a culture, a way of doing things. If people see the leader deviate, they'll deviate. If the boss gets his toes on the chalk line they'll get their toes on the chalk line. It all begins up there."

Recently, I came across a "My Turn" feature titled "Money for Morality" in *Newsweek* magazine. Written by Mary Argulles, a freelance writer, the article began with a tale of an eight-year-old boy who finds an envelope containing $600. The money is returned to the rightful owner, who rewards the boy by giving him $3. True, not a lot, but then there is no set amount for good samaritanship. The youngster's teachers took up a collection on his behalf and ended up giving him a $150 savings bond for the good deed. Thus Argulles concluded, "Evidently the virtues of honesty and kindness have become commodities that, like everything else, have succumbed to inflation." But she goes on to make a far more cogent point: "It seems the role models these days—in this case, teachers—are more confused and misguided about values than their young charges." Has the promise of the Golden Rule—Do unto others as you would have them do unto you—become worthless collateral? If so, what does that say about our society?

Ethics is the theory of human conduct, the study of moral values. Yet there is no single standard of morality, because each philosopher chooses his or her own. Many criteria are in use. Some are more widely known than others; the Golden Rule, for example, is found in the teachings of Confucius, Jesus, Hillel, Aristotle, and Plato and in the scriptures of the Buddhists, Zoroastrians, and Hindus. "Values," author James Michener once said, "are the emotional rules by which a nation governs itself. . . . Without values, nations, societies and individuals can pitch straight to hell."

Not since the scandals stemming from the great crash of 1929 has American business felt the fires of hell. Just when the insider trading scandals of Wall Street—with the convictions of Drexel Burnham, Michael Milken, Dennis Levine, Ivan Boesky, and others—were beginning to ebb, another tidal wave of scandal drenched the business landscape in 1991. The headlines said it all: "The Salomon Shocker: How Bad Will It Get? Federal investigations into possible T-bond manipulations are rocking the Street and Washington," blared *Business Week*. Well, it got pretty bad. Salomon Brothers, Inc., one of the nation's major investment banking firms, admitted its bond traders illegally violated bidding rules at auctions of the U.S. Treasury securities. Transactions are carried out over the telephone with billions of dollars traded based on the "good word" of people in the market. Salomon had been a privileged and trusted trader. The scandal occurred in an environment in which federal regulators had believed that the good faith and trust of the participants of that market would be a sufficient form of regulation. At the same time, an ocean away, the Japanese were coping with their own ethical problems. "Japan In The Dirt," stated the *Economist*, which went on to note, "A week without a fresh Japanese scandal would be like a meeting without swapping business cards: disconcerting, because it would be so unusual." Japanese political officials had bought at low prices in Recruit Cosmos and made huge profits when an offering of the company's stock was made to the public.

Not a day goes by, it seems, when a scandal hasn't denigrated the ethics of some segment of our society: politics, religion, sports, education, business. In one three-week period in 1991, resignations were tendered by the president of Stanford University, the chairman of Salomon Brothers, and the president of the U.S. Olympic Committee—all because of ethical improprieties. On top of this, investigators and Congress were still digging through the savings and loan (S&L) crisis, the Iran-Contra affair of arms for hostages, and the Bank of Credit and Commerce International scandal, which tarnished the sterling reputation of Clark Clifford and led to his resignation as chairman of First American Bank.

The disease is obvious. The prognosis fuzzy. A cure for our moral ills begs the question: How can we teach people about ethical behavior—without a stick or a carrot? In his study of what makes leaders tick, James McGregor Burns discovered that moral behavior is more closely related to affective response, such as degrees of love and affection for parents, than to external factors, such as expectations and practices of concrete reward and punishment. If, as Michener suggests, values are indeed the cumulative folk wisdom by which a society organizes and disciplines itself, then leaders and role models need to make positive statements instead of dispensing fables. Moral character, of course, is shaped by family, friends, religion, and education long before a person joins a company. "In the real world," observes Kenneth Andrews, professor emeritus at Harvard Business School, "moral development is an unsolved problem at home, at school, at church—and at work."

In other words, there is overlap. It's impossible to maintain one set of values at home and quite a different set in the workplace. "When you cut right through it," says Columbia's Kirby Warren, "so many of these ethical dilemmas are not ethical if you grow up in a halfway decent family. You know what is right and what is wrong." Echoing that sentiment is Robert Allen, chairman of American Telephone and Telegraph. "A high standard of integrity has been part of this business for so long that it really sheds itself of people who do not match up to those standards," Allen says. "It is instinctive for me, partly because of who I am and the values I had instilled in me as a child, but also in part because of the way we have run this business for so long."

It's not uncommon, as I pointed out in an earlier chapter, for leaders to carry their moral—and even religious—convictions with them into the business arena—despite the fact that most CEOs believe in separation of church and corporation. "I derive the human rules of the game from the Ten Commandments," says Motorola's former chairman Robert Galvin. "Should one's faith make a difference that goes beyond mere compliance with law and commonly accepted standards of business ethics?" muses attorney Elmer

Johnson, former executive vice president at General Motors. "I believe it should." Brunswick CEO Jack Reichert believes that values drive a company and the numbers merely reflect how good the values are.

Now that the greed of the 1980s is behind us, that doesn't mean there are not going to be plenty of prototypical bad guys in the 1990s. All heroes have clay feet. Even the gem of the ocean is suspect: "Will the hero of 1492 be the villain of 1992?" asked *Time* magazine of Christopher Columbus, who has come under fire for bringing European arrogance, brutality, and infectious diseases to the indigenous peoples of the New World. We know the only real heroes are those in mythology. Actually, it boils down to a simple fact: No one will follow a leader who isn't trusted. Followers don't want to think their leader is manipulating them.

"The most significant period of ethical development for businesspeople is when they are first engaged in business," believes Michael Josephson, head of the Institute for the Advancement of Ethics. "When they have the opportunity and authority to test their ethics and they define for themselves the line between go and no go."

Go and No Go

In a society where words are becoming "politically correct" there is no reason why management decisions can't be "business correct" and "ethically correct" as part of the corporate culture. Josephson explains: "If I'm an employer, I can create an atmosphere in my company where a person would not lie because lying is so inconsistent with what is approved in that organization that a person can't lie and succeed." What Josephson is talking about is a code of conduct and the fact that a corporation is a way of life that should shape values like any institution that attracts a following.

At PepsiCo, Inc., for instance, the pillars that support the whole system, insists D. Wayne Calloway, CEO and chairman, are "results and integrity." Calloway orchestrated a major restructuring of PepsiCo's operations in the mid-1980s, leading the company into three fast-growing consumer markets: soft drinks, snack foods, and restaurants. In the process, PepsiCo was ranked by *Fortune* magazine as one of America's most admired corporations. And Calloway developed some very definite ideas about the trigger of success and failure of managers. He sums it up in a word—*values*. PepsiCo had done an in-house study focusing on the careers of recruits, many of them bright MBAs full of potential. Yet some of them failed. Some who had been destined for a divisional presidency had topped out as vice presidents, nothing, of course, to be ashamed of. Nevertheless, Calloway wanted to know why they fell short of expectations. "We studied this phenomenon a good bit and found out something that was quite surprising," said Calloway.

The executives failed because of what Calloway described as "an overabundance of characteristics" that didn't allow them to operate in a large, freewheeling organization. "You see," Calloway explains, "as managers develop in their careers, they're increasingly confronted with issues that are less technical and skill oriented, and more people oriented—managing, leading, and negotiating. Values become increasingly important."

To be specific, the single biggest reason for failure at Pepsico was arrogance. "Arrogance is the illegitimate child of confidence and pride," said Calloway. "Arrogance is the idea that not only can you never make a mistake but no one else can ever be right. . . . Arrogant, dishonest executives can't sustain long-term results. They may succeed for a short time or in a specific situation but over time, victory goes to businesspeople who work hard and are consistent, fair, open, and candid."

That's where integrity enters the picture at PepsiCo, which doubles its business roughly every five years and where every full-time employee has stock options. "If you are only going to see your boss occasionally, there had better be hefty candor, openness, and trust. . . . With lots of freedom and a strong emphasis on results, you would have anarchy pretty fast if you didn't have integrity as a beacon."

There in the synthetic environment of the corporate culture, the leader becomes both role model and social architect, shaping the value system that governs the corporate denizens. To do so, the leader draws on the collective aspirations and shared values of the followers. "If you're going to build a team," says CEO Steve Lazarus of Arch Corporation, "you have to have a capacity to reach into people and find out what their true expectations are for themselves, what it is they really want, and manage in ways that make them believe that it is in your interest to help them find what they want."

The message seems clear enough. Power and empowerment need mutual purpose, coupled with the glue that binds individuals together and in turn the organization: trust. At the same time the leader acts with confidence, consistency, and a standard of ethics that conforms to the shared values of the organization. The hope here is to inspire consistent behavior on the part of the followers without resentment and anger. People do not necessarily have to like a leader. In fact, they generally won't when a company is undergoing dramatic change.

What happens without trust? "Too many companies have measured success without regard to how someone became successful," says Josephson. "As a result, deceit, lying, unfairness, and unaccountability have been allowed to succeed." A case in point is the January 1986 disaster involving the space shuttle *Challenger*. The cause of the accident was due to the failure of the pressure seal, or so-called O-rings, in the aft-field joint of the right solid-rocket motor. The O-rings were supplied by Morton Thiokol. On the chilly morning of the *Challenger*'s scheduled launch, Morton engineer Roger Bolsjoly advised Morton management not to proceed because of the cold weather and its possible adverse effect on the O-rings. Bolsjoly's immediate superior agreed. NASA officials, however, wanted to go through with the launch and were ready to bring in a second supplier. That would have meant the possibility of losing an exclusive contract for Morton Thiokol, a situation the company wanted to avoid. NASA also wanted to meet the scheduled liftoff without a hitch because it was seeking to expand its $7.3 billion annual budget from Congress. Morton Thiokol's management ended up overriding the engineering advice and gave NASA the okay to fly. Subsequently, Thiokol would admit it made a "nonengineering" decision to launch. The result: Safety rules and procedures were stretched. The outcome: The death of seven passengers.

In language that was dry, yet painfully clear, the thirteen-member commission appointed to investigate the *Challenger* accident concluded that "neither Thiokol nor NASA responded adequately to internal warnings about the faulty seal design. . . . There was a serious flaw in the decision-making process." The commission, headed by former Secretary of State William Rogers, had interviewed more than 160 people, held hearings that generated twenty-eight hundred pages of transcript, and summarized it in a 256-page report that met the deadline set by President Ronald Reagan. Although there were few surprises in the report, some of the findings did not come easily. Both NASA's Marshall Space Flight Center in Huntsville, Alabama, which supervised the rocket boosters, and Morton Thiokol initially were stingy in cooperating with the commission. It took an FBI agent working for the commission to discover, while gathering documents at Thiokol, that a "flight constraint" had been declared on July 10, 1985, for the booster-joint seal. Then the constraint was routinely waived for seven successive launches, including the *Challenger*'s last one. The commission found that the booster-seal problem was not merely a low-level worry. Top NASA officials were aware of it, even though they were never told of the recommendation by Thiokol engineers against launching the *Challenger* in cold weather. The Rogers commission report cites a briefing on the booster seals that took place on August 15, 1985, of key NASA staff members by managers of both Thiokol and the Marshall Space Flight Center. The briefing paper had urged action to correct the faulty seal, but also it concluded that the shuttle was safe to fly until the situation was corrected. Of the briefing paper, the Rogers commission declared that it had been "sufficiently detailed to require corrective action prior to the next flight."

While the commission excoriated NASA's "flawed process," it

found that the organizational structures, policies, and regulations were all in place to avert a disaster. Why, then, did the worst happen? Why were procedures and standards violated and then covered up? And why was the coverup covered up? Because both NASA and Morton Thiokol were in defensive postures, according to organizational psychologist Chris Argyris, author of *Overcoming Organizational Defenses*. There is a breakdown in the value system of organizations on the defensive, Argyris believes, that will not permit them to "detect and correct the errors that are embarrassing and threatening because the fundamental rules are to bypass the errors and act as if they were not being done; make the bypass undiscussable; and make its undiscussibility undiscussable." Translation: Ignore the problem. Don't talk about it. Mum is the word. Thus the *Challenger* incident was caught up in a culture that nurtured the sins of omission as well as the sins of commission.

What keeps a corporate culture constantly on the defensive? At least two factors, argues Argyris. First, individuals feel helpless and hopeless because they see the cure as making the illness worse; an attitude akin to chemotherapy destroying healthy cells along with the cancerous ones. Second, they don't want to come off as whistle-blowers who open the proverbial can of worms. "The result," Argyris concludes, "is something equivalent to an underground economy— namely, a gray organization that is alive and flourishing yet officially considered dead or nonexistent. This, of course, makes it possible for the gray organization to remain alive and to flourish. We now have the underground management managing the aboveground."

Look what happened at Salomon Brothers, Inc., the Wall Street investment banker with the squeaky clean reputation that dominated the world of U.S. government bond trading almost as completely as Drexel Burnham Inc. dominated junk bonds. When the junk-bond and insider trading scandals washed over the Street, Salomon was untouched. As one of a handful of primary bond dealers, Salomon belonged to a select club considered by its exclusivity to be highly honorable. The government bond market—where the Treasury borrows money to finance the deficit—is a huge market based on trust because of the high quality of the players. None was as big as Salomon, long known for its swagger; rough-and-tumble culture; and deep, deep pockets—some $3.5 billion of its own equity capital. Salomon could throw its investment weight around the Street.

In April 1991, Salomon's chairman and CEO John H. Gutfreund found out that his firm had manipulated the bond market. But the disclosure was kept under wraps for four months. In a statement issued on August 9, 1991, Salomon admitted it had committed "irregularities and rule violations in connection with its submission of certain auctions of Treasury securities." By then two of its managing directors had been suspended and the firm was being investigated by the Securities and Exchange Commission and the Antitrust Division of the Justice Department. A week later, on August 14, Salomon issued another statement conceding that it had failed to take prompt action and could be barred as a government-appointed bond trader. Not long after, Gutfreund, the aggressive hands-on CEO and chairman whose desk was out front in the open on Salomon's massive trading floor where everyone could see him, resigned. As did President Thomas Strauss and Vice Chairman John Meriwether. Gutfreund was replaced on an interim basis by Omaha billionaire Warren Buffett, who owned $700 million of Salomon's preferred stock.

Of the Salomon scandal, the *New York Times* mused: "Why not? Why haven't dealers in the Treasury securities broken the rules so flagrantly in the past? No one had a definitive answer, but there are various theories. The main one is disregard of moral standards coupled with Salomon's pay incentive system—a sort of 1980s Wall Street mentality reaching the Treasury security market . . . traders receive annual bonuses tied to profitability of their operation and in pursuit of bigger bonuses they cheated, many analysts say."

Salomon's squeeze produced short-term profits, but long-term problems in terms of its public image and trust among clients, associates, and competitors on the Street. As a primary dealer, Salomon had to stand ready to buy bonds, provide a secondary market for them, and was a source of bond market information.

Clearly the scandal had grown to menace the health of the eighty-one-year-old firm, whose major misdeed was to violate federal rules against acquiring more than 35 percent of Treasury notes and bonds at a government auction. The ceiling is designed to prevent powerful firms like Salomon from buying up a bond issue and then dictating the price when the bonds are resold to smaller buyers. But Salomon reached well above the ceiling by rigging bids in at least three Treasury auctions over a nine-month period. In one auction it had bought the 35 percent limit of an $8.5 billion, four-year-note sale and then submitted an additional $1 billion bid that was ostensibly for a customer, but was really for Salomon's own account. The combined transactions ended up giving Salomon 46 percent of the overall auction.

Now the once-aloof Salomon was being compared with the likes of Drexel Burnham, which had fallen from its reign as junk-bond king in the wake of the insider trading scandals. The first thing Buffett did when he appeared before the House subcommittee that oversees Treasury bond trading was to apologize on behalf of Salomon's management and its eight thousand employees. "It may become explainable, but never excusable," said Deryck Maughan, who became chief operating officer and the likely successor to temporary chairman Buffett. The failure of Gutfreund and company to report the transgression immediately was, as Maughan put it, "a failure of character, the misjudgment of the culture." And as for its impact on the securities industry, "It's an industry under a shadow," Maughan told Adam Smith in a television interview in November 1991.

The new Salomon management began to change the culture immediately. The freewheeling, unaccountable nature of the trading room was drastically altered. Management put in place a compliance director—sort of a cop on the trading desk—to oversee each day's activity. At the same time, Salomon would move toward a broader partnership structure—increasing partnership holdings from 10 to 30 percent of the Salomon stock—that would align producers with the interests of the stockholders. After all, said Maughan, "There are more important things in life than money." It was a far different attitude than that described by Michael Lewis in his 1989 best-seller *Liar's Poker,* in which the gruff-talking, cigar-chomping Gut-freund was said to exhort traders to come to work every morning "ready to bite the ass off a bear."

Maughan would probably agree with Harvard's Kenneth Andrews, who believes an adequate corporate strategy must also include noneconomic goals. In *Ethics in Practice: Managing the Moral Corporation,* Andrews contends a firm's economic strategy should be humanized and made attainable by deciding what kind of organization the company should be—"its character, the values it espouses, its relationship to customers, employees, communities and shareholders." To this end, the personal values and ethical aspirations of an organization's leaders must be a part of the strategic decisions. "Management's total loyalty to maximization of profits is the principal obstacle to achieving higher standards of ethical practice," writes Andrews, adding, "Defining the purpose of the corporation as exclusively economic is a deadly over-simplification which allows over-emphasis on self-interest at the expense of the consideration of others."

Code of Conduct

The lesson from Wall Street in recent years is clear: You can't teach ethics in a classroom or a boardroom. Joseph Neubauer, chairman of ARA Services, strongly believes that:

> it is very difficult to teach ethics. I think you can heighten people's consciousness of certain elements of behavior that might or might not be appropriate in certain instances. In our own organization, we have a very formulized business conduct group to ensure fair and faithful enforcement of our code of ethics. It's like a peer group review. Sometimes people are so anxious to succeed that they will bend a rule so you have to make sure people understand the conse-

quences of their actions. The other thing that you have to remember is that organizations are nothing more than microcosms of the world in which we live. So what you try and do is use the environment around you and your corporation to try to instill some controls and systems to do what you think is correct.

A number of companies have a written code of ethics worth reviewing. For instance, IDEX Corporation, a maker of industrial products, has adopted its "Standards of Conduct and Business Ethics," which is a booklet introduced by its chairman, Donald Boyce. "We are in the midst of rapidly changing times," states Boyce. "Industrial firms face increased competition from around the world, and not every company will continue to grow during these times. We believe strongly that IDEX will be a growth company, but we also believe strongly that one of the essentials to growth is adherence to the highest standards of ethical conduct."

Recognizing the ambiguities of business, Boyce continues to outline a tough ethics policy: "You should know that we are very serious about compliance with this policy. If anyone disregards any portion of the policy, that person will not only be subject to dismissal, but may also face civil or even criminal penalties."

The IDEX statement largely focuses on each employee's responsibility. *"No policy can be written to cover all eventualities. In the final analysis, each individual's own best judgment is likely to be what is required to comply with the policy."* At IDEX *"the buck stops at each individual person's ethical judgment"* and cannot be delegated to someone else. For a code of conduct to work, individuals must see it in their own best interest and consequently take personal responsibility for their own acts.

Often codes of conduct are stated as a corporate credo. At Chicago's Harris Bank the credo is direct: "The core of our corporate value is honesty and fair dealing . . . integrity, professionalism and honorable, moral conduct." Johnson & Johnson's credo describes its responsibility to doctors, nurses, patients, mothers, and the users of its products as well as to its employees, the community, and stock-holders. Baxter Laboratories declares: "PRINCIPLES: What We Stand For: We are committed to serving: Customers Employees Stockhold-ers—Through: Teamwork Quality Business Excellence."

At San Francisco-based Levi Strauss & Company, whose jeans have become an icon of American pop culture and a symbol of the Old West's rugged individualism since the company's founding in 1850, management appeals to the aspirations of its employees:

> We all want a company that our people are proud of and committed to, where all employees have an opportunity to contribute, learn, grow, and advance based on merit, not politics or background. We want our people to feel respected, treated fairly, listened to, and involved. Above all, we want satisfaction from accomplishments and friendships, balanced personal and professional lives, and to have fun in our en-deavors.

Levi Strauss, in fact, calls its credo its "Aspiration Statement." "What type of leadership is necessary to make our Aspirations a Reality?" the statement rhetorically asks. The answer is expressed through six points:

> *New Behaviors:* "Leadership that exemplifies direct-ness, openness to influence, commitments to the success of others."
> *Diversity:* "Leadership that values a diverse work force at all levels of the organization."
> *Recognition:* "Leadership that provides greater rec-ognition—both financial and psychic—for individuals and teams."
> *Ethical Management Practices:* "Leadership that epitomizes the stated standards of ethical behavior."
> *Communications:* "Leadership that is clear about company, unit, and individual goals and performance."

Empowerment: "Leadership that increases the authority and responsibility of those closest to our products and customers."

There are corporations—AT&T, Motorola, Waste Management, and IDEX, to name a few—that have gone that extra step of making sure every manager literally signs on to a code of ethics. Managers are required to certify that not only have they not been involved in any illegal activities but also that they are not aware of any inappropriate actions of associates. Often managers and officers sign these statements under penalties that include termination. Various financial publications such as *Forbes* and *The Wall Street Journal* require officials, editors, and reporters to fill out forms that indicate what positions, if any, they hold in the various financial markets these publications cover. More and more companies have set up employee hot lines for anonymous reporting of potential improprieties so that management can identify these problems in early stages and save money, people, and public embarrassment.

There are times when the business leader, like a politician, has to take his or her case to the people. AT&T's Robert Allen dealt with that situation when he handled a major network failure in January 1990. During that month, AT&T's long-distance lines had failed, causing hundreds of thousands of calls to be interrupted and millions more from being made for a period. Instead of stonewalling and using a lot of "uhs," Allen faced AT&T's customers candidly through newspaper ads and press interviews, explaining the technical glitches in the system and apologizing for the inconveniences. He recalls, "It just never occurred to me to do anything other than say exactly what happened, what we knew and what we didn't know and what we're going to do about it—just tell the facts." As it turned out, Allen's forthrightness was a wise public relations decision. "I got praise for that with letters by the thousands," Allen said. "Apparently, it is a bigger issue in the minds of some people than I would have guessed, because they appreciate that fact that what we said was just like it was." Allen had also sent a message to AT&T

employees as well: They too are stewards that manage the company for its owners.

Allen had publicly set forth a code of conduct that made the handling of future problems less stressful for AT&T management. Or so it seemed. It happened again in September 1991 when an electric-power failure at an AT&T switching center knocked out the company's long-distance telephone service to more than one million customers. The outage also severed communications links between air traffic controllers and airline pilots, grounding more than five hundred planes in the area and causing delays as far away as Boston, Los Angeles, Paris, and Amsterdam. Another major glitch in the system. More inconveniences. More flared customer tempers. More embarrassment for the premier U.S. provider of telecommunications services. " 'Apologies are not enough,' " stated the boldface headline of the full-page AT&T ad in the *New York Times*. The headline was the beginning of a personal letter from Allen to AT&T customers. "I am deeply disturbed that AT&T was responsible for a disruption in communications service that not only affected our customers but also stranded and inconvenienced thousands of airline passengers," Allen began. "We feel a deep sense of obligation not only to our customers, but to the public at large. . . . We built our business, in a far simpler day, on an unyielding ethic of service. . . . I have great confidence in AT&T people. . . . You can count on our people's commitment." Not only is prompt disclosure the preferred ethical policy to follow but it is the only practical policy that protects the company's most treasured assets: its reputation and it goodwill.

Motorola's Bob Galvin (who said, "I find the issue of ethics to be terribly simple, and that is the Golden Rule") remembers the ethical dilemma his company faced back in the early 1950s when Motorola's annual sales were $200 million (in 1991 they were some $12 billion). The company had received a $10 million order from a South American government for a microwave radio system, a much-needed major sale for Motorola at the time.

Today Galvin recalls that particular sale as if it were yesterday. He relates it as part of Motorola's folklore:

An official from the South American country told our salesman to rewrite the proposal to raise the price to eleven
million dollars and that about nine hundred thousand dollars
of the increase was to be paid to some generals. The demand
was a serious breach of ethics, but the sale represented five
percent of our total volume. Considering overhead and such,
about half of that five percent meant pure profit on our
bottom line. Suddenly the issue was big. If we assumed our
first responsibility was to our shareholders, to public relations, and to increases in sales and earnings, we could ra-
tionalize the deal by telling ourselves, "When in Rome do as
the Romans do." I was second in command at the time and
the order would have meant even more responsibility. I didn't
have to think twice. I told our salesman to tell the government officials the entire deal was off. We wouldn't sell the
system for ten million dollars even if they came back to us
and said it was all a misunderstanding. Furthermore, I decided we would take no more business from that country.
Why did I take that position? Because now we knew what
that country's principles were and anyone else who had done
business there also knew. And if they saw we were doing
business there, they would equate A to B and would view us
as a payoff company. That would have set the stage for
contaminating our reputation. I was comfortable with the
decision and so were my associates. That incident, nearly
forty years ago, became an historical role model for our
company.

By maintaining a long-term outlook and foregoing a short-
term economic gain, Galvin was able to establish an ethical standard at Motorola that guided all future dealings in a rational and
consistent manner. *There are indeed profits in ethics and integrity.*
Repeatedly, the CEOs interviewed for this book were asked how
they resolved the potential conflict facing them and other business
managers of satisfying the needs of stockholders and meeting the
ethical standards of the corporation. Repeatedly we were told that
a corporation's long-term profitability is maximized when the com-

pany acts ethically and with integrity. Moreover, these business leaders generally applied their personal ethical standards in making decisions.

While most CEOs concede that it's possible to achieve short-term gains by violating ethical standards, such actions end up hurting the corporation and alienating valuable employees and shareholders in the process. Says Waste Management's Dean Buntrock, "I don't think that unethical practices keep the earnings up. I suppose you can make a case for a quarter or so, but I can't imagine in the real world that would last longer than a quarter." Edward DiCorcia, CEO of The Unoven Company, uses society as the reflection pool of ethics. "We can't continue to prosper by cheating the public," he says. "Ultimately, there is no such thing as right or wrong. There are only judgments of society. And no business organization can do its job efficiently, which is to provide goods and services that are demanded by the public, unless that enterprise reflects pretty closely what those judgments of right or wrong are."

Other executives such as AT&T's Bob Allen see the ethical struggle as a classic conflict in which good wins out over evil. "In the long run, ethically or morally incorrect or wrong behavior will get punished, and I just believe that," Allen says. "You can't win out in the long run by capitalizing on a short-run advantage that is ethically or morally wrong. You err on the side of being absolutely pure. I do business with almost anybody as long as they are willing to negotiate on moral and ethical terms."

Another Allen, by the first name of Woody, depicted the moral struggle through the angst of two characters in his classic bittersweet film *Crimes and Misdemeanors*. One fellow is Jonah, a doctor of high standing in society who in his desperation to cut off an adulterous relationship has his mistress murdered. The second person is an unhappy documentary filmmaker, trying to woo a female producer while making a film about his self-centered boss, a man whom he despises. Both men have compromised their lives, each living his own respective lie. Actually, they are two separate stories tied together in the last scene of the movie, when both characters are drawn into a discussion of morality that ends with the narrator's epilogue:

> Moral choices. Some are on grand scale. We define ourselves by the choices we have made. We are exactly the sum total of our choices. Events unfold so unpredictably, so unfairly, human happiness does not seem to have been included in the design of creation. It is only we, with our capacity to love, that gives meaning to the indifferent universe. And yet most human beings seem to have the ability to keep trying and even to find joy in simple things like their families, their work and from the hope that future generations might understand more.

Reflections: Ethics and Integrity Are the Foundation of the Weft

Leadership mandates ethics and a high standard of morality. Integrity is the very foundation of leadership because no one will follow you as a leader if they don't trust you.

We learn ethical behavior from those we admire and respect, such as parents, teachers, coaches, leaders, and heroes we encounter in life and even in fiction. We also learned that there are organizational cultures that nurture the sins of omission as well as the sins of commission. Predictably, the results in those organizations are disastrous.

Although we define ethics as moral conduct, we must never forget that ethics is human conduct. People and companies fail when they begin to have such thoughts as:

> "What isn't really illegal is okay."
> "It's safe because no one will ever know."
> "The company will protect me if I should get caught."

It's up to the leader to send a clear message to employees that good ethics is good business.

8

Vision Becomes Reality Through Communication

> People are generally better persuaded by the reasons which they have themselves discovered than by those which have come into the minds of others.
>
> —BLAISE PASCAL

*T*he typical large organization, such as a large business or government agency twenty years hence will have no more than half the levels of management of its counterpart today, and no more than a third of the number of managers," predicts Peter F. Drucker.

To business leaders, this prediction from the maestro of modern management is music to their ears. Corporations across America are downsizing, streamlining, and excising layers of managerial hierarchy. Eventually these hierarchies, Drucker believes, will give way to something resembling a symphony orchestra with scores of specialists reporting directly to the CEO.

Once again, we are back to the need for solid communication, back to information flow among people and machines. Computers will shape a company's strategy and structure to fit new information technology, changing the corporate rhythm to a livelier beat. Product development will be quicker, decisions faster. That means more than quick repartee at a finger-snapping pace. And the process involves more than mere talking and listening, too. Rather, it is an interactive process, the kind you find between a conductor and the musicians he or she is leading. Think of it this way: each member of

159

the symphony is a soloist reporting directly to the conductor. In Drucker's vision, employees will know what has to be done without a gaggle of vice presidents feeding them facts, figures, and flow charts. One conductor—the CEO—will be enough to keep everyone on the same beat.

The communication is direct and specific. There are no excess layers of bureaucracy. The conductor looks at each orchestra member and conveys his or her vision in a clear and forceful manner. The musicians respond, each playing his or her part in a creative burst of self-expression that shapes the composition. Yet everyone is playing the same tune, in the same key, in the same beat.

"Each musician must learn to play, on the one hand, as if he were a soloist and, on the other, with the constant awareness of being an indispensable part of a team," the great cellist Pablo Casals once said. "It is this quality of human teamwork ... that has always afforded me a joy as a conductor that no solo performance can duplicate."

Thus the symphony orchestra demonstrates the essential elements of leadership style and organizational structure, highlighting the conductor as a metaphor for tomorrow's business leader, who with the help of information technology will guide a company far different from the hierarchical model adapted from the military a century ago.

The orchestra—like the corporation—has a separate existence with music and laws of its own. The orchestra can only function if each performer accepts the responsibility to be accountable for his or her performance and contribution. This requires high self-discipline from the performers and strong, decisive leadership from the conductor.

Something else is also required: information that is relevant and purposeful. One of the basic problems of the current business scene is that most of the managers don't know which score they are playing. By that I mean they lack focus. They maneuver in one direction while the other departments go in another direction, not because they wanted to deviate from the plan but because they misread the strategic goals or long-range plan.

For example, in a boom year for Sealy the profits of its Florida manufacturing unit dwindled to almost nothing while at the same time ten other Sealy plants operated with moderate sales growth and solid profit increases. All managers had received the same planning and operating instructions: "Focus your attention on preserving your market share taking into account the corporate profit threshold of 18% return on equity." Nine other plants did a splendid job of reaching the annual sales goal. Florida, however, posted record sales as profits tumbled to near zero.

To me it was obvious that the Florida unit was playing in a different key than its counterparts. It played the "volume growth" score while the rest of the units played the "volume growth at normal profits" score. Simply because the Florida operation did not follow the complete score, the profits disappeared and the team became demoralized, disoriented, and played off-key for three more years.

In contrast, an orchestra's musicians are playing from one score, written by a single composer, led by a conductor who creates a musical vision. If indeed business information is data charged with relevance and purpose, then the gathering and interpretation of this information becomes critical in today's competitive environment as well as tomorrow's.

Who will gather and process the nuggets of information that flow like notes from the pen of a master composer? Now comes the new majority, as Drucker describes them, or the "knowledge workers"—the performers, in symphonic terms—who are the value creators of the future organization. They collect and interpret the information with skill that's portable, as opposed to a job to which they are anchored. Thus the knowledge workers have high mobility. As they organize feedback from colleagues and customers, their own performance becomes more disciplined.

"The only way to know is to listen to a host of sources," says George H. Conrades, senior vice president and general manager at IBM, the giant, some analysts believe, that has remained stuck in the present while clinging to a corporate culture bound to past glories. Yet from 1986 through 1991 the company slashed forty-seven thousand workers from its payroll and today realizes that speed is a competitive weapon for the company of the 1990s. Part of IBM's strategy, Conrades explains, included a reduction in cycle times. For instance, IBM has cut the development time for its main frames—IBM's bread-and-butter product—from three years to eighteen months. The Japanese had already realized the advantage of speed: Automakers Toyota and Honda were churning out cars from design to market in a three-year cycle compared with five years for General Motors. "There is no room for ego. It's not what you think is best for the customer, it's what the customer wants," Conrades adds. "You have to be careful though in determining customer's requirements. It's more than just listening; it's an interactive process. This is critical because the customers may also not always understand or know what they want."

As competitors square off across the battlements of the 1990s, the trick will be to create a linked chain of disciplines across a company. The challenge, Conrades believes, is to identify and integrate a company's "horizontal processes" such as design, marketing, manufacturing, and research. "American companies today are just beginning to work on these horizontal linkages," he says. "Japanese companies are far ahead of us on that. Rarer still is the American company today that can transfer innovations from one part of their organization to another."

Attitude is also part of the new equation. Leaders have to be open-minded and willing to take the best ideas wherever they find them. That means, in essence, to listen in order to read the customer correctly. Conrades illustrates the point with his local grocer, Stew Leonard, who owns two independent supermarkets in western Connecticut. Leonard's stores sell almost three times more per square foot than the major national chains. "He has two rules by which he runs his company," Conrades said. "They are painted on the large sign in front of his stores: 'Rule 1: the customer is always right. Rule 2: if the customer is ever wrong, read Rule 1.' " Leonard, which bills itself as the world's largest dairy store, is not too big to take customer suggestions. One suggestion he kept pulling out of the box: "Instead of prepackaging your strawberries, lay them out in a flat bed then let us pick out the strawberries." Both the store manager and produce manager objected to such a suggestion. It would, they assured Leonard, lead to a loss. The customers would become highly selective, picking out only the biggest and ripest berries, leaving behind the small blemished ones that no one would buy. But Leonard believed in listening to his customers. The strawberries were laid out for the picking. The produce manager was right. Predictably, the customers left the small, damaged berries behind and every night the store had to throw them away. How much did Leonard end up losing? To the contrary, within three months he ended up tripling his revenues—and doubling the profits on his berry business. The customers, it turned out, were buying three times more strawberries than before because they could select the best ones. "That comes from listening," said Conrades.

Information technology will enhance the numbers of people reporting to a single manager. Some experts say corporate staffs will disappear and dozens of managerial layers that now exist will be reduced to a half dozen front-line supervisors. Dartmouth's professor John Quinn argues that a good information system will stretch the numbers even more. The number of subordinates one CEO can command will give way to what Quinn calls "spans of communication" in which as many as two hundred people could report to a single manager. That's one heck of an orchestra.

Know the Score

Here's how Jack Reichert conducted his symphony orchestra in tune with the times shortly after he was named CEO and chairman of Brunswick Corporation:

I decided to change the company dramatically from a highly centralized company to a highly decentralized one. There is a fundamental difference between people who create wealth and people who preserve wealth. The role of the corporate staff is to preserve wealth and the role of the divisions is to create wealth. You don't want these entities to get in the way of each other. I cut corporate staff by fifty percent, doubled their severance pay, and created an outplacement service. We placed ninety percent of the people and engaged in massive decentralization programs. We increased capital investment authority at the operating level by five to ten times of what it had been; we fixed what needed to be fixed and got done what needed to get done. We had ten or twelve levels of supervision and I cut them down to five. From the first-line foreman to the president, there couldn't be more than five levels of supervision. I was either sixth or first in line; it didn't matter which one I was. I elevated the division presidents to report directly to me so the response time was cut dramatically. We were more efficient and we saved twenty-five million dollars. At the operating division level we also reduced expenses by six to seven million dollars. We decentralized and cut division expenses as well as corporate expenses; when the top of the pyramid was fat, the bottom of the pyramid, namely operations, also had to be fat to support it. We focused more people in research and development, manufacturing and less on the administrative part of the business. The company was changed permanently. Today, the corporate staff is about one hundred and forty, about one-third of what it used to be. Our sales, when I was appointed CEO, were one billion dollars and in 1988 they were three billion dollars. We have sixty-six percent fewer people generating three times the sales.

Reichert had started off with a plan like the conductor who begins to work on a score, erasing previous interpretations in an effort to give each performance freshness and new meaning. (The conductor's copy of an orchestral score contains all the parts, whereas the individual players have only the part to be played by their instruments.) It's the conductor's responsibility to spark the musicians' enthusiasm with new ideas for old works. Yet, unlike the orchestra, the corporation is more spontaneous, more improvisational as it were, sometimes composing as it goes along. "A business has no score to play except the score it writes as it plays," Drucker observes. "And whereas neither a first-rate performance of a symphony nor a miserable one will change what the composer wrote, the performance of a business continually creates new and different scores against which its performance is assessed."

Charles Kaye, executive personal assistant to Sir Georg Solti, music director laureate of the Chicago Symphony, describes how Solti would communicate his vision to the orchestra. Explains Kaye:

> Once he's learned a work, he's built up a picture in his mind—a sound picture—of how he wants it to sound. When he gets up in front to conduct the work, he will control the tempi. He's a very clear man of the beat—that's always been his gospel. But with a great orchestra like this you go beyond that. You've got to achieve an artistic conception. He rarely will stop the orchestra on a first read through. He will be listening to what they're producing and his brain will compare what's coming out with what he imagines—and what he wants. After years of experience he has the ability when he comes to the end of the movement to say "Right. Now let's go back. Bar five. Let's concentrate on that a bit. What you were doing is this. What I feel we need is this. Let's work on it." . . . So bit by bit he's trying to achieve an interpretation of the work—his sound picture—by comparing what's actually coming out with what he wants.

In other words, Solti's vision is becoming reality through a process that produces constant refinements in the music. So business leaders have the responsibility to both create the vision and guide the management to its realization. We are back to the essence of change, however subtle or radical. In bringing about the coordination of all the players, the conductor shades the dynamics of music, changes the mood and numerous other details of the performance. It is the conductor's leadership style that distinguishes one from another.

There stands the conductor on the podium, a notch above the

others. He is the true participant-observer, able to direct the orchestra, yet be a part of its collective musical soul. He achieves
distance and intimacy at the same moment, while he strives for a
delicate balance between the music and the senses without eroding
the attention of the audience, the customers as it were. And much
the same as the corporate leader, a conductor's confidence comes
through a blend of learning, experience, and technical capability.
Thus the great conductor develops the confidence to be bold. It is
that very boldness that leads to the refreshed interpretations of the
orchestra's repertoire.

As he walks the path between self-discipline and self-
expression, the conductor's confidence in his own skills and his
deep belief in what he is doing gives him the ability to stand before the orchestra, communicating tempos, style, feeling, a sense
of direction and his interpretation of the overall composition. From
the musicians he elicits their absolute best because they trust in
the leader. Thus the conductor encourages the performers and
shows them what is necessary in their performances to achieve his
vision, a vision they too can see.

"Solti is an unbelievable leader," said Samuel Magad, co-
concertmaster of the Chicago Symphony. "I mean, whether you like
it or not, you would follow him over the cliff. What he really has is
the ability to persuade you to do what he wants the way he wants it
done. You may like it, you may not like it, but you will do it his
way."

Solti's true talent, and that of every competent leader, then, is
to bring out the best in every player. If he were the CEO of a big
corporation, he would be the model of poise. And he knows full well
that up on the podium, there's nowhere to hide and no room for
arrogance. "I am never afraid to say to an orchestra, even today, that
I don't know, maybe I made a mistake," Solti has said. "It is essential that you not act infallible. I have learned during the last
twenty years . . . that you encourage. You don't discourage. You
don't criticize or be negative. You build up, not down. No imperti-
nence, no hysteria or screaming. If anything, I make jokes."

Solti's aggressive, raw energy, at times bordering on athleticism, was also communicated through body language. "Throughout the performance, Solti's body language is dramatically explicit," observed *Time* magazine as if it were covering an athlete in motion. "The violins are brought in with huge lefthanded scoops to the floor. The trumpets are cued by the riveting spear of an arm and index finger. A starburst of fingers summons the crash of the cymbals. . . . His gestures may at times seem overlarge, but they are no mere sideshow to titillate the audience. Solti is all business on the podium, his energies totally focused on the orchestra."

Communication

Solti's ability to communicate came not only from his tremendous confidence in his own capabilities but also from his very deep and close knowledge of what his performers could do technically on their instruments. The basis of Solti's knowledge of the orchestra: He had appointed 70 percent of the players who have performed over the past twenty years. Thus the great orchestras built over the years are composed of performers who come to know each other's styles so well that the communication is almost telepathic. And through intuition and a heightened sense of perception, the relationship between them and the conductor grows much like a marriage of love rather than convenience.

Another powerful tool of communication is the metaphor, a word or phrase applied by analogy to another. It gives worn and stale language new life, emotional impact, and sharpness of detail, espe- • *cially sensory detail.* "I often use analogies with the orchestra," said Elaine Scott Banks, conductor and artistic director of Chicago's City Musick orchestra:

> Sometimes these analogies have nothing whatsoever to do with music. I am reminded of a very wonderful one apparently used by Erich Leinsdorf when he was conducting Ravel's *Daphnis et Chloe Suite.* . . . The music is an evocation of

sunrise over the sea. Leinsdorf asked the orchestra to give him a "blinding" sonority at the climax of this marvelous opening passage. . . . Giving players something to think about which has a physical or tactile impact is so effective because they never forget it. They get to that place in the score and they know exactly what feeling the music should have. . . . To take a disparate body of people and give them the same vision and commitment that you have, I think this is the key to an exciting performance.

Armed with a baton, the conductor-leader stands tall—imperious, tender, parental, demanding, guiding, attention getting, threatening, surrendering, and compassionate—among the instincts, habits, and feelings of character. His or her technical know-how is a prerequisite for achieving, as is a business leader's who is capable of carefully filtering the noise of data to come up with facts. The conductor is a person for all reason. "You have to try to elicit their best, inspire them, encourage them, teach them," says Dale Clevenger, principal horn of the Chicago Symphony. "You have to be a psychiatrist and you have to sometimes not only know when to push, but when to back off. Leaders have to learn to deal with people."

In truth what we learn from the performance of a symphony orchestra is a simple lesson: Out of vastly different components can come a blend of sounds that create a greater unity. The leader brings it all together, using every available resource to communicate his or her vision. Through the use of visual and tactical images to invoke the appropriate musical response, conductors must teach, inspire, encourage, and persuade. They must use a certain amount of psychology not only in understanding themselves but in bringing the best out of each individual player. They must not only be technically competent but possess an inspired artistic point of view. They are the pathfinders, the role models, and the wizards who can turn trepidation into enthusiasm with the wave of a wand. As Solti's successor, Daniel Barenboim, who has also led operas, sums it up: "Opera, when it works, is the most complete of all arts. It has everything in it: instrumental music, vocal music, staging and theater, and lighting. Every possible discipline of artistic expression is included in the opera—this is what makes it so difficult. Often the singers are very good and the orchestra and staging less good, and other times the staging is wonderful and you have wonderful actors whose ability to sing is more restrained. All of this is what makes opera so difficult and so fascinating. As a conductor, you have to really immerse yourself in all these different aspects." When it works the entire ensemble has created something much larger than the sum of the individual parts.

So, too, in business the leader creates something that is larger than the sum of its individual parts. And like an expert in any field, a business practitioner or a symphony musician knows just how much of himself or herself to surrender for the good of the ensemble. It is not enough that each musician in an orchestra is a brilliant virtuoso or, in a business setting, that the leader has excellent workers; rather the conductor-leader takes the best of each player and builds something of even greater value that's larger than the ability of an individual to be brilliant. Likewise, the business leader builds the team in the quest for a goal that is larger than either the leader or any single manager of the team can achieve on his or her own.

As corporations write their scores for the 1990s, the composition of management will change to accommodate a new type of performer, one who is motivated by increased responsibility rather than lofty title as the traditional career ladder loses many of its rungs. Since 1980, some experts estimate, American companies have eliminated nearly one out of every four middle-management positions. Fewer management layers, however, could mean fewer promotions for promising younger managers eager and hungry to make a difference in a company. Since the 1960s and 1970s, the boom years for business expansion, fast-rising young executives were promoted every eighteen to twenty-four months, according to management professor Ross A. Webber at the University of Pennsylvania's Wharton School. Today, believes Webber, the length of time has at least doubled. So job satisfaction will become even more important for the twenty-first-century manager. "In an era of layoffs, fear becomes a powerful motivator," observed *Business Week* in a 1990 cover story titled "Farewell, Fast Track." But fear, as we all know, is not a particularly useful motivator. "Fear," *Business Week* continued, "stifles innovation and risk-taking while prompting inertia, caution, and buck-passing." Thus the business leader is responsible for figuring out creative ways for managers to do their jobs differently and perhaps even better. For example, at Hughes Aircraft, which cut fourteen thousand jobs, or 17 percent of its total, and shed two management layers between 1985 and 1990, some managers are encouraged to seek lateral moves. An electrical engineer might switch to quality control. At Hyatt Corporation staffers are encouraged to become entrepreneurial by starting their own businesses instead of impatiently waiting to run a hotel or being lured away by a competitor. Some firms are offering transfers abroad or offering mid-career breaks during which promising executives attend business schools to sharpen their skills. One of my recent students had a doctorate in education administration and was sent by the university she works for to get an MBA. She will return to her job a more rewarded and skilled person, she says, with a better understanding of general management. Small wonder the U.S. executive track is beginning to look more like that of the Japanese, a sort of zigzagging path that gives younger managers a wide latitude of experience first and ends up with senior managers who know their craft and companies far better than their American counterparts.

What these companies are doing is what the great conductors do: playing variations on the established themes with authority, freshness, and new meaning. Remember, the vision has to be clear. You can't play an uncertain chord. Banks sums it up: "A conductor should bring a unique vision to a musical ensemble. I've never thought that being a traffic cop was what a conductor was all about . . . the point is not just to avoid fatal collisions, but to produce something distinctive. A conductor's most central mission is shape a clear concept of the score at hand, and then to devise methods, however unorthodox, to realize that concept in sound. The idea must excite and sound fresh and new, and it should produce, in a very real sense, a compelling experience for the listener."

Whether a CEO or a conductor, the creative leader faces the challenge of providing meaningful alternatives. "As you start quantifying the differences between alternatives," muses Peter G. Peterson, chairman of the Blackstone Group, "you understand that certain choices have a lot more impact than others. All this, in turn, leads one to understand that the rare person is the one who can invent alternatives, who can conceive the product or market that hasn't existed before. Just think of Xerox, a Polaroid, or a General Motors in Alfred Sloan's time. The people behind these products conceptualize what an industry could be, what the consumer's problems really were. *They are thought of as having invented the solutions, but in some ways they did something more fundamental. They invented the questions.*"

An innovative corporate model that already has captured the envy of such giant companies as Du Pont Company is Gore & Associates Inc., a Delaware-based family-owned supplier of textiles that has been experimenting with a free-form management structure for thirty-five years. The $700-million-a-year company that ranks in the top 5 percent of major companies in return on assets and equity was never big on titles, and consequently, each of its thirty-five hundred employees is an "associate." And instead of bosses, "leaders" head teams in plants and staff departments. Leaders share the power to hire, discipline, or fire associates with peer committees, personnel staffers, and "sponsors." Every employee has a sponsor, a mentor who serves as a counselor and advocate. Again, it's a variation on a management theme that's been around for decades, but to the Gore employees it's sweet music to their ears.

The Humanities

Practicing one's profession is not enough. As a knowledge worker you've got to grow yourself. Yet staying on top of things technically shouldn't retard your growth as a human being. Business is not a technical science, but a liberal art "after one is promoted beyond the level of technician," observes Princeton University President Harold Shapiro in his insightful book *Tradition and Change*. More harm has been done by graduate students believing that they truly are masters of business administration when they truly are custodians of the tools of management and have yet to be apprenticed in the business world to gain the skills necessary for such a distinguished and entry-level designation of craftsperson.

The humanities can prepare us for the transition. Shapiro sees the study of humanities, together with the natural and social sciences, as helping us define truth, intellectual integrity, encourage imagination, consistency, simplicity, and coherence. Thus the humanities satisfies a powerful human need by offering an individual who has grown beyond the technical level ways to organize personal experiences so the world becomes more intelligible—to get a handle on objective reality through reason. "How can I learn?" you ask yourself. From the collective past. Study the humanities, which provide broad knowledge—history, modern languages, literature, the arts, and of course, the classics—because they recharge us and rejuvenate us from the toils of the mundane world.

Attorney Elmer Johnson, managing partner at Kirkland & Ellis and former General Motors executive vice president, recalls his encounter with the humanities, which helped shape his personal leadership tapestry:

> I had not been a great student up to the seventh or eighth grade, at which time I lost a sister to polio two years younger than I. I turned more religious, more introspective, and ended up being a much better student because of that. I took my studies more seriously.
>
> At the same time I was getting into the trumpet. The trumpet became very important in my life. I had to get on the stage and perform solo, and if you make mistakes with a trumpet it's very noticeable, unlike other instruments. It gave me a certain self-assurance because I ended up being quite good at it. For some people it was athletics, but for me it was my trumpet.
>
> Then I met with the chairman of the Yale scholarship committee and he ripped me apart for not having a better background in English literature and history because I de-

voted most of my time to science and math. I decided he was right. When I got to Yale I realized that the prep school guys were much more steeped in the classics. I didn't know Chaucer, Shakespeare, Milton, Dante, and Homer. Right then and there, I decided that even though I had gotten top grades in physics and math without working too hard, I had to work like a slave in English and history. I ended up majoring in English with a minor in history, and that's why I still thank him for this turn in my life.

While at Yale, Johnson also ended up as first-chair trumpet in the Yale band and orchestra and second chair in the New Haven Symphony.

Johnson's devotion to the humanities as a path of self-discovery is often lacking in today's undergraduate student. The University of Chicago's Allan Bloom points out that "what we see today is young people who, lacking in understanding of the past and a vision of the future, live in an impoverished present. And our universities, entrusted with their education, no longer provide the knowledge of the great tradition of philosophy and literature that made students aware of the order of nature and of man's place with it."

"The essence of commerce does not reside in spreadsheets or flowcharts," said senior executive Luigi Salvaneschi, for whom hamburger and humanities were serious business. "Rather it springs from culture, communication, education, and philosophy." While at McDonald's Corporation, Salvaneschi was responsible for planting the golden arches in Holland, France, and Japan. Before opening these new territories, however, he spent a great deal of time reading up on each country's history, government, and civilization as well as learning the basics of each country's language. "I do not think I would understand the markets if I didn't understand the inner thoughts of the people that formed the markets," he said. "The best long-term business strategy ever articulated was Dante's *Divine Comedy* ... demonstrating [his] ability to create with proportion and balance."

In this technological age, the importance of humanities is still as valuable as the newest generation of computers. Not only does it provide a basis for linking us with our past, while portending the future, but it gives us a sense of complexity, variety, and the rate of change in ourselves and the institutions we create. There is wisdom in the humanities as surely as there is beauty in a sunset. If anything, the humanities give us balance, a chance at seeing how the pieces of the complex and dynamic tapestry of life might fit. "In the early periods," writes Shapiro, "legends, myths and later traditional religions interpreted the origins of both the earth and life on it. An ethical code of individual and social behavior accompanied these accounts of creation. Thus science was knit together with moral and social behavior into a single fabric."

Although science, as Jacob Bronowski tells us, is the search for unity and hidden likeness, *the humanities offer a means of organizing our experiences by teaching us what we can learn from our collective past, the meaning of morality, the essence of art, and how we should be governed.*

When you've got hard decisions to make, say, on morality, and everyone is watching you with magnifying glasses, you can't just act on your instinct and intuition alone. You have to know what the practice of morality is, the common denominator. What did the philosophers think? The theologians? The historians? How do you grasp moral perspective? The goal of the study of humanities is to enable us to judge what we are doing in a larger context; to gain insight into reality; to obtain intellectual discipline; to develop depth of understanding; to facilitate better judgment; and to reward us through personal enjoyment, personal enlargement, and personal enlightenment.

In short, the study of humanities is the study of the wisdom of humanity.

Reflections: A Lifetime of Adding Weft Threads

I've used the metaphor of the symphony as a word picture of the emerging corporate structure in which the leader, manager, and follower will interact in a more cooperative and cohesive manner.

The weaving metaphor, however, is a personal metaphor for self-development, emphasizing the necessity of continued personal growth and the nurturing of the individual's potential. We all have unique and creative solutions, waiting to be discovered within us, to long-standing professional problems. University of Chicago philosopher Allan Bloom could very well have been talking about close-minded businesspeople of all ages when he observed that "young people who, lacking an understanding of the past and a vision of the future, live in an impoverished present."

Corporations are filled with executives who have a relentless drive to get an edge, and in the process many are pushed over it, freefalling without an open parachute. They have forgotten to listen to new ideas in an age of mass communication where ideas are easily exportable. For example, several years ago as I toured Japan with the Sealy licensee, I discovered one of my own ideas in use. There in a Yokohama furniture store was a mattress point-of-sale device I had created back in the mid-1960s. It had been patented by Sealy, but never used. When the patent expired seventeen years later, a competing Japanese mattress manufacturer copied the device and introduced it as a new idea in Japan. Later I learned that it is common practice for Japanese companies to patent watch: to closely review the list of expired patents in the United States and glean creative solutions to some of their thorny business problems.

"The main reason I seek the ideas of others is for help—the diagnosis and treatment of my own isolation and enlargement of my understanding," writes Bill Moyers in the book *A World of Ideas*. "If you have ever hiked in the Rockies and seen the vistas change as you move from one plateau to another—revealing peaks, contours, crests, colors, and vegetation previously hidden—you know what I am trying to say. I have had a career of discovery and feel compelled to share it."

The lesson is simple: *For help in nurturing personal growth and spiritual renewal, study the humanities, which can provide the balance between intellectual discovery and the day-to-day grind of life.*

Total Quality Management Mandates Total Quality Leadership

There go my people, I must follow them, for I am their leader.

—MOHANDAS K. GANDHI

*B*ecause you've read this far, you know that I firmly believe leadership has nothing to do with a genetic role of the dice. Leaders are not born to lead. They are made through a combination of formative factors in one's upbringing, tempered by time, circumstance, and events they are caught up in. Thus leadership is not a matter of biological destiny but one of choice. And once that choice is made, need takes over: the need to prove oneself, to believe in oneself, to trust one's own feelings.

It pays us to listen to David Ruder, the thoughtful, philosophic professor and former dean of Northwestern University law school, who in 1987 left the ivory tower for the rigors of chairmanship of the Securities and Exchange Commission (SEC). Ruder, a Phi Beta Kappa at Williams College and number one in his law school class and editor-in-chief of the *Law Review* at the University of Wisconsin, practiced corporate law before going into academia in the 1960s. In August 1987, he was chosen by President Reagan to replace John Shad as SEC chairman. Ruder had been on the job about two months when the nation's financial sky fell down—the greatest stock market crash in American history—thrusting him into the national and international spotlight. Almost overnight he was faced with the role of leader in a management crisis that had spread worldwide like some unchecked virus as the stock, options, and futures markets began to unravel. Eventually, of course, the markets settled down and went on to set new record highs. In 1992, back in Chicago teaching at Northwestern and practicing law, he took time to reflect on leadership as the retired SEC chairman:

> I think the world is full of people who are capable of exercising leadership. The opportunity to exercise that leadership involves a great deal of fortuitous circumstances. When a person who has the capability of leadership gets put into the leadership role, then the job does indeed create the leader. You have to have both elements: the capability of leadership and the events that cause the leader to exercise that capability. I can, for example, take my own experience. I had a chance to exercise leadership as the opportunity presented itself.
>
> At some point you begin to think that solving problems is not accidental. You gain self-confidence. You begin to think you do have talent. I had always believed that the overly ambitious people were the ones who succeeded. But that characteristic, I have since discovered, is not likely to make as great a leader as the individual who is competent, able, and can rise to the occasion. Often ambition gets in the way of leadership. I frankly think that's what wrecked former President Richard Nixon. He was extremely ambitious. He finally got to the point where he thought he *was* the president, not a person in the office of president. There is a difference, believe me. I think that once you get that into your head, you're going to lose a lot of rationality about your job.
>
> I once wrote an article titled "Bang—You're a Freshman." I have since reflected on that idea—that you are continually a freshman in life: energetic, capable, ambitious,

and interested in progress and success. But you always end up being in a unfamiliar situation, like a freshman starting anew.

You can sense a bit of that freshman in GE's chairman Jack Welch when he outlines his company's new strategy for the twenty-first century in three words: speed, simplicity, and self-confidence. Throughout the 1990s and beyond, he promised, GE will turn its management away from "serving the system and fighting the system" to serving the customer and competing more effectively.

It sounds as if Welch were intent on turning GE into a symphony orchestra with clear lines of communication between the players and conductor. "Our business with tens of thousands of employees will not respond to visions that have subparagraphs and footnotes," said Welch. "Simplicity means plain speaking, directness, honesty and simplicity itself is the media for communicating the vision and with an impact."

Speed and simplicity are the boogeymen of deep-layered organizations, or as Welch put it, "Bureaucracy is terrified by speed and hates simplicity." To compete in the European and Asian markets in the years ahead, however, GE's objective is clear: to get there faster and first. To accomplish that will require a collective sense of self-confidence throughout the GE organizations. But Welch knows full well that companies can't distribute self-confidence and that "self-confidence breeds simplicity and the best way to earn self-confidence at GE is by people contributing to the success of the enterprise." Welch's message to GE workers from the executive suite to the production line is also clear: Winning in the marketplace is the ultimate job security.

So what kind of business climate are the Jack Welches going to face in the decades ahead? A tough formidable one in which more subordinates will report to each manager and where overseas duty will be important to executive advancement as jobs grow slower than the labor force.

As for those who predict that future companies will evolve into unstable collections of people, resembling firms in the toy industry that expand rapidly when they have a winner and shrink with a passing fad, they need only see what is anchored in today's reality. There is nothing faddish about the new economic realities taking hold across oceans and the collapse of a political system that viewed business managers as exploitative. Renegade capitalism in Eastern European countries that once thrived underground (and under the nose of the state) will receive amnesty.

Fortress Europe will not be coming about to enhance the economic well-being of North Americans. The Europeans seek economic protection, synergy through combined common markets, and efficiencies from lower transaction costs and fewer trade barriers. It isn't exactly a wall like the Chinese once built to keep out enemies and foreign exploiters; think of it more as a rain forest canopy—an overarching cover—that allows just enough light and moisture to filter through the tree crowns for healthy growth. The EC grows not out of a common language or a common heritage but out of a common need in a rapidly changing world. It also grows out of the recognition that in a borderless world, some type of rationality has to be derived from the European cultural diversity.

There too is the emergence of the Asian Rim's economic bloc, not yet a formerly developed entity. But the prospect of some kind of economic federation of Japan, Taiwan, Singapore, Thailand, South Korea, and Hong Kong has impressive economic potential. Co-prosperity leads to co-dependency. Japan itself is going through an economic restructuring with the Bank of Japan trying to force out inefficient firms through high interest rates and governmental policy that focuses on emerging technology. Moreover, most of the shareholders of Japanese firms do not care about dividends, allowing the companies to focus on the long run instead of short-term profits. Roughly every four and a half years Japan grows with a volume equal to the gross national product of France. At that growth rate Japan will overtake the United States as the world's largest economy early in the next decade. And all the while, China looms as a piece of Asia's economic puzzle that one day will be in place to form what some futurists are already calling the Pacific century.

Meanwhile, America is shaking off the indulgence of the leveraged buyouts of the 1980s to face the 1990s and a new reality: slimmed-down capitalism. As corporate America sheds the layers of managerial fat that have accumulated since the late 1940s, it isn't doing so to reach back with nostalgia to the simple life. The new engine driving our industry is necessity. It is simple necessity that begs for vision and redefined mission to protect our economic turf and to seize the productive initiative. It is likely you will get to look the leader squarely in the eye and have the opportunity to interpret the vision as you sit in the business symphony of the future. You will be expected to produce results, to be personally responsible for your performance. But simply doing more of what worked in the 1980s won't be enough in the 1990s when speed and information technology will become part of the winning strategy.

That was the case in the Gulf War in which the United States fought smarter than it ever had before. Take, for example, the air power. While the Iraqi Mig-15 accelerated faster, climbed more rapidly, and could turn tighter, it had a restricted view compared with the U.S. F-86, which had a plastic-domed bubble that allowed enemy activity to be more easily observed. The F-86 could thus maneuver more easily, decelerating and diving while switching directions. Clearly, better intelligence and faster maneuvering canceled out the Mig's superiority. To operate at a faster tempo than an adversary, Colonel John Boyd told *Forbes* magazine, was to get inside the enemy's "time/cycle loop." Added Boyd, "This is exactly how the Japanese use flexible manufacturing to out-compete us." In the auto industry, for instance, the Japanese can develop and make new products in one-half to one-third the time it takes any other nation. Honda's Acura and G.M.'s Saturn were announced at about the same time. Yet, by the time Saturn began arriving in the marketplace during 1991, Honda had already made three model changes in the Acura.

Deming: The Japanese Prize

The United States may be hanging on to its shaky edge in innovation, but it's losing time and money in new product development compared with the Japanese. It's been said that American companies often attempt to hit home runs but often miss the ball, whereas the Japanese try to hit as many singles as possible, maintaining a higher batting average. The statistics are beginning to bear out that observation. For instance, a 1991 *Fortune* survey showed that Japanese manufacturers spend more time planning, suffer fewer development setbacks in a smaller portion of products, and waste less of their time debugging finished products than their American counterparts. At the same time, Japan's nondefense research and development expenditures as a percentage of gross national product is far outpacing that of the United States. The payoff isn't surprising: Japanese companies invest more of their managerial time in new products—and receive more revenues from them.

Along with speed and information technology, communicating new strategies from CEO to manager will be streamlined as well, bringing us back to the conductor and the symphony orchestra.

"An example of a system well managed is an orchestra," W. Edwards Deming told *The Wall Street Journal* in 1990 when the guru of Japanese business was eighty-nine years old. "The various players are not there as prima donnas—to play loud and attract the attention of the listener. They're there to support each other. In fact, sometimes you see a whole section doing nothing but counting and watching. Just sitting there doing nothing. They're there to support each other. That's how business should be. . . . The system must be managed. It will not manage itself. The components cannot manage themselves. And so many companies have separate business plans for separate departments. That's not management. That's foolishness. That's the kind of thing that only makes things worse."

Deming, ignored in his own country for more than forty years, is the father of Total Quality Management (TQM) and today is sought by U.S. companies for advice. Courses around his ideas are being taught at some of the nation's major business schools. But the Japanese have been in awe of Deming's theories that have become practice in numerous Japanese companies. Since 1951, the Union of Japanese Scientists and Engineers has awarded the highly regarded annual Deming Prizes to those Japanese companies excelling in quality control.

In the foreword of Mary Walton's book *The Deming Management Method,* Deming himself writes: "The biggest problems [of American business] are self-inflicted, created right at home by management that are off course in the competitive world today."

There are fourteen steps in the Deming methods to TQM. I prefer to call them "Deming's Fourteen Commandments." There is little doubt that TQM is a powerful idea. But without leadership, TQM will die at the middle management level in most American companies, because it requires a long-term view. Total Quality Leadership (TQL) is the fundamental element that can transform American companies into world-class competitors, for TQL puts the focus on the long run and gives industry and its workers the time to modify behavior and perfect TQM principles in the workplace. Long term is the time-frame of leadership. Thus TQM can be more than a theoretical set of practices that become muddled in the hard realities of such American economic ills as an indifferent work force, declining international competitiveness, and undereducated candidates for the job market.

With this in mind, I've reviewed Deming's fourteen steps to quality production and applied our leadership insights to each.

1. Create consistency of purpose for the improvement of product and service.

It is the leader's role to nurture an environment where short-term results support the long-term improvements that are required in today's dynamic business environment. Product and service improvements generally come very slowly. However, the culture must support the long run, which in turn supports a commitment to constantly refining what we do so that we do it just a little better every day.

2. Adopt the new philosophy. The company can no longer live with delays, mistakes and defective work.

Product and process innovation requires dynamic responses to marketplace shifts. In order to commercialize new technologies, leaders must empower the organization to try to take risks—to try and succeed or try and fail—but not to be afraid to try.

3. Cease dependence on mass inspection to achieve quality. Use statistical process controls to get it right the first time.

The culture of the company defines what is important:

"Attention to details."

"Quality first; inspection second."

"Fix the cause of the defect, not the defective part."

Since the leader defines the culture and is the custodian of what we do and how we go about doing it, it is the leader's role to incorporate statistical process controls, as defined by Deming, into the culture.

4. End the practice of awarding business on price tag alone. Minimize costs by working with a single supplier. Make quality a prerequisite.

Like promoting from within, supplier relationships thrive on long-term support and mutuality of interests. It is the leader's role to send the signals indicating that, in a TQM environment, it is the corporate policy to maintain continuity with suppliers in order for supplier and company alike to learn from each other's strengths and get the most responsive reaction to each other's needs.

5. Improve constantly the system of production and service.

The leader aligns people to the task of doing things better, not to that of putting out fires. He also links long-term performance with management compensation. It is the leader who initiates the programs that mandate that it is each individual's responsibility to improve quality and productivity.

6. Institute on-the-job training.

The leader requires that all employees from the very top (himself) or bottom must be involved in an ambitious training and retraining program. The leader takes the position that training is a necessity in which all departments and divisions have a mutual interest and a mutual stake.

7. Institute leadership.

The need to empower people—to create teams that focus on everything from product development to production process to customer satisfaction—and to allow people to manage themselves in an integrated and flexible system is the goal of the business leader in a TQM environment.

8. Drive out fear.

A responsive company is an open company—one open to achieving its full potential. Fear closes an individual down and limits a person's willingness to take risks. Fear nurtures the idea that what is "safe" is the proper conduct rather than what is "best." For both the short and long run, an open corporation without fear is the one most likely to prosper.

9. Break down barriers between departments.

Deming, too, views the well-managed business system as a symphony orchestra in which each musician supports the others. At the same time, there are no communication barriers between the members of the ensemble and the conductor. Likewise, many companies are striving for a model that permits more performers to report directly to their leader. Communication becomes the catalyst between leader and follower as information flows back and forth.

10. Eliminate slogans, exhortations, and numerical targets.

Telling people what to do from the top down doesn't work. Each department should maintain its own initiative. "Goals are like hay somebody ties in front of the horse's snout," says Deming. "The horse is smart enough to discover no matter whether he canters or gallops, trots or walks, or stands still, he can't catch up with the hay."

As the leader develops the mission statement—a road map to the future—he is careful to avoid the dead ends. Dead ends are goals that are unobtainable and a strategy that does not fit the culture. The mission statement is far more than a mere slogan. Besides defining long-term objectives, it should serve to match the personal values and aspirations of the employees with the goals of the organization. Vision and mission become relevant only when everyone has a stake in the outcome.

11. Eliminate work standards (quotas) and management by objective.

Deming tells us that as long as you have managers who are trained to manage by objectives; to set numerical goals that force different departments and their people to compete with one another; to evaluate, grade and rank people and thereby demoralize them; the transformation of American corporations will be close to impossible.

12. Remove barriers that rob the worker, engineers and managers of their right to pride of workmanship.

Only the leader can create the culture that allows workers to redefine themselves and their values. Only the leader can give back to the worker what so many companies have crushed for so long— eagerness to learn, dignity, self-esteem. Quality products help a company grow and encourage workers to have a personal stake in the results. Workers no longer should be perceived as a commodity, but as an asset with valuable skills, pride, dedication, and needs that require satisfaction in the workplace.

13. Institute a vigorous program of education and self-improvement.

In today's business world, the investment in education is as valuable a corporate asset as the latest high-tech machine or computer. When we look at improvement as a process, we see that education is a necessity in today's chaotic business world.

14. Put everyone in the company to work to accomplish the transformation.

To accomplish these Deming steps takes a "critical mass" of senior management with a solid plan to implement the program. Total Quality Management is said to be simple—but not easy. It can't be accomplished overnight and its success depends on everyone's job. The keys to mastering the quality steps are long-term commitment, a clear understanding of the leader's role, a belief that people at every level of a company can make a difference, and the courage to take the first step.

"You must think of the company as a system and manage it as such. The function of every component, every division under good management is to adjust its contribution toward optimizing a system of profound knowledge," explains *Chicago Tribune* writer Ronald Yates in his provocative article on Deming, "Messiah of Management." "Good management, impeccable quality, efficient and proper use of resources and of people, continual improvement and transformation, optimization of a system of production and services—these are not pie-in-the-sky ideals for Deming. To him, they are the very keys to America's survival.

Baldrige: The American Prize

American business is finally listening to Deming. And so are the business schools. Why now? Because industry has told the schools they haven't done enough with the standard B-school menu of finance, accounting, economics, and statistics. They want graduates who have a feeling for the philosophy of Total Quality Management. Only in recent years have the academicians focused on the way American industry operates. In order to teach TQM, they had to reeducate themselves, first learning how the Japanese do it. At the University of Chicago Graduate School of Business, for instance, associate professor George S. Easton teaches courses in statistics and quality management. Since 1989, Easton has been on the board of examiners for the Malcolm Baldrige National Quality Award—the equivalent of Japan's Deming Prize—sponsored by the U.S. Department of Commerce. "Business schools are talking about total quality management," says Easton. "While they talk a lot about it, most are not in a position to teach it very well because it is cross functional and process oriented in nature rather than oriented toward functional specializations." Likewise, senior executives support the Baldrige Award with public relations, speeches, and so on, but they are troubled by their own leadership roles in the process of designing the system that will improve quality. They fall short of creating the decision-making process to accomplish quality control. Says

Easton: "I have never seen a truly well thought out leadership plan that responds to a company's real needs."

Easton's observations are borne out in a 1990 survey by the General Accounting Office (GAO) titled *Management Practices— U.S. Companies Improve Performance Through Quality Effort.* In a survey of twenty companies that had competed for the Baldrige Award, the GAO found no standard approach to implementing TQM. Each company used different practices and techniques, relying heavily on customer focus, senior leadership, commitment to worker training, empowerment and involvement, and a systematic means of gathering information that led to a decision-making process to foster improvement.

In short, many of today's business leaders have yet to devise a management system that creates and sustains clear and visible quality values in line with excellence. Among the names on the Baldrige Awards, which were first presented in 1988, are Motorola, Xerox, Cadillac Motor, IBM, Federal Express, and Procter & Gamble. In August 1991, American Express, Ford, IBM, Motorola, Procter & Gamble, and Xerox sponsored The Total Quality Forum, a three-day meeting that drew more than two hundred academicians to discuss Total Quality Management and its role in business schools and engineering schools across the nation's campuses. One point everyone seemed to agree on: Our system of higher education is the nation's most powerful competitive weapon.

To deliver on the package of Total Quality Management, however, you've got to have total quality leadership. If, as Deming puts it, transformation is everybody's job, someone has to have the vision to know what the company is transforming itself into. Creating the new mission and vision is the singular job of the leader—no one else can do it. Adopt the new vision, says Deming, and create consistency of purpose.

Reflections: Quality Champions through Quality Leadership.

The role of the leader, then, is to be a quality and consistent communicator, which leads to driving out fear and breaking down the barriers that Deming so deplores. That process empowers the followers to buy into the new vision. The leader asks each person to redefine himself or herself in a new productive way that facilitates the new vision. Leaders need to create a risk-taking environment without fear. *To get people to change, leaders must put the focus on the individual just as the conductor depends on each individual in the ensemble to be a virtuoso and member of the team at the same time.*

10

Gordon Segal Weaves the Warp and Weft of Leadership

What's in a Plate? Gordon Segal saw his future in one as he was drying it back in 1962. As the beads of water slid down a piece of Arzberg china he held from a set of dinnerware he and his bride, Carole, had bought on a shopping trip in New York City, the bulb of inspiration lit up. Shortly thereafter, the twenty-three-year-old Gordon and Carole opened their first store, despite the fact they knew nothing about retailing. Their enthusiasm had canceled out their naïveté as they took the entrepreneurial risk by betting their savings of $10,000 on themselves. The money (along with another $7,000 borrowed from Segal's father) went to convert a derelict elevator factory in the Old Town area of Chicago into a specialty store called Crate & Barrel to sell imported tableware, culinary utensils, and pots and pans—all stacked on the makeshift crates and barrels they had arrived in from the European factories the Segals had prodigiously shopped. And all affordable for the city dwellers setting up housekeeping who wanted clean-lined, contemporary, European-style table goods.

"We were young kids, it was a counterculture store," Segal recalls. "We wore open shirts and sold on an informal and casual basis. It was niche marketing."

That was nearly thirty years ago. Today thousands of shoppers buy an array of silverware, dishes, glasses, cutlery, pots, pans, and even sheets and furniture from thirty-six Crate & Barrel (C&B) stores in ten markets nationwide—from Kittery, Maine, to San Francisco—and through the sixteen million C&B catalogs mailed out each year. Annual sales for the privately owned "the Crate," as Segal calls it, are more than $170 million and climbing. In 1990, the Crate took its place on Chicago's Magnificent Mile—the posh retail and high-rise strip along North Michigan Avenue—in a new forty-five-thousand-square-foot building clad in shimmering white aluminum and glass, replete with escalators in a glass rotunda, skylights, and an outdoor terrace. The off-beat shop had grown into a plush emporium. But the philosophy never changed. "We work for the customer, not the manufacturer," Segal says.

These days Segal, who sees the Crate paternalistically, depends heavily on the more than one thousand employees, attributing the Crate's track record to their performance. "We have a tremendous group of people that make it happen," he says. "If I do have a talent it is for attracting and keeping together a unique group of artists." For employee and customer alike, he says, "We had to create a vision people could buy into."

The hardest thing Segal had to cope with over the years: delegating authority. A tall man with dark penetrating eyes, a gracious smile and an infectious sense of humor, Segal admits it took him almost fifteen years to make the transition from entrepreneur to business leader, a process that at times was painful for Segal and those around him. "Stay humble, stay nervous," he advises. "No one individual has all the wisdom." And with the verve of a risk taker he adds: "You can't say you're a leading edge retailer and play it safe."

The objective of this chapter is to present a slice of leadership reality in an almost stream-of-consciousness format to capture the color, struggle, change, passion, and growth of an entrepreneurial CEO. I've annotated the reflections of Gordon Segal as a critic would

Shakespeare or *Alice in Wonderland.* But my purpose, of course, is neither scholarly nor academic pursuit but to sort out the stuff of leadership by picking through Segal's fluid thoughts.

No one ever accused Gordon Segal of playing it safe. On a crisp fall evening in 1991 Segal, in a breezy, candid, and rambling style, shared his recollections of a remarkable career with my class.

What does it take to be an entrepreneur?[1] Well, I think it takes somebody who's a little bit crazy today. I think you have to have an obsessed personality,[2] along with being somewhat neurotic. You also have to be somewhat driven and even a little bit of an egomaniac. It takes a great deal of burning desire. Besides being very risk orientated, you've got to be a bit of an actor because obviously you're putting your neck on the line. You're out there on the stage, especially in retailing; I always believe the best retailers are actors and actresses, because they're really out there performing every day. I think one has to have all these attributes. And, of course, you've got to be hungry and want to really work hard, especially if you're going to be in any entrepreneurial role. When you're starting up a business you virtually have to do it all. You can't say I'm very good at this but I don't want to do this or that.

Working for a big company, you can specialize. But when you start up your own company, I guarantee you, you need a breadth of skills. If you don't have them, then learn them damn fast because you can't afford to hire someone for everything you'll need to know.

Let me go into a bit of personal history, along the path I traveled over the last thirty years. My wife and I married in 1961. Like other young couples, we looked around and everything we loved for our home we couldn't afford and everything that we could afford, we didn't like, so we said there had to

[1] Entrepreneur: Organizes an economic venture; owns, manages, and assumes the risk

[2] Personal factors of Gordon Segal's leadership restated:
· Hungry/driven
· High energy level
· High capacity to manage detail
· Focused (obsessed)
· Insecure (actor/neurotic)
· Enthusiastic (good communicator)
· Very creative

[3] Family restaurant business taught importance of being "great" every day

[4] Real estate experience was valuable later in negotiating leases and selecting locations

[5] Reflective of the core motivation of most leaders: to make a difference

be other young couples like us with good taste and no money. I had traveled to Europe right after I graduated with a degree in political science. I thought I was going to go into the restaurant business and I wanted to tour all the great European restaurants. It was natural since I had grown up in the restaurant business. But deep down it wasn't something I wanted to do.[3] I decided, instead, to venture into the real estate business. For me it was an easy business, too easy. I really didn't find real estate very creative, even though there was big money to be made. There were few ethics in that business and that was no fun for me.[4] My motivation in life from early on was to be creative and do something unique. I didn't want to just go out and make money. I figured if I was good, I'd make money; if I wasn't so good, I'd starve. Rather, I wanted to really be noticed and really contribute.[5]

The idea for Crate & Barrel occurred one night while I was washing dishes. My wife and I had been on a honeymoon in the Caribbean and I had traveled in Europe. While I was in New York where I had some business to conduct, I realized that there were a lot of great little stores in all of these places that had great Scandinavian and European merchandise that you didn't see in Chicago in those days. In the 1960s there were a few contemporary furniture stores offering beautiful and wonderful designs, but everything was quite expensive, quite elitist. After doing a little more research, one night I said, "Carole, there are all of these wonderful household products out East and overseas, but you can't buy them in Chicago." Maybe, I wondered, could there be a market in the Windy City? True enough, after browsing and investigating, I concluded there were no stores selling reasonably priced, uniquely designed cookware, china, and glassware in Chicago other than department stores.

I also concluded that this could be a fun business. I could travel to Europe. I could meet a lot of people, which is my secondary interest, and maybe find merchandise that was well designed and beautiful and sell it to customers.[6]

We took the plunge. Not knowing a thing about merchandising, I decided to become a retailer. I tried to capitalize the store by plunking down the ten thousand dollars we had saved up since graduating from college. But we needed twenty thousand. So I did what any budding entrepreneur worth his salt does. I scampered. My idea wasn't worth ten thousand dollars to an outsider. Nobody wanted to invest ten grand for even half of Crate & Barrel before the startup. I finally found one very rich guy for whom I had done a lot of real estate work. After thinking about it for a month, he said, "Gordon, I want to tell you something—if I'm your partner and you're not successful, you're going to be very unhappy that I'm your partner. And guess what, Gordon, if I'm your partner and you're not successful, I'm going to be very unhappy that I'm your partner. Why don't you get some money from your family?" And so, tail between my legs, I went back to my dad who wasn't a very wealthy man, and he gave me all the money that he probably had saved in his life which was seven thousand dollars.[7] He really had faith, he gave me the money and with seventeen thousand dollars we started the Crate & Barrel.

You've got to realize why my wife calls me the luckiest guy alive. We had to come up with innovative ways for building the store. We finally found an old and torn-up elevator factory in Old Town. We couldn't afford to buy Sheetrock so we hammered up crating lumber on the walls to finish the interior and sanded the old wood floors for three days straight. We didn't have any money for fixtures

[6] The creative vision comes from knowledge of where we are now and seeing the possibilities (the economic opportunity from within the niche) and acting on the information.

[7] Timing and external events often dictate the form, substance, and execution of a new venture: 100 percent owned with 100 percent of the risk. Low-cost interior design and display made a statement that captured the spirit of Crate & Barrel.

so we took the packing crates and barrels, pushed them over, spilled out the wood excelsior, stacked up the merchandise, and we opened the doors. Imagine if we would have had money to buy real fixtures, imagine if we would have had money to put Sheetrock on the walls, buy fancy lighting fixtures, Crate & Barrel would not have been the same kind of store. Necessity had forced us to use the crates for display and everybody thought, "What a clever idea."

All of a sudden there was a little store with this young couple, twenty-three years old, selling china and glass out of packing crates. Now we began to think about going directly to Europe and visiting all the small factories that made glassware in Sweden, Belgium, Denmark, and Germany and finding the porcelain factories and small craftsmen making wooden pottery and flatware. Buying directly from the factory and selling directly to our customers would enable us to eliminate the whole importer distributor channel.[8] The usual method at that time was for small shops to buy from an importer-wholesaler who would be in New York or San Francisco or Baltimore or Boston. A factory might sell an item for one dollar to the importer. It would cost fifty cents to import the product or a landed cost of a dollar fifty, and the importer would sell it to a retailer for three dollars. The retailer would then sell it to a customer for six.

Now our idea was to buy the merchandise directly from the factory, pay a little more, but save on importing and handling and eliminate the importer's markup. We could then sell that item for three fifty or four dollars, a price thirty to forty percent below market for that quality of item. We could also find better designed items, exclusive items for Crate & Barrel. Besides, when we went to Europe ourselves, we'd find a product that wasn't import-

[8] By buying direct, Segal had to function as his own wholesaler and importer. He was willing to take these risks too, so that he could offer lower prices as well as good design. This gives us more dimension to his creative vision.

ed.[9] We'd find little guys with small factories making beautiful things. That's pretty exciting. It is the search that is really the best part of retail, searching for that product and then deciding whether that product is right. The table, the glass, the bowl, the vase—are they the right shapes, dimensions, colors? Are they priced right? Are they the right products for the types of consumers who shop your store? Anticipating correctly was the thrill of the game and, of course, being able to travel in Europe on business was very exciting also.

I was very fortunate, I became bored with real estate at the same time my wife became bored with teaching elementary school. She had a great deal of talent in display and design. I had great energy and a sense of organization. Both of us were very good at salesmanship.

Well, we were just so excited. We jumped into the store, opening it on December seventh, 1962. That first Christmas between December seventh and December thirty-first we had an eight thousand-dollar month. We were ecstatic, eight thousand times twelve months equaled ninety-six thousand dollars; we had it made. According to our pro forma we needed only sixty-five thousand dollars to break even for the year. We were the most brilliant retailers around, so brilliant we had forgotten to buy a cash register. By mid-January, we found out we had mispriced most of the merchandise we sold in December. We sold most of it for cost because we had no time to look up the invoices, we just said, what do you think it's worth?[10] So we opened up the store with absolutely a total lack of retailing management skills. Now this is important to understand: That is, retail is a very forgiving business, if you have the right instincts and passions.

Then February 1963 came and we had a two-

[9] The warp threads of industry and the weft threads of creative vision unify to become the Crate & Barrel concept.

[10] Mistakes don't make a new venture fail most of the time. Lack of learning from mistakes and failure to make correc-

tions are the un-
forgiving sins.

[11] Fear of failure
is also a fear of
diminishing one's
image.

[12] Today's stores
are well lighted,
with lots of mer-
chandise individu-
ally arranged,
piped-in music,
and cheerful and
knowledgeable
employees who all
wear aprons.

[13] They were vi-
sionaries who
translated the val-
ues and aspira-
tions of young
people into a re-
tail atmosphere.

thousand-dollar month. In fact we had one day we
had such a bad snowstorm that only one customer
walked into the store; we sold her eight dollars'
worth of goods, and that was it for a whole day.
Now every time my staff gets a little depressed by
a sales report, I say remember February 1963,
nothing has ever been that bad!

There's nothing that motivates you like fear
of failure.[11] We were terribly excited and terribly
anxious, and we worked like hell to make the store
work. We learned our business and figured out
how we were going to buy and sell our product.
Fortunately, we had several good things going for
us. One, we had a unique way of selling household
goods and a unique way of thinking—in essence,
the idea of going to Europe, bringing the stuff in
directly, and not having a very fancy store. It's
nothing like our stores are today, by the way, we
literally had packing crates of merchandise, bur-
lap backdrops, no spotlight, plain incandescent
lighting.[12] We weren't these great visual merchandisers we are today. We were just excited young
kids in a very simple, rough-hewn store. In fact we
called that first store in Old Town a counterculture
store.[13] We also were not very polished, wearing
open shirts, selling customers in a very informal,
very casual manner. However, we've never made
the mistake of buying products that we didn't like.
We always bought something we loved so that we
had sincere enthusiasm.

To give you some perspective, we didn't know
that we weren't supposed to go to Europe and buy
directly. We didn't know that we weren't supposed
to display the way we did. We didn't know that
this was an incorrect way to go into retail. But
because we had this desire to be successful and
because we had this interest in searching for and

finding products, we started this company and went at it with a great deal of hard work and a very sincere manner.[14] I think that one thing I'm very proud of at the Crate is that we've never made a mistake of getting caught up thinking that we can sell anything at any price because it was done by a neat designer or a neat manufacturer. We're not really selling for the manufacturers; we're not their sales agents. We are the consumer's buying agents. It's always critical to remember who you're working for. We're working for the customer and we never forgot that.[15] So that means we've got to go over to Europe and Asia and find beautiful things at great prices. We felt that there was a fairly thin market at first and had to keep broadening that market, educating our customers in terms of the product we'd find and the way we developed the company. But we loved what we were doing, we truly loved our business, we truly enjoyed what we were learning to do and we grew the business very carefully because we had no capital. We had to grow the business by doing a broad range of jobs ourselves. I was doing the accounting and the bill paying and besides the key job of selling I also was doing the unpacking of the crates and counting the merchandise and doing the inventory. This went on for nearly six years until we slowly accumulated enough capital.[16] Probably that first year we did better than break even, about ninety thousand; second year, one hundred and ninety thousand; the third year, two hundred and ninety thousand dollars; and then our landlord said our lease was up as we only had a three-year lease. Luckily the little bit of real estate I had done earlier was to clean up bad real estate titles. Our landlord owned a vacant lot twenty-five feet away, a lot with a bad title. I was able to convince the landlords that

[14] Sincere commitment means total commitment to the vision, mission, and execution of the idea.

[15] He did not say he was working to make a profit. He did say he was in retailing to satisfy the customer. This is how value is created.

[16] Doing all the jobs during the startup served them well when they started to delegate and became more observers than doers.

if I would clear up the title, I could build a building on the land and we would pay the mortgage on it over ten years. This is the first store we built ourselves, and we occupied it from 1965 till September 1990. [The store had been an outlet for selling end-of-season and closeout merchandise in recent years. In November 1990, a new and bigger outlet store opened about a mile from this Old Town location.] When we built this first store, however, we got the concept of doing wooden beam ceilings, solid oak floors, and brick walls. We played with the idea of fixturing and we started our first spotlighting of merchandise and all of a sudden we learned about the art of merchandising, not just being a retailer.[17] We learned to take pitchers and line them up on a shelf and take all the glasses and mass them on a pedestal. And we slowly evolved the kinds of merchandising techniques that have made us quite successful. We were young, energetic, experimental, and willing to change so we slowly evolved this merchandising technique along with creating great fabric backgrounds, having music in the stores, and spotlighting displays. We learned by traveling around Europe; picking up ideas; focusing on what made those shops so charming, so wonderful; learning about the personality of a company, learning about the style of different stores and what made them work.[18] We learned from each one of them, melding our observations into our psyches and then creating something unique.

Like growing children, nothing happened very quickly. Day by day, week by week, we learned by experimentation. Everything was an evolution of something we had seen. We focused and slowly built the business. By 1968 we reached the five-hundred-thousand-dollar mark. We really

[17] They did not stop developing the Crate & Barrel concept with the success of their first store. Vision and mission must be refined with new knowledge and new insights.

[18] Creativity is evolutionary.

didn't want to open a second store and by no stretch of the imagination had we ever considered building a chain of stores. I just loved being a retailer; buying merchandise and inspecting it when it got to the store. I loved running a small business, being on the sales floor, talking about my product. I loved managing one store. In 1968 when I was thirty, it was very hard for me to imagine anybody else being able to run a store as well as I could run it.[19] It was very hard for me to imagine delegating a store to somebody, even if we had a store manager to run the store on a day-to-day basis. I couldn't imagine not being in that store every day, giving it a critical overview. I mean I really loved being a shopkeeper. I've learned that it's very hard for a founder to delegate, to give away these jobs, these functions, these unique talents and to believe that other people can do the job as well or better than they've been doing it. I probably wouldn't have ever built the second store but when Martin Luther King was assassinated, they were burning down all the neighborhoods around us. The National Guard was called out, streets were going up in flames, and I thought now's the time for diversification. We'll go to Wilmette (a northern Chicago suburb along Lake Michigan), take the safe course and have two stores, one a suburban store and one a downtown store. That was the only thing that motivated us. We never would have expanded otherwise.

So our first suburban store opened up in June 1968 in Plaza del Lago in Wilmette. Now there were two stores and a warehouse and all of a sudden I had to learn how to be a different kind of a manager. Oh, was that hard. I'd run back and forth between Plaza del Lago and Old Town and I was working six and a half days a week. I was making sure everything was just right in Old Town, then

[19] Delegation is a crisis that must be surmounted by all managers, leaders, and entrepreneurs. Delegation required creating a new role for Gordon:

· He had to learn to compromise.
· He had to learn to be approachable.
· He had to learn the power of
· the team versus that of one individual.
· He had to learn to empower others.

200 THE TAPESTRY OF LEADERSHIP: CREATING THE WEFT

going to Plaza del Lago, making sure everything was just right there. Then off to the warehouse in Wilmette. I was doing everything you could imagine. I would walk into a store and if it wasn't right, I'd scream and shout and yell. I made every management error you could make about not delegating properly, not giving authority or empowering people, because I didn't want to let go. What I was really doing was still trying to do it all myself. I'd run from one store to the other, trying to dominate the place I had been two days before.[20] In every case I was wrong in the way I handled the management in those early days because in a sense I expected everyone to function just the way I functioned with exactly the same neuroses, with the same idea of how things should be, with the same management style. I even expected staffers to have the same critical eye that I had, even though no two people are alike. Eventually, you've got to come to a point where you start recognizing the problem and tell yourself that perhaps there's another way of doing things.

That happened about 1969 or 1970. As I started to wear myself out, I realized I couldn't do it all myself or expect people to emulate my style.[21] So I hired some very good people, trained them myself and told them to go run the store. I went to Europe for three weeks and when I came back and walked into the store they had totally changed some displays. I went berserk because nothing looked the same. I had one of the most talented designers, who still happens to work for me, amazingly enough, and I asked him why he was displaying the merchandise differently. "Why?" I demanded. "Who gave you permission?" I was going crazy. Well, luckily I've always been an approachable sort of a guy after I let off steam.

[20] This behavior is not unusual in a startup business under a detail-oriented owner. Even in a big corporation, delegation is difficult for most.

[21] After some trigger events forced the issue of delegation.

I retreated to my office and shortly thereafter this designer sat down and told me how hard they had all worked and how unhappy they were with my reaction. They had busted their buns and while I'm gone three weeks, they've run the store and business was looking good. "Gordon," the designer said, "you said be creative and you just cut the rug from under us." I went home that night, and I was really devastated, realizing that I essentially had done something very wrong.[22] You know what? I came back the next day and said, "We're going to leave it this way, your way, and we're going to try it." Well, the way they had done it worked. About eighty percent of what they had done ended up to be what we still do today. You see, it wasn't me who created all the merchandising techniques that made Crate & Barrel. It was all these young people whom I had at that time not empowered. But since then I learned to empower with a sense of letting people do their own thing.

> [22] It's hard to modify your behavior . . . but not as hard if you are approachable and sensitive to the feelings and needs of others.

If you are going to take young people and work them hard with very little pay in the beginning, and you ask them to be creative, be part of the process, you truly have got to let them do it. You've got to sit back and cheer. Some things you're going to like and some things you're not. No matter, let them do it and then critique it.

I guess having an open door and encouraging them to talk to me was one of my better attributes.[23] In a sense that incident taught me an important lesson in management.

> [23] Leaders are good listeners and are approachable. Unless a leader is in touch with the nitty-gritty of the business, he or she loses touch with reality.

I had great young management people. Barbara Turf (now our executive vice president) could sit me down when I was really off base and say to me, "Hey, Gordon, you're really upsetting the staff, they're working like hell for you, you're coming in here and you're cutting the people to shreds. It's pretty hard to have them work this hard anyway and now look what you're doing to them." I'm telling you at thirty-one I thought I was failing. I really thought I just didn't have the personality to deal with multistores and different people. All of a sudden I learned that I had to compromise. I had to let down a little bit and I had to be a little easier. I had to accept the hard fact that other people could do things well, but differently. You know, I also started learning that perhaps they could do things better than I could. And maybe I started learning the fact that these people also had great creative ideas and could offer a significant contribution to the Crate's future. All of a sudden I started pulling back and not being so uptight, not being so critical. I slowly stepped back from that precipice where I could have gone over the other way and been absolutely ruthless and said, "You're out of here," or "This is the way I want to run this shop and I'm going to run it my way and don't you criticize the way I come in and talk to the staff because I'm right and you're wrong."[24] That would have been the other option and the Crate would have been a one- or two-store business. That's all I could have managed with that technique and that's where my story would have stopped.

[24] This is Gordon Segal *the boss* speaking—not Gordon Segal the leader.

Barbara Turf, Crate's executive vice president of merchandising and marketing, is one of the most unusual human beings around. She is a great leader and has a better sense of people than anyone I've ever met. For openers, she has a great sense of humor, a great sense of merchandising, and a great tolerance for me. She really deserves most of the credit for the past ten years of our success. She has earned a great deal of respect from our factories in Europe and designers from all over the world. She has built a solid team of buyers, merchants, and advertising people who love creating for Barbara.[25] She's very difficult, as difficult as I was but in her own way. Her style is different and our strengths so complemented each other that as a team we grew the company. One of my frustrations in life is that I keep getting all the honors and it's Gordon this and Gordon that but honestly it's really a team effort and Barbara has as much to do with it as I ever had to do with creating this company. She's not a numbers-oriented manager but she has a great sense of merchandise, style, and people.[26] We slowly grew together, melding our ideas into a vision of what Crate & Barrel should be and why we were in business. The ability to pick up a working partner, like Barbara, and to attract people who want to work with you is very critical. Around us we built a team of six key people and most of these people have been with us since the early 1970s. That's remarkable in retail, because it's a very fast in-and-out business with high turnover. We have only lost one buyer to a competitor in our thirty years.[27]

People who join the Crate love the concept of the way we do business. They work so hard for us because of the sensitivity we have to people and our vision of the business. They become neurotic over how a store should look and be run.[28] In the beginning we didn't have a strong strategy but by the time we got our third store we developed one. We really didn't want more than one store, as I said. Then we had two stores. And three stores. At that point, I said, "No more." I didn't want to run around because I couldn't run any faster. I couldn't do any more. I thought I had to run around and supervise all of these people and all of these details. Who else would supervise them? That's the

[25] Barbara gets the power to run the business not by ownership but by being empowered by her staff. When Gordon delegated or relinquished some of his power and authority, Barbara used it to build a team of stars, to build relationships, and to build internal and external networks.

[26] The team of talented people is always stronger than one individual. "No one of us is as smart as all of us" is proven here by Gordon, Barbara, and the Crate & Barrel team.

[27] People stay with Crate & Barrel because they like themselves better as they see themselves as contributors to a winning team.

[28] The difference between a job and a career is when a person so identi-

fies with the vision of the enterprise that he or she starts to define personal success in terms of the achievement of the company; such a person has made a career commitment.

[29] Networking helps one get a handle on tough decisions, gives one the understanding that most businesspeople share similar problems, and helps put problems in focus.

[30] New role models and mentors gave Gordon a performance standard by which to judge his own performance.

narrow vision I had in the early 1970s. I then was lucky enough to join a group called the Young Presidents Organization [YPO]. The YPO is an organization of young men and women who become presidents of their companies before the age of forty. I joined in 1976 and I think that the requirement then was that the company had to do five million dollars a year and have about fifty employees. Everybody in the organization is under fifty and leaves when they reach that birthday. We heard a lot of great lectures at YPO, a lot of great speeches, and attended a lot of great conferences. But I also learned something invaluable. There were other businesspeople like me who had the same business problems that I had;[29] I had always thought all my problems were unique. I thought all these issues of personnel, finance, delegation, and growth were Gordon Segal issues and I thought these were issues that I either created myself or issues that in a sense were insoluble. Through the YPO contacts and network, I could sit around a luncheon table and talk about these issues that had been nagging me for years with peers who understood because they had the same problems. Misery loves company notwithstanding, that made me feel good. And over time I went through a metamorphosis.[30]

Even though I did have a degree in business, I had no one around me with advice on how to run a business. Sometimes it was trial, other times error. I had become isolated in a sense; not withdrawn, but out of touch with the experience of other businessmen. No wonder I thought Crate & Barrel problems were all my problems. When I realized that they were the same kinds of problems that others were dealing with and solving, I changed my focus. I began to read more, to ask more questions, and to listen more carefully. I had gained a new burst of confidence and realized that I could be bigger than I was. I could be bigger than a five-million-dollar company. I was only thirty-one. Why not ratchet up my goals? I could be a little more successful without struggling to run a three-store business. If I applied myself and figured it out, I could have four, maybe five stores. The YPO experience had become a real breakthrough for me psychologically as well as intellectually.[31]

    The biggest obstacle that prohibits a person from doing something can be his or her own psyche. There I was making fifty thousand a year. It was all the money in the world, I thought, and I didn't want any more. So why go through the agony and the risk of opening new stores, building a new warehouse, and hiring new people? I certainly couldn't work any harder. That's when I started stepping back another level and began consulting with my management team about planning, hiring, organizing, and managing. I now have people who do the job well, and I feel good about it. It was a great part of our success the day I realized we could grow and I was able to mentor people like Barbara Turf who turned out to do things better than I ever could.[32] She has a great deal of style and is a much better merchant than I ever was.

    When I look around Chicago, I see other creative merchants like restaurateur Rich Melman, the founder of Lettuce Entertain You. He loves to create things. He's in the restaurant business, and he'll go out and open new restaurants with all the risks that are inherent in terms of creating a new format. There isn't a more dangerous and risky business than creating new restaurants. And when you have a successful one, most

[31] Managers control details and focus on the short run—leaders see possibilities and focus on the long run. Gordon now could think about long-run issues rather than short-run details.

[32] The successful leader has a management team that can do most things better than the leader.

restaurateurs just duplicate it. But not Rich Melman. Rich doesn't want to do that, he just wants to create another new restaurant, another new idea, another risk, he just loves it.[33]

[33] Rich Melman is a role model for Gordon.

When we decided to open up a store on Chicago's famous Michigan Avenue in 1975, it was a calculated risk. While this would anchor the reputation of Crate & Barrel, it also could jeopardize its future. If Crate & Barrel didn't work on Michigan Avenue, we were out of business. It was big rent in those days. We kept asking ourselves, should we take the risk? Over the next nine months I couldn't sleep thinking about how the store was going to come out, hoping it would be successful. Of course, history shows it was and Crate & Barrel became a popular place on Michigan Avenue. Now we had eight or nine stores and had reached yet another level. Once again my role changed. I had to step back and assume the position of the true leader—that of the visionary coach and creator.[34]

[34] Gordon is doing a job that only a leader can do. He has progressed from originator, to manager, to delegator, to visionary leader. He is still the owner, but so are his employees who have invested a part of their emotional selves in Crate & Barrel.

We have now grown to thirty-six stores; we'll do about one hundred and seventy million dollars' worth of volume. How did we take it from our single-store beginning in Old Town to a thirty-six-store chain? We couldn't have done it by running around any faster. We couldn't have done it by screaming any louder. We did it by creating a vision that people would buy into. And the vision had to be far more than Gordon Segal wanting to make more money. What we had to do was to have young people working in the stores because they enjoyed doing it. They enjoyed doing it because they enjoyed being creative merchants and running the most outstanding stores in the country. We don't hire people because they are high-powered salespeople but because they love being at Crate & Barrel. We want a staff who enjoys dealing with customers and understands enough about the product to complete our mission: to educate the customer about our product. We keep telling our people that their goal is to be a merchant, not just another salesperson. Yes, they have to sell, that's why they're here and how we earn our bread and butter every day. But our goal is truly to create young people who want to be merchants. We set our goals to bring great merchandise to the consumer and make sure that when they buy something at Crate & Barrel, it's a great purchase for them. Because we have this motto: If it's not a good purchase for the customer, it's not a good sale for the store.

After all these years, there are still plenty of tough questions to tackle. How do you keep it fun? How do you keep enjoying it? How do you keep searching for merchandise and presenting it in a unique way? How do you enable your people to take on more responsibility? How do you grow the company?[35] I believe you do it by hiring and training people who help create an environment that a customer can palpably feel as they walk into a store. An environment that makes the customer feel terrific and the customer may not know why, but they feel it's because somebody loves the store. The personnel in the store are smiling and energetic and they're running around and it's clean and the merchandise looks fresh and there are new things that they have never seen before and they say to themselves, "Boy, I like this place." You have to do it day in and day out by growing your people, especially in our kind of business, because what makes our business unique is the craziness we have for detail and the attention to the customer.

[35] Retailing has changed, the company has changed, Gordon has changed, but the basic mission and values of Crate & Barrel (although modified) are still the same.

Reflections: Weaving the Tapestry of Leadership

There are universal lessons to be learned in this chapter, one of which is a primary theme of this book: Most of us possess the threads of leadership—but often don't realize or understand them. There's a remarkable story here of a man, low on financial resources but high on creativity, who transformed a rather mundane retailing category—dishes, glasses, pots, and pans—into a highly innovative enterprise that in 1991 drew customers to thirty-six Crate & Barrel stores in ten markets across the country. The key to Segal's success? *The ability to anticipate change—and the willingness to take risks, a sense of urgency, the skill to synthesize, optimism, confidence, curiosity, empathy, intuition, creativity, good role models, and strong mentors.*

The culture of Crate & Barrel, which channels anxiety into creativity, fosters sound industry knowledge, outstanding merchandising skills, being in touch with the marketplace where each C&B store is located, a strong ethical foundation, a high energy level, and a participant-observer's insight into what is possible.

Mastering the Craft of Leadership

*N*o leader has perfected the art of weaving the leadership tapestry and no leader gets straight A's in their career journey from start to finish. Life is too full of ups and downs, starts and stops, interruptions and unforeseen events for one to devise a universal road map to leadership.

Why do leaders challenge the status quo? Why are leaders dissatisfied with things as they are? Why do leaders have an intuitive feeling that they can make a difference? The answers lie in the search for self-esteem. To that end I heartily agree with Dave Ehlem, head of Wilson Learning Corporation, that "self-esteem is a basic building block on which personal effectiveness is based." In a business context (and likely in a political context) the leaders' need to redefine themselves and grow while at the same time growing in self-esteem also carries through in redefining the enterprise. Leaders need to expand the environment in which they operate and change the forces that inhibit their personal growth. To do so improves their environment, too.

A number of years ago when I went to work for Sealy Inc., I felt uneasy about the company's future. But I had a good opinion about

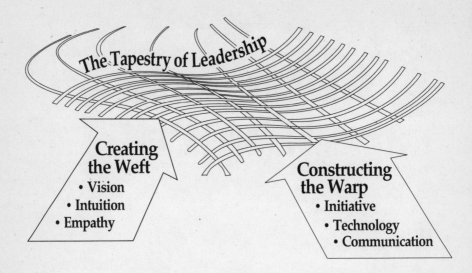

The Tapestry of Leadership

Creating
the Weft
• Vision
• Intuition
• Empathy

Constructing
the Warp
• Initiative
• Technology
• Communication

myself and the participant-observer skills needed to change the context. I told myself I would never work in a second-rate environment and gave myself two years to change Sealy's environment—or get out. The changes took place and I ended up staying twenty-seven years. Research clearly shows that leaders need to redefine themselves as even our mythic hero Luke Skywalker did, in the quest for self-esteem.

In my classroom, I try to simplify the entire business process to make this point: There are three types of people in business—value destroyers, value creators, and people who move the sand around the beach. The custodians, administrators, and other overseers are the bean counters, the product watchers, the foot soldiers of business who require little vision. The value destroyers, unfortunately, make up the largest segment of the American business population, essentially wear out capital, exploit people, and manipulate events for short-term goals. Now come the value creators: the makers of goods and services who lay the foundation for improved productivity that creates wealth and new possibilities and gives an enterprise its economic vitality.

Leadership is the ultimate creative business skill that is rewarded with premium compensation—not to be confused with entitlement—and genuine psychic satisfaction unmatched in other roles and tasks. A leader is a visionary whose creative effort matches the test of inquiry and challenges from informed followers. Robert Greenleaf says it best: "Framing all of this is awareness, opening wide the doors of participation so as to enable one to get more of what is available of sensory experience and other signals from the environment than people usually take in. Awareness has its risks, but it makes life more interesting." Value creating and vision go hand-in-hand in every successfully led company.

And what does creativity require other than an open mind?

Technical Competence—I've called it information leverage in this book and also in the classroom. Any would-be leaders must demonstrate to colleagues that they are exceptionally proficient in at least one phase of the business that they are engaged in. Knowledge is the currency of future achievement.

People Competence—There are two competencies that are especially important to leaders: communication and listening. Being part of an informal network that broadcasts the "news" is most helpful. There cannot be any kind of transformation without excellent and consistent communication. Leaders also understand the unspoken feelings of their colleagues, particularly the rank-and-file followers who are someday going to be asked to refocus their view of the future in line with that of the leader's new vision.

Conceptual Skills—The leader is able to cut to the heart of complex issues. The ability to integrate and create simplicity out of complexity is a crucial leadership attribute. "I would not give a fig for the simplicity this side of complexity," said Justice Oliver Wendell Holmes, "but I would give my life for a simplicity on the other side of complexity."

Participant-Observer—Everyone who has passed through the trauma of adolescence has survived a born-twice experience. How we deal with trauma, the dislocations, anger, and anxiety prepares us for our role as participant-observer—that unique ability that allows us to gain perspective on our own life, like the artist who paints a self-portrait and then steps back from the easel with a critical eye. By understanding the context we operate in, we can project ourselves into a more rational and predictable future. And that's precisely what leadership is all about—creating a vision that creates value.

Judgmental Skills—The crucible of real life is the classroom for leadership learning. Leaders learn by failure and mistakes. "Ready, fire, aim, fire again" is a favorite Tom Peters phrase that describes the way leaders learn from acting and from correcting errors. In effect, they see their entire life as a learning experience.

Character—What the leader says, the leader must do. The organization must be able to count on the leader or it won't take the risks the leader asks it to take in the future. A clear, strong point of view is helpful, but it is essential that the leaders stand for something that is different from consensus. The successful company—based on whichever yardstick you choose to apply—consists of high-caliber talent, a shared vision and mission, open and honest communication, and subordinates who have power and freedom to act. A corporate culture with such elements must be built on a foundation of high ethical standards that extend from the mailroom to the boardroom. These standards shape the reciprocity of trust that binds follower to manager, manager to leader, leader to follower in a ring that circulates the common goals of the organization.

Optimism—Leaders have hope. "I have found that people who know that they are preferred or favored by their mother(s) give evidence in their lives of a peculiar self-reliance and an unshakable optimism which often seems like heroic attributes and bring actual success to their possessors," wrote Sigmund Freud in his seminal work *The Interpretation of Dreams.* Whether or not you agree with Freud, our research demonstrates that leaders are optimists and purveyors of hope. Leaders listen to the "still, small voice inside" and trust their gut to help them unravel the complex issues that lead to new vision and value creation. The final character trait of a leader is that they trust others and are trusted by their peers. They know that trust is the emotional glue with which a business enterprise is held together.

Balance—The need for self-esteem, technical competence, people competence, conceptual skills, judgmental skills, integrity, optimism, and trust is vital to the leader. But each want and need must be kept under control so that a balance is reached and an individual does not tilt in one direction and favor it at the diminution of another. We define ourselves by the choices we make, carrying with us defeats as well as victories. Pragmatically, we are the sum total of those choices. They become part of each person's tapestry of leadership that is woven with life's threads—natural endowments, education, nuances of personality—into a montage that is unique, self-expressive and valuable.

A Believer in Change—Leaders believe. They not only have seen the new possibilities, but they present them to the organization and others at whatever risk might follow. Leaders not only are risk takers but believe in change and, therefore, are facilitators of change. Not only does the enterprise change but the leader changes and all of the followers change, too.

I was recently refreshed by a visit to the newly restored Ellis Island, where I saw a moving film on how Ellis Island symbolized the gateway to a new adventure. I was reminded again how millions of immigrants took the risk by separating themselves from their cultures that had nurtured (and in many cases smothered) them. Through all the trauma, the immigrants eventually discovered that America's streets weren't paved with gold as they had been told. Yet they found something even more valuable: a dynamic society that offered opportunity. The trip from their roots changed the immigrants spiritually rather than physically as each tried to carve a new path in strange territory using the attributes they brought with them and those they would eventually acquire. The voyage in this book will, I hope, guide you on a journey of personal transformation, with new insights and the understanding that there is a leader within you who can be enhanced as you travel the path of self-discovery.

Appendix

Leaders Interviewed in Alphabetical Order

Hall Adams, Jr.   Retired chairman and CEO, Leo Burnett Company

Robert Allen   Chairman, AT&T Corporation

Takashi Aoki   Chairman and CEO, Fujisawa Pharmaceutical USA

Robert Baker   Vice president, Field Operations—Midwest Section, Xerox Corporation

Wayne Baker   Assistant professor, Business Policy, University of Chicago

Elaine Scott Banks   Musician

Robert Barnett   Ameritech Bell Group

James Bere   Former chairman and CEO, Borg-Warner Corporation

Earl Bird   President, Metropolitan Chicago Health Council

Delmar Bloem   ICS Medical

William Bolinder   President and CEO, Zurich-American Insurance Company

Edward Bottum   Continental Bank

Donald Boyce   Chairman and president, Idex Corporation

Bernard Brennan   Chairman, president, and CEO, Montgomery Ward

William Brodsky   President and CEO, Chicago Mercantile Exchange

L. Don Brown   Vice President, Operations, Kraft General Foods—Canada, Inc.

Willard Brown, Jr.   Chairman and CEO, Rubloff, Inc.

John Bryan   Chairman and CEO, Sara Lee Corporation

Dean Buntrock   Chairman and CEO, Waste Management, Inc.

Robert Cadieux	Executive vice president, Amoco Corporation
Wayne Calloway	Chairman and CEO, Pepsico International
Pat Canavan	Vice president and corporate director, Human Resources, Motorola
Barry Chase	Chairman and CEO, TFI Incorporated
Weston Christopherson	Retired CEO, Northern Trust Company
W. H. Clark	Chairman and CEO, Nalco Chemical Company
Dale Clevenger	Principal horn, Chicago Symphony Orchestra
Robert Cohn	Octel Corporation
George H. Conrades	Former executive vice president, IBM
Stanton Cook	Chairman, Tribune Company
Philip Corboy	Partner, Corboy & Demetrio
Walter Cornett III	Chairman, president, and CEO, WGC Enterprises
James Cotting	Chairman and CEO, Navistar International Corporation
Dr. Lourdes Cowgil	Headmistress, Pine Crest Preparatory
James Cozad	Chairman and CEO, Whitman Corporation
Joseph Cramblit	President, Geldermann, Inc.
Don Davis, Jr.	President, Allen Bradley Co.
Art Decio	CEO, Skyline Corporation
Bruce DeMaeyer	President, Ameritech Mobile Communications
Richard DeSchutter	President, G. D. Searle
Edward DiCorcia	President and CEO, Unoven Company
James DiMatteo	CEO, Dominick's Finer Foods
Charles Doherty	President and CEO, Midwest Stock Exchange
Donald Druyanoff	CEO and president, Pacific Coast Trane Corp.
John Dugan	Managing partner, O'Connor Partnerships
George Easton	Associate professor, Quality Management, Graduate School of Business, University of Chicago
Guy Eberhart	National manager, Public Affairs, Sears Roebuck and Co.
Patricia Engle	President and CEO, Mileage Plus
Dan Fabian	Station manager, WGN Radio
Eugene Fanning	Founder, Fanning Cadillac
Richard Ferris	Former CEO, United Airlines

Paul Fireman	Chairman and CEO, Reebok International Ltd.
Ernest Fleischer	Former chairman, Franklin Savings Association of Ottawa, Kansas
John Fox	Managing director, Deloitte & Touche Midwest Consulting Group
John Frazee, Jr.	Chairman and CEO, Centel Corporation
Gian Fulgoni	CEO, Information Resources Inc.
Joel Futterman	Musician
Jack Gallagher	President, Gallagher Asphalt Company
John Gallagher	Former CEO, Chemetron
Christopher Galvin	President, Motorola, Inc.
Robert Galvin	Chairman emeritus, Motorola, Inc.
Edward Gardner	Chairman, Soft Sheen Products, Inc.
Sheldon Gilgore	Chairman and CEO, G. D. Searle
Alfred Goldstein	President, Sears–Specialty Merchandising
Ruben Gonzalez	Co-Concertmaster, Chicago Symphony Orchestra
Ellen Gordon	President, Tootsie Roll
Jerome Gore	Former CEO, Hartmarx
Chet Gougis	President, Duff & Phelps Financial Consultants
Karl Granitza	Soccer player
Hanna Gray	President, University of Chicago
John Hall	President, Goose Island Brewery
Robert Hamada	Director, Chicago Board of Trade
Alan Hamilton	Managing senior partner, Hamilton Partners
John Hammerschlag, Jr.	President, General Parking Company
Claire Hansen	Former chairman, Duff & Phelps
Dan Hansvick	CEO, Logic Plus
Michael Harper	Chairman and CEO, ConAgra
Neil Hartigan	Partner, Gardner, Carton & Douglas
Warren Hayford	Vice chairman, Gaylord Container Company
Denis Healy	President, Turtle Wax, Inc.
Christie Hefner	Chairman and CEO, Playboy Enterprises,
Charles Henry	President, Chicago Board of Options Exchange
David Hinson	Former chairman and CEO, Midway Airlines, Inc.

Elroy Hirsch	Former professional football player
Jerome Hirsch	Executive vice president, Mid-Continent Screw Products Company
Tom Hodgson	President and COO, Abbott Laboratories
Takaaki Hosono	Director, Mitsubishi International
George Howell	Managing director, Pfingsten Partners
Blair Hull	Managing partner, Hull Trading Company
Elmer Johnson	Partner, Kirkland & Ellis
Henry Johnson	Retired chairman, Spiegel, Inc.
C. Paul Johnson	Chairman and CEO, First Colonial Bankshares Corporation
Dan Josephs	CEO, Dominick's Finer Foods
Charles Kaye	Secretariat to Maestro Georg Solti
Silas Keehn	President, Federal Reserve Bank of Chicago
George Philip Kelly	President, Mallards
Joseph King	Executive vice president, Molex Corporation
Arthur Knight, Jr.	President and CEO, Morgan Products Ltd.
Harry Kraemer	Vice president, Baxter Healthcare
Duane Kullberg	Former CEO, Arthur Andersen & Co.
Vincent Lane	Chairman, Chicago Housing Authority
Steven Lazarus	Director, ARCH Development Corporation
Elliott Lehman	Co-Chairman emeritus, Fel-Pro, Inc.
Lois LeMenager	Chairman and CEO, Marketing Innovators
Charles Locke	Chairman and CEO, Morton International, Inc.
Vernon Loucks, Jr.	Chairman and CEO, Baxter International, Inc.
William Lowrie	President, Amoco Oil
Ian MacGregor	Former chairman, British Steel/Coal/Amax
Samuel Magad	Co-Concertmaster, Chicago Symphony Orchestra
Richard Mahoney	CEO, Monsanto Company
John Malec	Chairman, CEO, and president, VideOcart, Inc.
Robert Malott	Former chairman and CEO, FMC Corp.
Bruce Mason	Chairman and CEO, Foote Cone & Belding
Mark McCabe	Former director, General Motors Europe
William McIntosh	Partner, Salomon Brothers
Andrew McNally IV	President and CEO, Rand McNally & Company

Leo Melamed	Chairman emeritus, Chicago Mercantile Exchange
Richard Melman	CEO, Lettuce Entertain You Enterprises
John Mengel, Jr.	CEO, Chicago Data Storage
Ray Meyer	Retired DePaul University Basketball Coach
John Michelman	Vice president and co-owner, Michelman, Inc.
Jack Miller	President and CEO, Quill Corporation
Susan Missner	Senior vice president, Kemper Lesnik Organization
Lee Mitchell	President and CEO, Field Corporation
Scott Moon	CEO, Res Manufacturing
Sanford Morgenstein	Dytel Corporation
Richard Morrow	Chairman and CEO, Amoco Corporation
Alan L. Morse	Partner, Arthur Andersen & Co.
Leo Mullin	Chairman, president, and CEO, American National Bank
Robert Nason	CEO, Grant Thornton, USA
Simone Nathan	President, Nathan & Nathan
Joseph Neubauer	Chairman and CEO, ARA Services, Inc.
Ralph Nichols	Dean of the College, University of Chicago
James O'Connor	Chairman and CEO, Commonwealth Edison Company
John Pacholick	Chairman and CEO, Rollins Burdick Hunter of Illinois
Scott Pardee	Chairman, Yamaichi International (America)
Homie Patel	Chairman, Men's Apparel Group, Hartmarx
Neal Patterson	CEO, Cerner Corporation
Roger Peterson	President and CEO, Ace Hardware Corporation
Richard Phelan	President, Cook County Board of Commissioners
Howard Pizer	President, Chicago White Sox
Derek Podobas	Former member, Polish Olympic Team
Marvin Pomerantz	Chairman and CEO, Gaylord Container Company
Robert Pritzker	President and CEO, Marmon Group, Inc.
Michael Quinlan	Chairman and CEO, McDonald's Corporation

George Rathmann	AmGen Corporation
John Rau	LaSalle National Bank
Jack Reichert	Chairman, CEO, and president, Brunswick Corporation
Warren Rhodes	President, Mercy National Purchasing Group
Sherman Rosen	Vice president, Human Resources, Hartmarx
Howard Ross	Holland Partners
David Ruder	Former chairman, Securities & Exchange Commission
Dave Runnels	President, Econ-O-Cloth
Glenn Rupp	Former CEO, Wilson Sporting Goods Company
Joseph Saunders	Founder, Household Card Services
Kit Saunders	Director, Women's Athletics, University of Wisconsin
William Schmidt	President, Precision Plastics
Thomas Schrader	Wisconsin Gas Company
James Schrager	President, Japan Capital Markets, Inc.
Larry Schulman	Partner, Boston Consulting Group
Joel Schultz	President, Presidential Mortgage
Gordon Segal	President and CEO, Crate & Barrel
John Semmelhack	CEO, Hammacher-Schlemmer
George Shaheen	Partner, Arthur Andersen & Company
John Shea	Vice chairman, president and CEO, Spiegel, Inc.
Gloria Shealy	President, Daniele Development
Hayao Shiraishi	Manager, Mitsubishi Bank
Burt Siegel	Former manager, Drexel Burnham Lambert
William Smithburg	Chairman, president, and CEO, Quaker Oats Company
John Staley	Managing partner, Ernst & Young
Bob Star	Former president, Manischewitz
Michael Stefanos	President, Dove International
Fred Steingraber	Chairman and CEO, A. T. Kearney, Inc.
Richard Strong	Investment manager, Strong/Corneliuson Capital
Charles Stroupe	President and CEO, Wesley-Jessen
Shinichi Sugiura	Manager, Mitsui Construction Company

James Taylor	President, Hometown Distributors
Richard Teerlink	President and CEO, Harley Davidson
Thomas Theobald	Chairman, Continental Bank Corporation
Richard Thomas	Chairman, president, and CEO, First National Bank of Chicago
John Thompson	Vice president and Midwest Area general manager, IBM
John Walter	Chairman and CEO, R. R. Donnelley & Sons Company
Lawrence Weinbach	Managing partner and CEO, Arthur Andersen & Co.
John Weithers	Midwest Stock Exchange
B. Kenneth West	Chairman, Harris Bank
Wes Westin	CEO, Westin, Inc.
Scott Whitlock	Executive vice president, Honda America
Walt Winding	Schweiger Industries
Linda Yu	Anchor, WLS Eyewitness News
Francis Yuen	CEO, Stock Exchange of Hong Kong
Fred Zucker	Former CEO, private *Fortune* 500 Company

Notes

Introduction

"The MBA explosion": See Robert J. Samuelson, "What Good Are B-Schools?" *Newsweek*, May, 14, 1990, p. 49.

"Leadership is the process": See John W. Gardner, *On Leadership* (The Free Press, New York, 1990), p. 1.

"the thinking man's Rambo": See Warren Bennis, "The Dreamless Society," *New Management*, Fall 1990, pp. 17–24.

"the change in leadership": See Ralph Strayer, "Johnsonville Food," *Harvard Business Review*, December–January 1990.

"intellectual capitalism": Ibid.

Chapter One

"The heroes and winners": See "The Mind of Jack Welch," *Fortune*, March 26, 1989, p. 30.

"Everywhere around us": See Burt Nanus, *The Leader's Edge* (Contemporary Books, Chicago, 1989), p. 53.

"No wonder General Electric": From a speech by Jack Welch entitled "Speed, Simplicity, Self-Confidence: Keys to Leading in the '90s," presented at GE's annual shareholders' meeting in Greenville, SC, April 26, 1989. To beat a bureaucracy the size of GE's, Welch keys his leadership to six rules: face reality as it is, and not as it was or you wish it were; be candid with everyone; don't manage, lead; change before you have to; if you don't have a competitive advantage, don't compete; and control your own destiny or someone else will. Says Welch, "Call people managers and they are going to start managing things, getting in the way. The job of the leader is to take the available resources—human and financial—and allocate them rigorously. Not to spread them out evenly like butter on bread. That's what bureaucrats do. It takes courage and tough-mindedness to pick the bets, put the resources behind them, articulate the vision to the employees, and explain why you said yes to this one and no to that one.": See "The Mind of Jack Welch," *Fortune*, March 26, 1989, pp. 39–50.

"Several years ago a Booz-Allen": See "1992: Ready or Not," *Intermarket*, May 1989, pp. 18–24.

"a boundaryless company": See *Fortune*, March 26, 1990.

"Sees the companies": Fred Steingraber on "Global Leadership in the '90s" at Reflections on Leadership symposium, University of Chicago, May 11, 1990.

"That initiative was": See John E. Jeuck, "Pride and Prejudice," Towers/Cresap Lecture Series, Selected Paper No. 64, 1986.

"the professional mercenary soldier": See Theodore Leavitt, *Corporate Pathfinders* (Penguin Books, New York, 1986), p. ix.

"Our management schools have": See Mintzberg, "The Manager's Job: Folklore and Fact," *Harvard Business Review*, July–August 1975, pp. 50–54. Mintzberg, notes Jeuck, defines a manager as the person in charge of an organization or one of its subunits. Besides the CEO, this definition can include vice presidents, bishops, foremen, hockey coaches, and prime ministers. All of these people have something in common: they are vested with formal authority over an organization. With such authority comes status, which leads to a host of interpersonal relations, and from this comes access to information. Information, in turn, enables the manager to make decisions.

"He succeeded me in our": Scott Whitlock on "Communicating Vision and Information" at Reflections on Leadership symposium, University of Chicago, May 11, 1990.

"With demand for MBAs wavering": See *Economist*, "Schools Brief," November 30, 1991, p. 53.

"The European business schools": Ibid.

"Frankly, I went to a lot": Students' interview with William Smithburg.

"the Age of Restructuring": See Walter Wriston, "The State of American Management," *Harvard Business Review*, January–February 1990, pp. 78–83.

"We all have motivation": See Mary Walton, *The Deming Method* (Perigee, New York, 1986).

"The kind of people who make": "Worthy of his hire," *Economist*, February 1, 1992, p. 19.

"All true leadership": See Peter Vail, *Managing as a Performing Art* (Jossey-Bass, San Francisco, 1988), p. 224.

"The language of the": See "Should Your Company Save Your Soul?" *Fortune*, January 14, 1991, p. 33.

"is behavior, because we all see it": See "The Year of the People," *Time*, January 1, 1990, p. 52.

"When Thomas Jefferson wrote": See *Chicago Tribune*, November 17, 1991, p. 37.

"Historians have since rated": See *Time*, April 5, 1991, p. 35.

"If anything is certain": See Robert E. Kelley, "In Praise of Followers," *Harvard Business Review*, November–December, 1988.

"If you fail in the": Students' interview with Steve Lazarus.

"Leaders must help people": See John Gardner, *Leadership Papers* (Prepared for Leadership Studies Program for Independent Sector, Washington D.C., 1986).

"Corporate dreams just": See Henry Johnson, *The Corporate Dream* (Carol Publishing, New York, 1990), p. 39.

"Your identity is what": See John Gardner, op. cit.

"Commitment rquires hard work": See Robert K. Greenleaf, *The Servant as Leader* (Maine, 1988), pp. 1–37.

"I love what I do": See Warren Buffett, *Fortune*, March 26, 1990, p. 30.

"This is the only country": See Wriston, *Harvard Business Review*, January–February 1990.

Chapter Two

"Come to work for Brunswick": Students' interview with Jack Reichert.

"It taught me what": Students' interview with Michael Quinlan.

"When you go to work": Students' interview with William Smithburg.

"Only people who believe": See Theodore Levitt, "Command and Consent," *Harvard Business Review*, July–August 1988, p. 5.

"A person may be": Ibid.

"The truth of the assumption": See James MacGregor Burns, *Leadership* (Harper & Row, New York, 1978), pp. 49–66.

"Did she succeed because of": Ibid., p. 60.

"Successful leaders are those": Students' interview with Robert Malott.

"A couple of years before": Students' interview with Derek Probas.

"based on eight classic stages": See Erik Erikson, *Children and Society* (W.W. Norton & Co., New York, 1963; with additions 1985).

"Much of the social savvy": See Howard Gardner interview with Daniel Goleman, "'Child Skills at Play," *New York Times,* October 2, 1990.

"Greenleaf's servant as leader": See Greenleaf, op. cit., p. 1.

"The paradox is that": Students' interview with Robert Galvin.

"In findings published nearly": See Howard Gardner interview.

"It must be considered that": See Niccolo Machiavelli, *The Prince and the Discourses* (Random House Modern Library edition, 1950; with introduction by Max Lerner), pp. 18–30.

"Some executives underestimate": See Keith Hammonds, "Why Big Companies Are So Tough to Change," *Business Week,* June 17, 1991, pp. 28–29.

"Change lies at the heart": Ibid.

"managers perfect the formula": See Richard Pascale and Anthony G. Athos, *The Art of Japanese Management* (Simon & Schuster, New York, 1981).

"We've got a problem": George H. Conrades on "Change and Effecting Change," at Reflections on Leadership symposium, University of Chicago, May 11, 1990.

"a network of compensation systems": See Hammonds, op. cit.

"Reebok is a company": Paul Fireman interview in *Babson Bulletin,* Spring 1990, p. 15.

"Was it dumb luck?": Ibid.

Chapter Three

"The history of business": Robert Galvin on "The Paradox of Leadership" at Reflections on Leadership symposium, University of Chicago, May 11, 1990.

"work at an unrelenting pace": See Mintzberg, *Harvard Business Review,* July–August 1975, pp. 50–54.

"Managing means that once": See Harold Geneen with Alvin Moscow, *Managing* (Avon Books, New York, 1984).

"Even managers don't know": See Mintzberg, op. cit.

"A number of important": See Mintzberg, ibid.

"few things as bad as": See Levitt, op. cit., p. 5.

"People skills are not my": Students' interview with Robert Malott.

"I want you to remember": Patton's speech from film *Patton*, released in 1970. Screenplay written by Francis Ford Coppola and Edmund H. North. Patton (1895–1945), who led the Third Army in the breakout after the Normandy landings in June 1944, was known as "Old Blood and Guts."

"Bosses are not necessarily": See Robert E. Kelley, "In Praise of Followers," *Harvard Business Review*, November–December 1988, pp. 142–148.

"That kind of thinking can": See "Leaders of the Most Admired," *Fortune*, January 29, 1990, p. 43.

"At Wal-Mart our philosophy": Ibid., p. 46.

"When Merck corporation hit": Ibid., p. 40.

"The runner of the business": Robert Galvin on "The Paradox of Leadership" at Reflections on Leadership symposium, University of Chicago, May 11, 1990.

"In communicating vision": Scott Whitlock on "Communicating Vision and Information" at Reflections on Leadership symposium, University of Chicago, May 11, 1990.

"Business communicates by the": Students' interview with Robert Galvin.

"managers favor the verbal": See Mintzberg, op. cit.

"Trust is the force that": See Warren Bennis and Burt Nanus, *Leaders* (Harper & Row, Perennial Library, New York, 1985), pp. 152–186.

"The capability to build trust": Arthur Knight, Business School Management Conference, University of Chicago, April 3, 1991.

Chapter Four

"The wizard of": See Walter Truett Anderson, *Reality Isn't What It Used to Be* (Harper & Row, New York, 1990), p. 29.

"Man is as old as": See Will Durant, *The Pleasures of Philosophy* (Simon & Schuster, Touchstone Books, New York, 1953), p. 399.

"through the looking-glass self": Two important figures in the development of this perspective, particularly as applied to early childhood, are Charles Horton Cooley and George Herbert Mead. There are three parts to Cooley's process in determining sense of self: presentation, identification, and interpretation. Thus identity is produced through the interaction with others. Mead followed a similar line of thinking. He, however, tried to show how "mind, self and society" blended through a process of symbolic interaction by emphasizing the role of language as the basic form of human symbolic communication.

"Business leaders have a professional": Joseph Neubauer on "The Importance of Leadership" at Reflections on Leadership symposium, University of Chicago, May 11, 1990.

"It was a concept": See William James, *The Varieties of Religious Experience* (Macmillan Publishing Company, First Collier Edition, 1961), pp. 80–81.

"For a once born personality": See Abraham Zaleznik, "Managers and Leaders: Are They Different?" *Harvard Business Review*, May–June 1977, pp. 67–78.

"My second life will then": See Abram Kardiner and Edward Preble, *They Studied Man* (Mentor Books, New York, 1961), p. 16 from chapter on Charles Darwin, titled "A Second Life," pp. 15–32.

"Leaders grow through mastering": See Zaleznik, "Managers and Leaders: Are They Different?" *Harvard Business Review*, May–June 1977, pp. 67–78.

"When movie director": Profile of Martin Scorsese, "Martin Scorsese Directs," American Masters series broadcast on PBS in Chicago, July 16, 1990.

"Leo Melamed, a pioneer": Students' and author interview with Leo Melamed.

"Anybody going on a journey": See Joseph Campbell: *The Hero with a Thousand Faces* (Princeton/Bollingen, Princeton, New Jersey, 1973), pp. 10–36. Though he never uses the term "born twice," Campbell writes brilliantly about the born-twice experience that every hero encounters on the journey of transformation.

"the rapture of living": Ibid.

"At forty-five jazz pianist": Author interview with Joel Futterman.

Chapter Five

"The breakdown in communications": See David Evans, "How Iraqi brass rendered troops deaf during war," *Chicago Tribune*, July 1991.

"networks are designed to build": See Ram Charan, "How Networks Reshape Organizations—For Results," *Harvard Business Review*, September–October 1991, pp. 104–115.

"Agreement without alignment": Ibid.

"in a strong culture, the network": See Terrence Deal and Allen Kennedy, *Corporate Cultures* (Addison-Wesley Publishing Inc., Reading, Massachusetts, 1982), pp. 85–103.

"The first task of an executive": Ibid., pp. 86–87.

"The value of networking": Author interview with Ira Levin.

"At Intel Corp": See "Farewell, Fast Track," *Business Week*, December 10, 1990.

"of what goes on": See Deal and Kennedy, *Corporate Cultures*, p. 86.

"Networks are faster, smarter": See Charan, *Harvard Business Review*.

"It is back to": See Elizabeth M. Fowler, "When You Can't Get in Front Door," *New York Times*, August 20, 1991, p. C-5.

"Some corporate cultures": See "Managing," *Fortune*, July 15, 1991, p. 54.

"We're considering you": Author interview with James Bere.

"Likewise Commonwealth Edison": Author interview with James O'Connor.

"Typical perhaps is the": See "Big-City Village," *Business Month*, February 1988, p. 43.

"For instance a number": See "Weaving a Network of Mentors for Young Women," *New York Times*, September 11, 1991, and "Working Smart—Times Have Changed and So Have Networks," *Chicago Tribune*, September 17, 1991.

"She terms such networks": See Sally Helgesen, "Grace Pastiak's 'Web of Inclusion,'" *New York Times*, May 5, 1991.

"A second wave of women": See Judy B. Rosener, "Ways Women Lead," *Harvard Business Review*, November–December 1990, pp. 119–125.

"it helps to have": Students' interview with Robert Galvin.

"He was a remarkable": Ibid.

"I'm privileged": Ibid.

"James Bere inculcated": Author interview with James Bere.

"Qualities of leadership": See Burns, *Leadership* (Harper & Row, New York, 1978), p. 78.

"The mentorship of a": Students' interview with John Bryan.

"Another executive who": Students' interview with Elmer Johnson.

"There are lessons": Students' interview with Robert Galvin.

"Allowed yourself to be": See Peter Schwartz, *The Art of the Long View* (Doubelday/Currency, New York, 1991).

"We can also learn": See "CEO Disease," *Business Week*, April 1, 1991, pp. 52–60.

"Like Donald Trump": See "Myth vs. Man," *Business Month*, July 1990, pp. 52–60.

"as the gods once": See Joseph Campbell, *The Hero with a Thousand Faces* (Princeton/Bollingen, Princeton, New Jersey, 1973).

"These figures teach": See Donna Rosenberg and Sorelle Baker, *Mythology and You* (National Textbook Company, Lincolnwood, Illinois, 1975), p. 274.

"It has to do with": See Joseph Campbell with Bill Moyers, *The Power of Myth* (Doubleday, New York, 1988), p. 145.

Chapter Six

"the most brilliant vision": See "The Most Fascinating Ideas for 1991," *Fortune*, January 14, 1991, p. 30.

"like a lamb": See *Fortune*, Special Issue, Spring/Summer 1991, p. 18.

"We're dedicated to": Scott Whitlock on "Communicating Vision and Information" at Reflections on Leadership symposium, University of Chicago, May 11, 1990.

"But it goes beyond": Ibid.

"If a leader is going": Students' interview with Robert Galvin.

"Vision is anchored": See Bennis and Nanus, *Leaders*, pp. 87–109.

"The key to Johnson & Johnson": See *Fortune*, January 29, 1990, p. 50.

"All too often": See Ram Charan, "How Networks Reshape Organizations—For Results," *Harvard Business Review*, September–October 1991, pp. 104–115.

"Information is critical": Whitlock, op. cit.

From BBA Group plc mission statement.

"From the time": See *Fortune*, January 29, 1990, p. 62.

From Coca-Cola mission statement.

"Bernie brought this": See *Crain's Chicago Business*, May 29–June 4, 1989, p. 62.

"Brennan came from": Background obtained from Bernard Brennan's appearance before class during fall of 1990.

From Montgomery Ward & Company mission statement.

"No one had yet": From remarks by Bernard Brennan at the Harvard Business School Club of Chicago, April 14, 1989.

"I learned the": See Don Frey, "Learning the Ropes: My Life as a Product Champion," *Harvard Business Review*, September–October 1991, p. 52.

"Nothing puts a": Ibid.

"Love at First Byte": See *Time*, July 15, 1991, pp. 46–47.

Chapter Seven

"a man of impeccable": See *Newsweek*, April 1, 1991, p. 45.

"Recently I came": See "Money or Morality," *Newsweek*, October 28, 1991, p. 15.

"Values are the": See James A. Michener, "What Is the Secret of Teaching Values?" Commencement speech, Swarthmore, 1989.

"The Salomon Shocker": See "The Salomon Shocker: How Bad Will It Get?" *Business Week*, August 26, 1991, pp. 54–57.

"A week without": See "Japan in the Dirt," *Economist*, August 26, 1991, pp. 75–78.

"In the real world": See Kenneth Andrews, "Ethics in Practice," *Harvard Business Review*, September–October 1989, p. 100.

"When you cut through": Students' interview with Kirby Warren.

"A high standard": Students' interview with Robert Allen.

"I derive the human": Students' interview with Robert Galvin.

"Will the hero": See "The Trouble with Columbus," *Time*, October 7, 1991, pp. 52–56.

"The most significant": See "Our Changing American Values," interview of Michael Josephson by Bill Moyers, *World of Ideas* (Doubleday, New York, 1989), pp. 15–27.

"If I'm an employer": Ibid, p. 17.

"results and integrity": See "Developing Managers with Values," *GSB*, Spring 1991, p. 14.

"We studied the": Ibid.

"as managers develop": Ibid.

"Arrogance is the illegitimate": Ibid.

"If you're going": Students' interview with Steve Lazarus.

"As a result, deceit": Josephson, op. cit., p 17.

"Neither Thiokol nor": See "NASA Takes a Beating," *Time*, June 23, 1986, p. 25.

"it found that": See Chris Argyris, *Overcoming Organizational Defenses* (Allyn and Bacon, Boston, 1989), p. 37.

"There is a breakdown": Ibid., p. 42.

"At least two": Ibid., p. 43.

"Irregularities and rule": See *Business Week*, August 26, 1991, p. 54.

"Why now? Why": See *New York Times*, July 15, 1990, sec. 3, part 2, p. 23.

"It may be explainable": Remarks from interview with Adam Smith on PBS broadcast, November 10, 1991.

"There are more": Ibid.

"its character, the": Andrews, op. cit., pp. 101–103.

"It is very difficult": See Joseph Neubauer profile, *Chicago Business*, September 24, 1991, p. 3.

"We are in the": See Donald Boyce, "Standard of Conduct and Business Ethics" of Idex Corporation.

"At Chicago's Harris Bank": See "Who We Are, What We're Trying To Be," Statements of Harris Bankcorp's "mission, values, and style."

"Johnson & Johnson's": See Harvard Business School case study (384–053) on Johnson & Johnson, prepared by Professor Francis J. Aguilar and Arvind Bhambri, 1983.

"We all want": See "Values Make the Company: An Interview with Robert Haas," *Harvard Business Review*, September–October 1990, p. 135.

"It just never": Students' interview with Robert Allen.

"Apologies are not enough": See *New York Times*, September 23, 1991, p. C3.

"I find the issue": Students' interview with Robert Galvi.

"I don't think that": Students' interview with Dean Buntrock.

"We can't continue": Students' interview with Edward DiCorcia.

"In the long run": Allen, op. cit.

"Moral choices. Some are": From the motion picture *Crimes and Misdemeanors*, an Orion production, 1989.

Chapter Eight

"The typical large": See Peter F. Drucker, *The New Realities* (Harper & Row, Perennial Library, New York, 1990), p. 207.

"Each musician must": See Pablo Casals, *Joys and Sorrows* (Simon & Schuster, New York, 1970).

"The only way": George H. Conrades on "Change and Effecting Change" at Reflections on Leadership symposium, University of Chicago, May 11, 1990.

"American companies are": Ibid.

"He has two rules": Ibid.

"spans of communication": See *Fortune*, September 26, 1988, p. 52.

"I decided to": Students' interview with Jack Reichert.

"A business has no": See Peter F. Drucker, "The Coming of the New Organization," *Harvard Business Review*, January–February 1988, p. 49.

"Once he's learned": Students' interview with Charles Kaye.

"Solti is an": Students' interview with Samuel Magad.

"I often use analogies": Students' interview with Elaine Scott Banks.

"You have to try": Students' interview with Dale Clevenger.

"Opera, when it works": See Jeremy Seatman interview with Daniel Barenboim, *Showcase*, Fall 1991, p. 42.

"In an era": See *Business Week*, December 10, 1990, p. 193.

"A conductor should": Banks, op. cit.

"As you start": See *GSB*, Spring 1991, p. 4.

"An innovative corporate": See "Farewell, Fast Track," *Business Week*, December 10, 1990, p. 197.

"After one is": See Harold Shapiro, *Tradition and Change* (University of Michigan Press, Ann Arbor, 1987), pp. 51–57.

"I had not been": Students' interview with Elmer Johnson.

"What we see": See Alan Bloom, *The Closing of the American Mind* (Simon and Schuster, New York, 1987).

"The essence of": See *Forbes*, 1992.

"While science as": See Jacob Bronowski, *Science and Human Values* (Harper & Row, New York, 1972).

"Young people who": Bloom, op. cit.

"The main reason": Moyers, op. cit.

Chapter Nine

"I think the world": Author interview with David Ruder.

"serving the system": From a speech titled "Speed, Simplicity, Self-Confidence: Keys to Leading in the '90s," presented at the General Electric annual shareholders' meeting in Greenville, South Carolina, April 26, 1989.

"This is exactly": See "The gospel according to Sun Tzu," *Forbes*, December 9, 1991, p. 155.

"An example of": See "Deming's Demons," *Wall Street Journal*, June 4, 1990, p. R41.

"The biggest problems": See Mary Walton, *The Deming Management Method* (Perigee, New York, 1986).

"You must think": See Ronald Yates, "Messiah of Management," *Chicago Tribune Magazine*, February 16, 1992, p. 19.

"Business schools are": Author interview with George S. Easton.

Chapter Ten

Chapter Ten is based on a three-hour presentation by Gordon Segal before my MBA class on May 2, 1991.

Chapter Eleven

"Framing all of": Greenleaf, op. cit. p. 19.

Index

Acheson, Dean, 3
Adaptive personality pattern, 72
Aeneas myth, 79–80
Alienation, 43–44, 74
Allen, Robert, 143, 154–55, 157
Allen, Woody, 157–58
Alternatives, development of, 54, 68, 171
Amadeus (film), 47
Ambition, 6, 7, 177
American Express, 187
Anderson, Walter Truett, 70
Andrews, Bernie, 129
Andrews, Kenneth, 143, 151
Apple Computer, 138
Argulles, Mary, 141
Argyris, Chris, 148
Armour, Philip, 94
Art, changes in, 13–14
Arthur (king of England), 2
Art of the Long View, The (Schwartz), 100
Asian Rim, 179–80
AT&T, 154–55
Australia, 18
Authority
    delegation of, 190, 197, 199–201, 203
    of knowledge, 53, 69
Automotive industry, 17–18, 180. *See also specific organization*
Autry, James, 28
Ayers, Thomas, 93

Baby-busters, 7
Back to Basics, 27, 50
Baker, Sorelle, 104
Baker, Wayne, 92
Balance, 213
Baltic states, 15
Bank of Credit and Commerce International, 140, 142
Bank of Japan, 179
Banks, Elaine Scott, 167–68
Barenboim, Daniel, 168–69
Barrett, Craig, 89
Baxter Laboratories, 153
BBA Group plc, 123–25
Beethoven, Ludwig von, 47, 48
Bennis, Warren, 6–7, 44, 67, 119
Bere, James, 93, 97
Bernstein, Leonard, 106
Biology. *See* Myths: that leaders are born; Physical/biological aspects
Bloom, Allan, 173, 175
Body language, 167
Boesky, Ivan, 142
Boiled frog story, 50–53
Bolsjoly, Roger, 146
Booz-Allen Hamilton, 16
Boundaryless companies. *See* Stateless/panglobal companies
Boyce, Donald, 152
Boyd, John, 180
Braque, Georges, 13–14

Brennan, Bernard F., 129–38
Brennan, Edward A., 130
Bronowski, Jacob, 174
Brunswick Corporation, 36–38, 163–64
Bryan, John, 98
Buffett, Warren, 32, 149, 150
Buntrock, Dean, 157
Burns, James MacGregor, 3, 42–43, 44, 97,
    143
Business education/schools
    change of direction in, 19, 20–21, 34
    criticisms of, 1–2, 19–23, 40
    European, 23
    financing of, 18
    in-house, 21
    and the integration of theory and practice,
        23
    popularity of, 18
    and short courses, 21–22
    and the teaching of leadership, 4
    and total quality management/leadership,
        186, 187
    and the training of managers, 18–20
Business plans, 51, 86. *See also* Mission
    statements; Strategic plans
Business Week, 17, 142, 169–70

Cadillac Motor, 187
Calloway, D. Wayne, 88, 144–45
Campbell, Joseph, 79, 80, 102–3, 104
Capitalism, 7, 23–24, 29, 33
Career
    commitment to a, 204
    definition of a, 32
    and diversity in career paths, 89, 170
    job *vis-à-vis* a, 32, 203–4
Carnegie Foundation, 18
Carnegie-Mellon University, 21, 23
Casals, Pablo, 160
Case studies, 23
CEO disease, 100–102, 107, 204
Challenger (space shuttle), 146–48
Change
    anticipation of, 208
    in art, 13–14
    and the boiled frog story, 50–53
    as characteristic of the 1990s, 14
    as characteristic of leadership, 68, 82,
        208, 209–10, 213
    and creativity, 51–52
    and culture, 51
    and differences between leaders and
        managers, 56, 71
    and the elk story, 51
    fear of, 14, 49–50
    and the leader-follower relationship,
        49–50, 66
    leaders as creators of, 71–72

and mission statement, 128–29, 207
and personality patterns, 72–73
process of, 49
and rewards, 51
and risk-taking, 71, 73, 74, 213
and self-improvement, 100
and short-/long-term, 24–29
as slow and painful, 49
and stages in corporations, 71–72
and structural reorganizations, 23–
    24
supports for, 51
and total quality management/leadership,
    188
and values, 207
vanguard of, 13, 15–24
and vision, 51
Character, importance of, 212
Charan, Ram, 90, 120
Chicago Club, 93–94
China, People's Republic of, 179–80
Christopherson, Weston, 79, 83
Chrysler Corporation, 17, 88, 101–2
Churchill, Winston, 2–3, 42
Circuit City, 134
Civic affairs. *See* Social/civic situations
Clevenger, Dale, 168
Clifford, Clark, 140, 142
Coca-Cola Company, 125–29
Code of conduct, 144, 151–58
Columbia University, 19
Commitment
    and creativity, 114
    and differences between leaders and
        managers, 56
    and identity, 35
    importance of, 8, 31–32, 38, 46, 53, 84,
        113, 114, 191
    and job *vis-à-vis* career, 32, 204
    and leadership in the future, 34
    and making a difference, 138
    and mission statement, 126, 127, 128,
        129, 136–37, 139
    and motivation, 32
    and surprises, 56
    and total quality management/leadership,
        182, 185
    and trust, 67
    and vision, 67, 118, 138, 197
Committees, and vision, 117
Communication
    and confidence, 167
    and the corporate culture, 212
    and credibility, 66
    and differences between leaders and
        managers, 57, 59–60, 63–66
    and ethics, 153
    and fear, 188

importance of, 12, 29, 38, 53, 59–60,
   61, 63–66, 69, 113, 159–60, 188,
   191
and impression, 65–66
and interpersonal skills, 211
and intuition, 167
and knowledge, 167
and metaphors, 92, 167–68
nonverbal, 65, 167
and number of people reporting to
   managers, 163
overview about, 167–71
and the Persian Gulf War, 85–86
and power, 66
and repetition, 64–65
and technical knowledge, 168
and technology, 159–60, 163
and total quality management/leadership,
   181, 184, 188
and trust, 67
and vision, 63–66, 69, 73, 119–20, 137,
   139, 178
See also Networks
Company knowledge, 109
Compensation systems. See Rewards
Competition, 12, 91–92, 134–35
Computers, 159–60
Concept of the Corporation (Drucker), 121
Conceptual skills, 211
Confidence
   and communication, 167
   and ethics, 146
   importance of, 113, 166, 177, 208
   and improvisation, 81
   and leadership in the future, 178
   learning, 177
   and myths about leadership, 41–42
   and networks, 107
   and vision, 106, 118–19
Congress, U.S., 140, 142
Conrades, George H., 51, 161–62, 163
Conrail, 90
Consensus, 139
Container Corporation, 132
Continuing education, 21–23
Control, 52, 56, 57, 67, 183, 205, 213. See
   also Total quality control/management
Cooley, Charles Horton, 72
Cornell University, 21, 94
Corporate alliances, 16
Corporate Cultures (Deal and Allen), 87
Corporations. See Organizations
Crate & Barrel
   beginnings of, 189–90, 192–96
   culture of, 201–7, 208
   expansion of, 197–200, 206
   mission of, 206–7
   See also Segal, Gordon

Creativity
   as America's greatest untapped natural
      resource, 35
   capitalism of, 24, 29
   and change, 51–52
   as characteristic of leadership, 12, 54,
      113, 191, 208
   and commitment, 114
   and control, 52
   and education/business schools, 40, 51–52
   as evolutionary, 198
   and fear, 170
   and job descriptions, 40
   and leadership as the ultimate creative
      skill, 210–11
   and minutiae, 91
   and mission statement, 139
   and networks, 91
   and participant-observers, 83–84
   and rewards, 113
   and risk-taking, 83, 113
   stifling of, 41, 51–52, 113, 170
   U.S. as an incubator of, 29–34
   and vision, 192–93, 195
Credibility, 66, 118–19
Crimes and Misdemeanors (film), 157–58
Crisis situations, 42, 46, 48. See also
   Trauma; Twice-born experiences
Culture
   artificiality of business, 92
   categories of business, 68–69
   and change, 51
   characteristics of a successful business,
      212
   defensive business, 148
   entrepreneurial, 68–69
   ethics and the business, 144–51, 158
   and incentives for leadership, 48–49
   in Japan, 33
   leadership, 68–69
   and leadership in the future, 178–79
   managerial, 68–69
   myths as the software of, 80
   purpose of business, 92
   uniqueness of business, 92
Cummings, Tilden, 98
Curiosity, 100, 113, 208
Custodians in organizations, 210

Daewoo Motors, 18
Dartmouth College, 19, 23
Darwin, Charles, 75
Deal, Terrence, 87, 89–90
Decision making
   and networks, 204
   and tough decisions, 74, 118
Declaration of Independence, 116
Defense industry, 16

Deming, W. Edwards, 26–27, 181–86, 187, 188
Deming Management Method, The (Walton), 182
Deming Prizes, 182
DiCorcia, Edward, 157
Discipline, importance of, 46, 106
Dobbs, Ella, 11
Drexel Burnham, Inc., 24, 142, 148, 150
Drucker, Peter F., 121, 159, 160, 161, 164–65
Dun & Bradstreet Europe, 90
Du Pont Company, 171
Durant, Will, 71, 80

Eastern Europe, 15, 179
Easton, George S., 186–87
Economist, 142
Education
    as continuous, 39, 45, 46, 53
    and creativity, 51–52
    and the humanities, 171–74
    and motivation, 45
    and myths about leadership, 39, 44–45
    self-, 40, 45, 91, 204–5
    and total quality management/leadership, 183–84, 185, 187
    See also Business education/schools; Learning
Ehlem, Dave, 209
Eight Stages of Man, The (Erikson and Erikson), 108–9
Elk story, 51
Ellis Island, 213
Emotions, 46, 54, 105
Empowerment
    as an object of leadership, 33
    and delegation of authority, 199–201
    and ethics, 146, 154
    importance of, 84, 121
    and leadership in the 1990s, 35
    and motivation, 4
    and power, 203
    and self-discovery, 35
    and total quality management/leadership, 183, 184, 187, 188
    and trust, 146
Energy level, 12, 46, 108, 191, 195, 208
Entrepreneur, definition of, 191
Entrepreneurial capitalism, 7
Entrepreneurial culture, 68–69
Erikson, Erik, 43, 46, 83, 108–9
Erikson, Jean, 108–9
Errors/mistakes
    admitting, 166
    learning from, 54, 118, 195–96, 212
    and myths about leadership, 54
    reasons for, 195–96

and total quality management/leadership, 183
and vision, 118
See also Failure
Ethics
    and characteristics of ethical behavior, 141
    and characteristics of leadership, 12, 208
    and a code of conduct, 144, 151–58
    and communication, 153
    and the corporate culture, 144–51, 158, 212
    definition of, 158
    and empowerment, 154
    and failure, 145
    and Japan, 142
    learning of, 151–52, 158
    and religion, 143–44
    and rewards/profits, 149, 153
    shapers of, 143
    and short-/long-term, 149, 156–57
    situations where there is a lack of, 146–51
    standards for, 141
    and strategic plans, 151
    teaching of, 151–52
    and Wall Street, 142
    and whistle-blowers, 148
    See also Integrity; Values
Europe
    business schools in, 23
    and Europe 1992, 16
    and the European Common Market, 35
    and the European Community Commission, 15, 16
    failure in, 30
    See also Eastern Europe; Fortress Europe; Western Europe
Executives
    and the CEO disease, 100–102, 107
    education programs for, 23
    salaries/perks of, 27

Failure
    acceptance of, 137
    and the emergence of leaders, 42
    and ethics, 145
    in Europe/Japan, 30
    fear of, 196
    learning from, 99–100, 212
    reasons for, 195–96
    and risk-taking, 113–14
    and total quality management/leadership, 183
    in the U.S., 30
    See also Errors/mistakes
Fairness, 128
Family, and the "international family" concept, 128
Family values, 97

Faraday, Michael, 52
Fear
    of change, 14, 49–50
    and communication, 188
    and creativity, 170
    of failure, 196
    and the leader-follower relationship, 67
    and motivation, 169–70, 196
    and risk-taking, 170
    and total quality management/leadership,
        184, 188
Federal Express, 187
*Female Advantage—Women's Ways of
    Leadership, The* (Helgesen), 94–95
Ferris, Richard, 141
Field, Marshall, 94
Field, Stanley, 94
Fireman, Paul, 52–53
First Steps in Weaving, The (Dobbs), 11
Followers
    art of being, 60
    challenging leaders, 62–63
    and change, 49–50, 66
    characteristics of, 61–63, 68
    effective/ineffective, 60–61
    as engineers, 61
    leaders as, 48
    leaders' relationship with, 49–50, 60–69,
        73–74, 118–19, 144, 158, 184,
        199–204, 206–7, 212
    and power, 74
    and short-/long-term, 62
    and total quality management/leadership,
        188
    and trust, 144, 158, 212
    and vision, 63–67, 73–74, 118–19, 206–7
Forbes magazine, 154, 180
Force for Change (Kotter), 56
Ford, Henry, 97, 102
Ford Foundation, 18
Ford Motor Company, 16–18, 88, 137, 187
Fortress Europe, 15, 16, 179
Fortune magazine, 7, 28, 115, 119, 125, 145,
    181
Fowler, Elizabeth, 90
France, 23
Freud, Sigmund, 212
Frey, Don, 137–38
Futterman, Joel, 81–82

Galvin, Paul, 96–97
Galvin, Robert "Bob," 48, 56, 63, 65–66,
    95–97, 100, 118–19, 143, 155–56
Gandhi, Mahatma, 2–3, 43
Gardner, Howard, 46, 47, 49
Gardner, John, 5, 31–32
Gender. *See* Women
Geneen, Harold, 55, 57, 107

General Accounting Office, 187
General Electric Corporation, 16, 17, 88,
    178. *See also* Welch, John
General Motors Corporation, 18, 23, 88,
    98–99, 162, 180
Genius, myths of, 47–48
Germany, 15, 16, 17, 35
Gettysburg Address, 116
Giamatti, Bart, 5
Gifted leaders, 48
Glass, David, 63
Global issues, 15–16, 23, 61–62, 179–80.
    See also Stateless/pan-global
        organizations
Goals, 49, 84, 116, 117, 184
Goizueta, Roberto C., 125–29
Gorbachev, Mikhail S., 28, 62
Gore & Associates Inc., 171
Great Britain, 16
Great man theory of leadership, 42–43
Great Northern Railway, 115
Greenleaf, Robert, 31, 32, 48, 211
Grove, Andrew, 89
Gustafson, James, 98–99
Gutfreund, John H., 149, 150

Hammonds, Keith, 49–50, 51
Harris Bank, 152
Harvard University, 19, 21, 23
Havel, Václav, 28–29
Health. *See* Physical/biological aspects
Helgesen, Sally, 94–95
Henahan, Donal, 47
Heroes, 102–6, 138, 144, 158
Hesse, Herman, 48
Hill, James J., 115
Holmes, Oliver Wendell, 114, 211
Honda/Honda of America Manufacturing,
    Inc., 20, 64–65, 117, 120–21, 162,
    180. *See also* Whitlock, Scott
Hong Kong, 179
"How-to" management books, 4
Hughes Aircraft, 170
Human development, 46, 108–9
Humanities, 171–74, 175
Human resource policies, 51
Hyatt Corporation, 170
Hyundai, 17

Iacocca, Lee, 101–2
IBM (International Business Machines), 23,
    92, 138, 161–62, 187
Identity
    and commitment, 35
    and elements of leadership, 12, 46
    and the leader-follower relationship, 67
    and the looking-glass self, 72
    need for a common corporate, 49

Identity (*cont.*)
  and stages of human development, 46
  and twice-born experiences, 74, 104
IDEX Corporation, 152, 154
Immigrants, 29–30, 76, 104, 105, 213
Improvisation, 80–83
Individual
  and the organization, 74
  and the team, 169, 205
Industry knowledge, 12, 84, 109, 117–18, 208
Information
  and differences between leaders and managers, 57, 58
  importance of, 44–45, 161
  and the leader-follower relationship, 184
  leverage, 211
  and participant-observers, 120
  and perspective, 120
  and power, 121
  and rumors, 121
  and total quality management/leadership, 184, 187
  and vision, 117, 120–21
  See also Communication; Networks
Ingersoll, Robert, 93
In-house business education, 21
Initiative, 46, 68, 109, 121, 128
In Praise of Followers (Kelley), 60–61
Inquiry, importance of, 44–45
In Search of Excellence (Waterman), 91
Insider trading scandals, 142
Instincts, 6, 12, 105, 212
Institutional investors, 25
Integrity
  as a "bruised value," 140
  and the corporate culture, 144–45
  as an element of leadership, 12, 158
  and the leader-follower relationship, 66
  and mission statement, 128
  and rewards/profits, 156–57
  and role models, 96
Intel Corporation, 88, 89
Intellectual capitalism, 7, 33
Intellectual vision, 117
Intelligence, 12, 49
Interactive leadership, 95
"International family" concept, 128
International Telephone and Telegraph Corporation, 107
Internships, 21
Interpersonal skills
  and business school curricula, 20–21
  as characteristic of leadership, 12, 46–47, 109, 113, 200–201, 208, 211
  and differences between leaders and managers, 58–59

  and motivation, 46
  and team building, 203
Interpretation of Dreams, The (Freud), 212
Introspection
  and differences between leaders and managers, 58
  and empowerment, 35
  and the humanities, 173
  importance of, 2, 6, 32, 44–45, 46, 53, 54, 84, 113
  and motivation, 46
  as an ongoing process, 46
  and self-esteem, 209
  See also Trauma; Twice-born experiences
Intuition, 113, 117, 137, 167, 208
Investors. *See* Shareholders
Iran-Contra affair, 142
Isuzu, 18

Jaguar, 17
James, William, 75, 83
Japan
  career paths in, 170
  collective mentality of, 33
  culture in, 33
  economic restructuring in, 179
  and ethics, 142
  failure in, 30
  and Fortress Europe, 15
  and leadership in the future, 179
  leadership in, 33
  people as greatest resource of, 33
  shareholders in, 179
  and the short-/long-term, 25–26, 179
  speed of production in, 162
  and total quality management/leadership, 26, 180, 181, 182, 186
  U.S. corporation partnerships with, 18
Jazz musician metaphor, 80–82
Jefferson, Thomas, 116
Jefferson Ward, 135
Jeuck, John E., 18, 19
Job
  career *vis-à-vis* a, 32, 203–4
  definition of, 32
Job descriptions, 39–40, 57
Johnson & Johnson, 119–20, 152–53
Johnson, Elmer, 98–99, 143–44, 172–73
Johnson, Henry, 31
Johnson, Robert Wood, 119
Jordan, Michael, 8, 33–34
Josephson, Michael, 144, 146
Journey to the East (Hesse), 48
Judgmental skills, 212
Judis, John, 101, 102

Kaiser Permanente, 89
Kay, Mary, 64

Kaye, Charles, 165
Kelley, Robert, 60–61
Kennedy, Allen, 87, 89–90
Kennedy, John F., 6
Keough, Donald, 125
Kia Motors, 17
King, Martin Luther, Jr., 6
Knight, Arthur, 67
Knowledge
    authority of, 53, 69
    and communication, 167
    and elements of leadership, 12
    types of, 12
    See also Industry knowledge; Networks
Knowledge workers, 161
Korea, 17, 18
Kotter, John P., 27, 56, 116
Kroc, Ray, 97

Land, Edwin, 97
Landsbergis, Vytautis, 29
Larsen, Ralph, 119–20
"Latchkey" children, 7
Latin America, 17–18
Lazarus, Steve, 30, 146
Leaders
    as architects, 61, 146
    basic strengths of, 46
    as born or made, 3–4, 34–35, 36–54, 108,
        176, 177
    characteristics of, 5–6, 32, 48, 53–54,
        56–59, 67, 68, 82, 83, 84, 113–14,
        158, 191, 199–201, 209–13
    as conductors, 159–61, 164–69, 170–71,
        174, 181, 184, 188
    evolution of, 206
    as followers, 48
    gifted, 48
    and the great man theory, 42–43
    in history, 2–3, 6–7, 42–43
    as larger than life, 47–48
    as role models, 106, 146
    as servants, 31, 48, 104
    and staying at the top, 91
    as team players, 33
    See also Followers: leaders' relationship
        with; Leadership; Leaders-managers
Leaders (Bennis and Nanus), 44
Leadership
    definition of, 5
    essence of, 36–41
    in the future, 34
    gender gap in, 95
    interactive, 95
    in Japan, 33
    myths about, 34–35, 36–54
    need to nurture, 33
    object of, 33–34

    as a role, 42–43, 54
    as spiritual, 28–29
    threads of, 12
    vacuum of, 34
Leadership culture, 68–69
Leaders-managers
    and business school objectives, 18–19
    and change, 71
    and control, 205
    differences between, 34, 55–59, 61–67,
        71, 82, 120, 205, 212
    and improvisation, 82
    as interchangeable roles, 69
    and overmanagement, 61–67
    and perspective, 82, 120
    and short-/long-term, 82, 205
    and trust, 212
    and vision, 63
Learning
    and confidence, 177
    and ethics, 151–52, 158
    from errors/mistakes, 54, 118, 195–96,
        212
    from failure, 99–100, 212
    from life, 44–45, 212
    and total quality management/leadership,
        185
    by trial and error, 106
    See also Education
Leavitt, H. J., 20
Leinsdorf, Erich, 167–68
Lenin, V. I., 43
Leonard, Stew, 162–63
Leverage, 19, 26, 27, 34, 62, 211
Levin, Ira, 89
Levine, Dennis, 142
Levi Strauss & Company, 153–54
Levitt, Theodore, 41, 42, 58
Lewis, Michael, 151
Liar's Poker (Lewis), 151
Limited, The, 134
Lincoln, Abraham, 116
Listening
    to customers, 135, 162–63
    importance of, 53, 113, 201
    and mission statement, 135
    and people competence, 211
    and self-education, 204–5
London Business School, 23
"Looking-glass self," 72
Lucas, George, 102–3

McDonald's Corporation, 38–39, 173
McKinsey & Company, 21
Magad, Samuel, 166
Mailer, Norman, 76
Major, John, 3–4
Making a difference, 29, 138, 185, 192, 209

Malamed, Leo, 83
Malamud, Bernard, 33
Malcolm Baldrige National Quality Awards, 119, 186–87
Malott, Robert, 45, 58–59
Management Practices—U.S. Companies Improve Performance Through Quality Effort (GAO), 187
Managerial capitalism, 7
Managerial culture, 68–69
Managerial mind-set, 50
Managers
    characteristics of, 55–59, 67, 75
    confusion among, 160–61
    decline in number of, 159, 169
    job descriptions of, 57
    number of people reporting to, 163
    as a personality type, 75
    power of, 58
    See also Leaders-managers
Managing as a Performing Art (Vail), 28
Market knowledge, 12
Maughan, Deryck, 150, 151
Mazda, 17
MBA graduates, 1, 2, 19, 20, 21. *See also* Business education/schools
Melamed, Leo, 77–79
Melman, Rich, 205–6
Mentors, 40, 94, 103–6, 171, 204, 205, 208
Merck Corporation, 63
Meriwether, John, 149
Merrill, Charles E., 97
Metaphor
    and communication, 92, 167–68
    jazz musician, 80–82
    orchestra, 159–61, 164–69, 170–71, 174, 181, 184, 188
    weaving, 10, 11–12, 108–9, 112, 113–14, 175
Meyers, Martin, 25
Michener, James, 141, 143
Milken, Michael, 27, 142
Miller, Herman, 28
Minority entrepreneurs, 23
Mintzberg, Henry, 20, 56, 57, 58, 66
Mission statement
    and change, 128–29, 207
    and commitment, 126, 127, 128, 129, 136–37, 139
    and consensus, 139
    content of a, 122, 139
    and creativity, 139
    examples of a, 123–37
    and fairness, 128
    and goals, 184
    implementation of a, 134–37, 138, 197
    purpose/characteristics of, 121–22, 138, 139, 184–85

and reality, 139
    refining the, 198
    responsibility for development of, 69, 184, 187
    and risk-taking, 128
    and shared values/identity, 49, 212
    and short-/long-term, 26, 128, 129, 139
    and strategic plans, 134–37, 138
    and technical knowledge, 119
    and total quality management/leadership, 187
    and values, 206–7
    and vision, 119, 138, 139, 184–85
Mitsubishi, 17
Mobil, 132
Montgomery Ward & Company, 129–38
Moore, Gordon, 89
Morton Thiokol, 146–48
Motivation
    and characteristics of leadership, 12, 45–48, 192
    and commitment, 32
    and differences between leaders and managers, 58
    and empowerment, 4
    and fear, 169–70, 196
    and responsibility, 169
    and role models, 96
    and trust, 96
Motorola Corporation, 21, 100, 118–19, 154, 155–56, 187. *See also* Galvin, Robert
Movie industry, 157–58
Movies
    and heroes, 102–3, 104–6
    and leadership as inspirational, 59–60
    and myths of genius, 47–48
Moyers, Bill, 175
Mozart, Amadeus Wolfgang, 47, 48
Mythology and You (Rosenberg and Baker), 104
Myths
    Aeneas myth, 79–80
    of genius, 47–48
    and the great man theory of leadership, 42–43
    and heroes, 102–6
    that leaders are born, 3–4, 34–35, 36–54
    as models for understanding life, 79
    purpose of, 80
    as the software of culture, 80
    and trauma/twice-born experiences, 79–80
    Wizard of Oz myth, 70

Naked and the Dead, The (Mailer), 76
Nanus, Burt, 14, 44, 67
National Aeronautical and Space Agency (NASA), 146–48
National Women's Network, 94

Natural, The (Malamud), 33, 76
Negative role models, 100–102, 107
Networks
  and competition, 91–92
  and creativity, 91
  and decision making, 204
  efficiency of, 90
  formal/informal, 86–87, 89–90, 107,
    211
  importance of, 88–95, 106, 107, 121,
    201, 203, 204
  and interpersonal skills, 211
  and knowledge accumulation, 109
  and organizational plan, 86
  and perspective, 92
  purpose of, 86–88, 107, 204
  and reality, 92
  and social/civic situations, 91, 93–94
  and staying at the top, 91
  types of, 86–87
  and vision, 89, 120
  and women, 94–95
Neubauer, Joseph, 60, 74, 151–52
Newman, Francis W., 75, 83
Newsweek, 24, 141
Nixon, Richard M., 177
North, Oliver, 7

O'Connor, James, 93
Olympic Committee, U.S., 142
On-the-job training, 183–84
Openness, 84, 139, 145, 212
Optimism, 113, 208, 212
Orchestra metaphor, 159–61, 164–69,
    170–71, 174, 181, 184, 188
Organizations
  characteristics of successful, 212
  downsizing of, 159
  and the individual, 74
  as a leader's client, 74
  and shared values/identity, 49, 146
  stages in, 71–72
  stateless/pan-global, 17–18, 35, 87–88
  structure of, 23–24, 35, 86–87
Oscar Mayer, 21
Overcoming Organizational Defenses
    (Argyris), 148
Overmanagement, 61–67

Palmer, Potter, 94
Participant-observers
  and change, 209–10
  characteristics of, 72–73, 83–84
  and creativity, 83–84
  examples of, 76–83, 166
  and heroes, 105
  and improvisation, 82
  and information, 120

  as a personality pattern, 72–73
  and perspective, 120
  and reality, 208
  and risk-taking, 73, 83
  and trauma/twice-born experiences, 72–73,
    74–84, 82–84, 98, 211–12
  and vision, 120
Pascale, Richard, 50
Passion, 7, 54
Patton, George, 59–60, 107
Patton (film), 59–60
People competence. *See* Interpersonal skills
PepsiCo, Inc., 88, 144–45
Persian Gulf War, 27, 85–86, 180
Personality patterns, 72–73. *See also*
    Participant-observers
Perspective, 82, 92, 120, 211–12
Peters, Tom, 91, 212
Peterson, Peter G., 171
Physical/biological aspects, 12, 44, 45–46,
    108. *See also* Myths: that leaders are
    born
Picasso, Pablo, 13–14
Pistner, Stephen L., 130
Planning, 56–57. *See also* Business plans;
    Strategic plans
Plessey Company, 16
Poland, 28
Portugal, 17
Power
  and communication, 66
  and differences between leaders and
    managers, 58
  and empowerment, 203
  and ethics, 146
  and information, 121
  and leader-follower relationships, 74
  of leaders, 60, 66
  and trust, 146
Probas, Derek, 45–46
Procter & Gamble, 187
Professional investors/fund managers, 25
Protectionism, 16
Proving oneself, 41, 53
Pullman, George, 94

Quaker Oats Company, 39–41
Quality control. *See* Total quality
    management/leadership
Quinlan, Michael, 38–39

Reagan, Ronald, 29
Reality
  and characteristics of leaders, 201
  definitions of business, 35
  leaders as creators of their own, 71
  and mission statement, 139
  and networks, 92

Reality (*cont.*)
    and participant-observers, 208
    and the Wizard of Oz myth, 70
Reality Isn't What It Used to Be (Anderson),
    70
Reebok International Ltd., 52–53
Recognition. *See* Rewards
Recruit Cosmos, 142
Reichert, Jack, 36–38, 79, 83, 144, 163–64
Respect, 61
Restaurant business, 205–6
Rewards
    and business education, 40
    and change/conformity, 51, 113
    and control, 52
    and creativity, 113
    and differences between leaders and
        managers, 58
    and ethics, 149, 153
    and leadership as the ultimate creative
        skill, 210–11
    and risk-taking, 40
    and total quality management/leadership,
        183
    traditional, 7
Risk-taking
    approval for, 113–14
    and beginning new organizations, 190,
        191, 194
    and business education, 40
    and change, 71, 73, 74, 213
    as characteristic of leadership, 12, 32, 68,
        82, 84, 113, 191, 208, 213
    and creativity, 83, 113
    and differences between leaders and
        managers, 56, 67
    and expansion of organizations, 206
    and failure, 113–14
    and fear, 170
    and heroes, 105
    and the leader-follower relationship, 66
    and mission statement, 128
    and myths about leadership, 53
    need for taking, 8
    and participant-observers, 73, 78, 83
    and personality types, 78
    in the restaurant business, 205–6
    and rewards, 40
    stifling of, 41, 170
    and total quality management/leadership,
        183, 188
    and vision, 194
Rockefeller, John D., Jr., 97
Rogers, William, 147
Role models
    and ethics/values, 141, 143
    finding, 6, 95–103
    function/purpose of, 106, 168, 204

    leaders as, 106, 146
    and leadership development, 106, 109,
        208
    negative, 100–102, 107
    See also Heroes; Mentors
Roosevelt, Eleanor, 43–44
Roosevelt, Franklin D., 2–3, 87
Rosenberg, Donna, 104
Rosener, Judy B., 95
Rothschild family, 82
Royal Bank of Canada, 90
"Rubbergate," 140
Ruder, David, 176–78
Rumors, 121
Russia. *See* Soviet Union

Saab, 18
Salomon Brothers, Inc., 142, 148–51
Salvaneschi, Luigi, 173
Samuelson, Robert J., 1
Savings and loan crisis, 142
Schlesinger, Arthur, 87
Schwartz, Peter, 100
Scorsese, Martin, 76–77, 79
Scott, George C., 59–60
Sealy Inc., 161, 175, 209–10
Sears, Roebuck & Company, 129–30
Segal, Carole, 189, 191–92, 195
Segal, Gordon
    and the beginnings of Crate & Barrel,
        189–90, 192–96
    commitment of, 197
    and delegation of authority, 190, 197,
        199–201, 203
    and the expansion of Crate & Barrel,
        197–200
    as a mentor, 205
    and networks, 91, 92, 204, 205
    personal background of, 191–92
    and personality factors, 191
    and risk-taking, 190, 206
    role models/mentors for, 204, 205–6
    self-education of, 204–5
    and short-/long-term, 205
    and vision/mission, 117, 189–90, 192–93,
        194, 196–97, 198, 206–7
Self, "looking-glass," 72
Self-determination, 41
Self-discovery. *See* Introspection
Self-education, 40, 45, 91, 204–5
Self-esteem, 12, 75, 84, 106, 109, 185,
    209–10
Self-expression. *See* Communication
Self-improvement, 35, 100, 185. *See also*
    Introspection
Sempel, Robert, 99
Servants, leaders as, 31, 48, 104
Shapiro, Harold, 171, 172, 173

Shareholders
  in Japan, 179
  and the short-/long-term, 24–26
Shevardnadze, Eduard, 62
Short courses, 21–22
Short-/long-term
  and business school objectives, 19
  and change, 24–29
  and differences between leaders and
    managers, 56, 57, 67, 82, 205
  and elements of leadership, 12, 68, 84
  and ethics, 149, 156–57
  and followers, 62
  and improvisation, 82
  in Japan, 179
  and leadership in the future, 35, 179
  and leverage, 62
  and mission statements, 26, 128, 129,
    139
  and morale, 62
  and overmanagement, 62
  and total quality management/leadership,
    182, 183, 185
  See also Vision
Siemens, 16
Simplicity, 34, 54, 178, 211
Singapore, 179
Sloan, Alfred P., 97, 102
Smith, Adam, 150
Smith, Roger, 99
Smithburg, William D., 22–23, 39–41
Social/civic situations, 91, 93–94
Social conscience, 8
Social skills. See Interpersonal skills
Socrates, 46
Solti, Georg, 165–67
South Korea, 179
Soviet Union, 15, 28, 29, 35, 62
Spain, 17
Speed
  and leadership in the future, 178
  and total quality leadership, 180
Spiegel, 31
Stalin, Josef, 2–3
Stanford University, 18, 142
Star Wars (film), 102–3, 104–6
Stateless/pan-global organizations, 17–18, 35,
    87–88
Stayer, Ralph, 7
Steingraber, Fred G., 5–6, 17
Stewardship, 96
Stewart, Potter, 5
Stewart, Thomas, 116
Stock market crash (1987), 27
Strategic plans, 134–37, 138, 151
Strauss, Thomas, 149
Structure, organizational, 23–24, 35, 86–87
Style, of leadership, 7, 12, 95

Success
  and the CEO disease, 100–102, 107
  and character, 212
  and characteristics of a business culture,
    212
Supplier relationships, 183
Surprises, 56, 57
Svete, Lee J., 90
Sweden, 18
Synthesize, ability to, 113, 208

Taiwan, 179
Teams/teamwork, 27, 33, 89, 169, 201, 203,
    205
Technical knowledge, 117–18, 119, 168, 211
Technological advances, and communication,
    163
Telecommunications industry, 16
Thailand, 179
Thatcher, Margaret, 3
Three I's, 44–45
3M Corporation, 62
Tichy, Noel, 50
Time magazine, 6, 27, 144, 167
Timing, 79, 193
Total Quality Forum, 187
Total quality management/leadership, 26–27,
    176–88
Toyota, 18, 162
Toys "Я" Us, 134
Tradition and Change (Shapiro), 171, 172,
    173
Transformational experiences. See Trauma;
    Twice-born experiences
Trauma
  and introspection, 73
  and leadership development, 43–44
  and myth, 79–80
  and participant-observers, 72–73, 76–84,
    211–12
  and personality types, 72–73, 76–84
  See also Crisis situations; Twice-born
    experiences
Treaty of Rome, 16
Truman, Harry, 3
Trump, Donald, 27, 101
Trust
  as a "bruised value," 140
  and commitment, 67
  and communication, 67
  and the corporate culture, 145, 212
  and differences between leaders and
    managers, 212
  and empowerment, 146
  and followers, 158
  and heroes, 104
  and human development, 109
  importance of, 67, 212

Trust (cont.)
  of instincts, 6, 105, 212
  and the leader-follower relationship, 60,
    66, 144, 212
  and leadership development, 46
  and motivation, 96
  and power, 146
  and role models, 96
  and self-esteem, 106
  situations where there is a lack of, 146–51
  and vision, 67, 118
  ways of building, 67
Turf, Barbara, 201–3, 205
Twice-born experiences, 74–80, 103, 104,
  109, 211–12

Union of Japanese Scientists and Engineers,
  182
University of Chicago, 18, 19, 20–21,
  186
University of Pennsylvania, 23, 94

Vagelos, Roy, 63
Vail, Peter, 28
Values
  and change, 207
  creating, 212
  definition of, 143
  family, 97
  importance of, 84, 141
  and mission, 206–7
  and motivation, 32
  shapers of, 143
  shared, 146
  and total quality management/leadership,
    185
  and value creators/destroyers, 210, 211
  and vision, 196–97
  See also Ethics; Integrity; Trust
Varieties of Religious Experience, The
  (William James), 75
Vision
  and the boiled frog story, 51
  and change, 51
  and characteristics of leaders, 12, 23, 41,
    82, 113
  characteristics of, 115, 119
  and commitment, 67, 118, 138, 197
  and committees, 117
  and communication, 63–66, 69, 73,
    119–20, 137, 139, 178
  and confidence, 106, 118–19
  and consensus, 139
  creation of the, 165
  and creativity, 192–93, 195
  and credibility, 118–19
  and differences between leaders and
    managers, 58–59, 63

and errors/mistakes, 118
examples of, 115–16
and goals, 116, 117
implementation of the, 138, 165
and improvisation, 82
and information/knowledge, 117–18,
  120–21
intellectual, 117
and intuition, 117
and the leader-follower relationship,
  63–67, 73–74, 118–19, 206–7
and leadership in the 1990s, 34
and making a difference, 138
and mission statement, 119, 138, 139,
  184–85
and networks, 89, 120
overview of, 116–21
and participant-observers, 120
refining the, 198
and responsibilities of leaders, 69, 165,
  187
and risk-taking, 194
of Segal, 189–90, 192–93, 194
and shared identity/values, 49, 212
and short-/long-term, 118, 120
as a statement of purpose, 117
and total quality management/leadership,
  187, 188
and trust, 67, 118
and twice-born experiences, 212
and values, 196–97, 210–11, 212
See also Mission statement
Volkswagen, 17–18
Volunteering, 100

Wagner, Richard, 47
Walesa, Lech, 28
Wall Street, 142
Wall Street Journal, The, 154
Wal-Mart, 63, 134, 135
Walton, Mary, 182
Warren, Kirby, 143
Washington, George, 2–3
Waste Management, 154, 157
Waterman, Robert, 91
Watson, Thomas, 97
Weaving metaphor, 10, 11–12, 108–9, 112,
  113–14, 175
Webber, Ross A., 169
Welch, John "Jack," 14, 15, 17, 51,
  178
West, Ken, 79
Western Europe, 15
Wharton School (University of Pennsylvania),
  23
Whistle-blowers, 148
Whitlock, Scott, 20, 64–65, 117, 120–21
Wizard of Oz myth, 70

Women
  and mentors, 94
  and networks, 94–95
  style of, 95
Workaholism, 7
Work ethic, 1, 123
World of Ideas, A (Moyers), 175
Wriston, Walter, 23, 24, 33

Xerox Corporation, 23, 116, 187

Yates, Ronald, 186
Young Presidents' Organization (YPO), 91,
  204, 205

Zaleznik, Abraham, 75
Zenith Corporation, 21